5/24

To Gayle,

God Bless your
journey of healing
& forgiveness.

Blessings,

Carrie
Sheffield

Motorhome
Prophecies

Motorhome Prophecies

A Journey of
Healing and Forgiveness

Carrie Sheffield

CENTER
STREET

Nashville • New York

Center Street

Hachette Book Group

1290 Avenue of the Americas, New York, NY 10104

centerstreet.com

twitter.com/CenterStreet

First Edition: March 2024

Center Street is a division of Hachette Book Group, Inc. The Center Street name and logo are trademarks of Hachette Book Group, Inc.

The publisher is not responsible for websites (or their content) that are not owned by the publisher.

The Hachette Speakers Bureau provides a wide range of authors for speaking events. To find out more, go to hachettespeakersbureau.com or email HachetteSpeakers@hbgusa.com.

Center Street books may be purchased in bulk for business, educational, or promotional use. For information, please contact your local bookseller or the Hachette Book Group Special Markets Department at special.markets@hbgusa.com.

Library of Congress Cataloging-in-Publication Data

Names: Sheffield, Carrie, author.
Title: Motorhome prophecies : a journey of healing and forgiveness / Carrie Sheffield.
Description: New York : Center Street, 2024. | Includes bibliographical references.
Identifiers: LCCN 2023036572 | ISBN 9781546004387 (hardcover) | ISBN 9781546004400 (ebook)
Subjects: LCSH: Sheffield, Carrie. | Sheffield, Carrie—Family. | Latter Day Saint fundamentalism—United States. | Poor—United States—Biography. | Children of sick parents—United States—Biography. | Adult children of dysfunctional families—United States—Biography. | Journalists—United States—Biography. | Ex-church members—Church of Jesus Christ of Latter-day Saints—Biography. | Anglican converts—United States—Biography. | LCGFT: Autobiographies.
Classification: LCC BX8695 .S55 2024 | DDC 289.3092 [B]—dc23/eng/20230821
LC record available at https://lccn.loc.gov/2023036572

ISBN: 9781546004387 (hardcover), 9781546004400 (ebook)

Printed in the United States of America

LSC

Printing 1, 2023

To Marty, Rachel, and Abinadi. Angels watching from heaven.

Contents

Author's Note: I limited the extent to which I profile my living siblings and have changed their names—they have their own stories to share and their own faith journeys.

Introduction

Do not repay evil for evil or abuse for abuse; but, on the contrary, repay with a blessing. It is for this that you were called—that you might inherit a blessing.

—1 Peter 3:9

This is a book about sabotage. Sabotage from my father, others, and sabotage from myself—the kind that almost killed me. It's about how putting up fake fronts of perfectionism is fatally toxic. This book is also about identifying and defeating sabotage, the kind that's destroying families and society. For many years, I expertly put up fake fronts, and most people were surprised to find out about my abusive, dysfunctional childhood. But all those fake fronts built enormous pressure that eventually burst and landed me in the hospital nine times from complications due to anxiety, depression, PTSD, fibromyalgia, and nearly two decades of episodic suicidal ideation. This book is about tearing down false fronts, healing from the inside out, coming to peace with God, and forgiving others.

I am not the hero of this book, but I am also not the villain; though, for many years I painted myself in these absolutist, black-and-white terms. God is the hero, and though I thought my father was the villain, I now see that he got crushed by severe religious zealotry, sparked by mental illness after suffering sexual assault as a toddler and enduring isolation and the death of his best childhood friend. He's just as deserving of God's mercy and compassion as I am. I love my father and am sorry I waited so long to forgive him. He gave me a deep love of our exceptional country, intellectual inquiry, and beautiful music. Though we've had many disagreements, I know his heart holds a deep desire to serve others through his work. I pray God's blessing on his life, especially during his struggles with Alzheimer's. I'm grateful to my mother for her decades of selfless prayers for me, even when I didn't appreciate them. I know God was listening.

This book is also about redemption, forgiveness, and separating the gold from the rubbish our families throw on us. I received loads of rubbish, though in the process of taking out the trash, I also threw out important treasures. If I'd taken the time to quietly heal from my trauma, I could have avoided many costly mistakes, failed relationships, and wasted years. Instead, I gave my trauma power over my life, blaming others for my own wrong choices.

I grew up one of eight children with a violent, mentally ill street-musician father, who believed he was a prophet that would someday become president of the United States and that Satan had "reassigned" lesser demons in order to personally torment our family. We lived a transient lifestyle, skirting authorities by constantly moving. Besides various houses, we lived in motorhomes, tents, mobile homes, and sheds. One of my five brothers was born in a tent when our family lived in the public campground woods of Greenbelt Park, Maryland.

When I was a bit older, my dad accepted some inheritance

money from his dad, and so we didn't starve like we previously had (child custody authorities loomed), but we still lived a dysfunctional gypsy lifestyle in our motorhome at truck stops and in Walmart parking lots while performing classical music on the streets and passing out religious pamphlets. I attended seventeen public schools and was partially homeschooled, all before college— yet somehow, I graduated with honors, landed a full-tuition scholarship to Harvard for a master's degree, and worked on Wall Street before returning to my first love, journalism.

With four older brothers, as the oldest girl I was the fifth child, but first to escape the motorhome. Leaning on a dear high school friend, I left home at age eighteen, despite my dad's "prophecies" of my rape and death. I was declared legally estranged from my parents, who would not allow me to visit home because they claimed I was satanic and would corrupt my siblings by urging them to leave. Dad said my blood changed when I left home, that I was no longer part of their family, and I was photoshopped out of family pictures. I wrongfully thought that bad things happening—my bike and purse getting stolen, breaking my glasses, getting bitten by a possibly rabid dog, losing my job in a round of layoffs, the terrorist attacks of 9/11—were all punishment from God for my evilness.

I believe my father's psychological abuse contributed to the schizophrenia of two of my brothers, including one who sexually assaulted me and attempted to rape me when I was seventeen. Later, my other schizophrenic brother accused me of attempting to seduce him to have sex. He claimed that, with his iron willpower, he fended off my incestuous temptations. Dad believed his lie and said I encouraged this by dressing like a slut.

I've seen firsthand how easily a child can fall through the social net meant to protect her from abuse. I've also seen how that same net can later buoy up a wounded survivor and set her on the path of success. Fortunately, most of my siblings later left our dysfunctional confines and pursued a range of fulfilling endeavors. We've suffered mental illnesses ranging from PTSD and depression to various personality disorders. Sometimes I wounded them, and sometimes they wounded me. Sometimes they've been a lifeline to me, and sometimes I've acted as a sounding board and offered a lending hand (at times a shaky one) to help them along the path of healing.

I hope my story can help liberate people who feel trapped, whether in abusive family situations, mental illness, poverty, or religious fundamentalism. Others first trapped me, then I mentally held myself bondage. I've met many others who also feel trapped, and I know each of us can live a healthy and productive life without becoming the drunken slut or coked-up drug dealer in a body bag that our families threaten about.

My dangerous inner programming, created by daily indoctrination sessions—that could stretch on for hours at a time about my evilness and failures—contributed to my self-destructive feelings and suicidal ideations later in life. I was set up for failure, and fail I did—big time. But in many ways, I failed my way up the food chain. There are barnyards full of self-help literature (heck, even hardheaded economic literature from the likes of statistician Nassim Nicholas Taleb) that tell you failure should be embraced and encouraged, that we should become, as Taleb says, "anti-fragile." That is, we're not afraid of hardship, we actually welcome it, because it helps us become strong.

Since "the unexamined life is not worth living," as Socrates told us, I've written out my journey of self-examination in hopes of generating some kernels of insight. I see my life as a case study in how religious abuse (or abuse of any type, whether physical, spiritual, sexual, or mental) can be intensely psychologically damaging, and how escaping its allures can lead to Stockholm-syndrome behavior. This could include replacing one false cult (like my father's home-made one) with another. Humans build cults around religion, sex, power, money—you name it.

I've no intent to destroy religion—I see its value and hope for billions of people, especially since my Protestant Christian baptism in 2017, and I attend church each Sunday. I still love many people who practice the LDS faith, and there are many treasured cultural parts of Mormonism I will always carry within my heart. What I have done is trace the roots of my family's Mormon-offshoot extremism and explore its heartbreaking impacts. Intolerance flows among religious people as well as those who remain unaffili-ated. This is not from God. One of the hardest lessons I've learned is that God is not religion, and my hope is this book makes the case for reconciling and striving for peace across denominations and nonbelievers.

After spending nearly twelve years as an agnostic, it took me much time and effort to believe in a God who 1) existed, and 2) was not vengeful, hurtful, or indifferent. Even now, as a practicing Christian, I still see numerous examples of the wrenching pain inflicted by religious people in the name of God.

Though it wasn't the case when I was younger, my faith in God is now unshaken by the heinous actions of "religious" people. I know that's not God—that's corrupted man. This book is for Christian believers and nonbelievers alike. It's for those who are abused and need help breaking free and recovering from trauma. It is for devout Christians to help us show greater empathy and instill higher emotional awareness for the suffering of others, especially those wounded by human-run religion.

We live in an age of soaring rates of mental illness and domestic abuse, combined with plummeting spirituality, communal trust, and individual sense of purpose. This poisonous cocktail is brewing to create new generations teetering on the brink of suicide and depression, plagued by social media–induced insecurities and a culture that sows division and self-doubt. Humans have always lived in a broken world, but each generation has its own unique toxic manifestations, and my life contained many of them here in the late twentieth and early part of the twenty-first centuries.

My purpose in writing *Motorhome Prophecies* is to help bring others out of isolation. To let them know that "death and life are in the power of the tongue" (Proverbs 18:21). My father prophesied my rape and death if I left his cult. I internalized those curses, and as a result, suffered many close scrapes with the demon of suicide. But to quote author Linda Schubert, "While my failures were 'legendary,' the love of God was even more legendary." I'm proud to say I've come through on the other side, and I'm thriving. I pray this book might help others thrive, too.

But he said to me, "My grace is sufficient for you, for power is made perfect in weakness." So I will boast all the more gladly of my weaknesses, so that the power of Christ may dwell in me. Therefore I am content with weaknesses, insults, hardships, persecutions, and calamities for the sake of Christ, for whenever I am weak, then I am strong.

—2 Corinthians 12:9–10

Chapter 1

Hardscrabble Start

"Before I formed you in the womb I knew you, and before you were born I consecrated you."

—Jeremiah 1:5

Grandpa Ralph Sheffield's death was perhaps the greatest gift he could have bequeathed; it likely saved my life. A one-time beau later pointed out this chilling reality, which made me offer silent gratitude to a man I'd never met. His son, Ralph Jr., later became the source of my red-hot ire, and Ralph Jr. almost accidentally killed both me and my mom during my birth.

During the burning anger phase of my adult life, for years I called Dad by his first name, Ralph, because I didn't consider him worthy of the intimate title, "Dad." I didn't speak to him for about seven years after I decided to disown him in 2013. Sometimes I felt my anger toward him was as intense as what Salvador Dalí felt toward his own father, Salvador Rafael Aniceto. I first fell in love with the art of this brilliant surrealist Spanish painter in 2011, during a visit to a museum dedicated to his work in sunny St. Petersburg, Florida. It's a futuristic, fantastical building filled with spacious, airy light flowing through the glass atrium entryway attached to eighteen-inch-thick concrete. The sun-filled skylight is oblong spherical and named "Enigma," with a seventy-five-foot-tall glass ceiling encompassing a conch seashell–shaped white spiral staircase. It's a captivating and fitting home for this revolutionary man who pushed the boundaries intersecting art, science, and metaphysics.

But Dalí clashed for decades with his father, a midlevel civil servant who didn't appreciate his son's creative, rebellious nature or his association with surrealists. Adding insult to injury, Aniceto disapproved of his son's muse and future wife, Gala. Dalí said he considered his true father to be psychologist Sigmund Freud, and later, quantum physicist Werner Heisenberg. Legend has it that Dalí gave his biological father a condom containing the artist's own sperm, exclaiming: "Take that. I owe you nothing anymore!"

Obviously, that's disgusting. But I confess, there was a time in my life when I might have considered buying a sperm sample from a donor bank and sending it to Ralph. I thought he'd die before I'd ever speak to him again.

Speaking of sperm and conception—I was lucky to get both a hospital and a doctor at birth. Other siblings weren't so fortunate. The brother just ahead of me was delivered in a tent—almost as though we lived in medieval times—with Ralph playing midhusband in the forest of a public campground in Greenbelt Park, Maryland. My sister Rachel entered this world while my mother was alone in a tiny apartment in the squalor of Roxbury, a Boston neighborhood then riddled with crime and poverty. Three other siblings were born at home with Ralph again acting as midhusband.

I entered our planet at a hospital in Fairfax, a town in the suburbs of northern Virginia, where doctors gave Mom an emergency Cesarean section because my umbilical cord coiled multiple times around my neck. Both Mom and I most likely would have died if Ralph tried to deliver once more. Ralph harbored a deep distrust of doctors and hospitals, not only because of how expensive they were (and because we didn't have health insurance), but because he said his firstborn suffered a head injury, his fragile infant face turning blue from a doctor's botched forceps. So Ralph checked out midwifery books from the local library and he was off to doula-town.

Ralph would later claim credit for the decision to have me in a hospital as one of his premonitions from God. The only problem with his 20/20 hindsight is he was more than two thousand miles away at Grandpa Sheffield's funeral in Utah. And this was in 1983, before ubiquitous cell phones, Skype, and social media. Breaking news was harder to send, especially with our vagabond lifestyle and difficulty paying phone or other utility bills. Ralph was understandably busy mourning, a luxury he wouldn't afford my mom when her own mother passed away many years later. (Mom refused to attend anyway, due to Ralph's brainwashing against her own family. She believed her mom was evil because Grandma had a baby out of wedlock. Mom also refused to attend her younger sister's funeral because of her sister's alleged sinfulness.) Ralph flew to Utah for the funeral on a flight paid for by his family. Mercifully, Ralph's absence on my birthday likely saved my life.

Mom started gushing blood, and no one knew why. Thankfully, Mom's sister became our heroine when Ralph dumped my family at her doorstep before jetting off to Utah. Mom's sister lived in nearby Fairfax, Virginia (her husband worked for the Secret Service—he had entertaining stories, like that Richard Nixon had the annoying habit of leaving his wallet lying around), and shuttled Mom to the ER. My family lived across the river in a trailer park in tiny Stevensville, Maryland, some sixty-five miles away from Fairfax. Mom required multiple blood transfusions to keep her alive. The C-section was successful, and both of us survived. Now and then, my mom rubs it in that I caused her biggest delivery hullabaloo. She's right. I praise her incredible sacrifice and endurance. She was fighting steep odds by the time I came around: she was living in poverty and already bore six other kids, including two who tragically died as infants. Mom has a beautiful, deep love for children.

Given the timing of Grandpa Sheffield's death, I can't help feeling a special kinship with the man I never met. Family lore calls him a gruff force of nature. His obituary in the *Deseret News*, a Mormon-owned newspaper in Utah, lists his date of death at age seventy-nine as February 8, 1983 (I was born seven days later on February 15), and ticks off an impressive résumé: attorney, chairman of the Salt Lake City Zoning and Planning Commission for twenty-five years, seventeen years on the Salt Lake County Planning Commission, and elected member of the Utah House of Representatives for fourteen years. He was also president and chairman of the board at the Credit Corporation of America.

His official lawmaker portraits over the years give off Harry S. Truman vibes. They show a serious man, a bespectacled gentleman with short, wavy hair (dark red, my family says, though you can't tell in black-and-white photos) parted down the middle, a thin mustache, and crisp suits with snappy ties and bow ties.

His obituary notes he wrote the Utah state law allowing drivers to turn right at a red light. So whenever you're driving in the

Beehive State—thank Grandpa Sheffield for making it just a little easier!

And he was a super Mormon.

Grandpa Sheffield spent time as a young man as a missionary in the US South. I wish I could have heard his stories. Because of deep theological differences, the Bible Belt is notoriously anti-Mormon—difficult proselytizing ground. I experienced a small taste of this while working as a summer journalism intern in rural North Carolina during college. Once, I returned from lunch and found anti-Mormon pamphlets on my desk. They were placed anonymously, with no accompanying note, and they bashed founder Joseph Smith Jr. I felt violated and angry. The move backfired. It was a textbook example of how to make your Mormon colleague even more entrenched in her beliefs. I'd say the same applies to any disagreement, political or otherwise. Loving communication and relationship, not hostile insults, win people over.

Another time that summer, I attended church with coworkers who promised to attend mine in exchange. I kept my end of the bargain, but (just as some Mormon friends in town forewarned) they lied and never joined me. I imagine it would've been much worse as a missionary for Grandpa all those years ago.

As a married man with grown kids, Grandpa Sheffield and my grandma Cora Sheffield did "couples missionary" work in Oakland, California, and Independence, Missouri. All told, Grandpa Sheffield devoted ten years of his life as a missionary for the Church of Jesus Christ of Latter-day Saints (aka the LDS Church, informally known for many years by the nickname "Mormon Church"). Occasionally, during my twelve years as an agnostic, I felt pangs of guilt for leaving behind his legacy of faith. Yet even though I've departed that faith, I do admire some amazing cultural attributes of Mormonism, including its focus on family and community. On balance, they weren't enough to keep me in the flock, and today as a Protestant Christian, I find major doctrinal teachings problematic. But I'm at peace now and seek to build bridges with my LDS friends.

I realize the appeal of Mormonism. After all, the founder Joseph Smith Jr. created a nirvana-esque, specific, and expansive description of our afterlife that inspired his followers to risk life and limb to practice his nascent religion. It was this Mormon interpretation of the cosmos that propelled my ancestors to cross oceans and settle in the middle of a desert wasteland that back then wasn't even technically part of the United States. My rebellious ancestors got expelled out of America into Mexico in 1847. It takes a heck of a payoff to make that sound like a good idea.

My parents met in 1975 at their local LDS singles congregation (aka "ward") and were engaged and married within a few months.

This is typical for many hormonal Mormon couples who are betrothed and wed at lightning speed to avoid committing fornication. Now, as a practicing Christian, I've returned to the biblical counsel against extramarital sex, but I felt angry because I thought my parents rushed getting married, and my mom's family could have sniffed out his abuse with more time. My parents were ancient singles by Mormon standards—Mom was twenty-seven and Ralph thirty-seven. They must have been chomping at the bit. (I hate picturing it, but this helps you get the idea.)

Mormons also believe you must be married to a fellow Mormon and "sealed" together within the walls of a Mormon temple to reach the highest level of heaven, "The Celestial Kingdom." They call this "eternal marriage." You're banished to a lesser Kingdom if you're single, non-Mormon, or married to a non-Mormon. If your children are not baptized Mormon and "sealed" to you in the Mormon temple, then you are separated from them for eternity. Eternal marriage and sealing is a double-edged sword. If you can be sealed for eternity, you can also be banished for eternity. If the basis for that separation is belief in the LDS Church, that's a powerful form of gatekeeping control.

I think this type of extreme bonding can be beautiful in the sense that it motivates LDS families to love each other and dream of spending eternity in heaven as an affectionate family. A dark, twisted interpretation of this helped normalize my dad's extreme rejection of me—he thought he was doing God's will. Banning me from returning home during college and refusing to provide the data I needed to fill out my college financial-aid paperwork were his way of warning me that if I didn't change my ways, I would be separated from my family in the afterlife. He was just providing a foretaste.

Thanks to extensive genealogical records, our family knows lots about our lineage. My mother's maiden name is Black (and yes, kids would sometimes joke we are technically half black), a common moniker from the Emerald Isle. Mom's Irish and British ancestors crossed the pond to join Mormon settlers in America.

My mother is a petite woman at 5'3" with brown eyes, auburn hair, and high cheekbones, which she likely got from her Native American ancestors on both parental sides. My own 23andMe DNA analysis shows 3.7 percent Native American ancestry. Mom's great-great-grandmother was a full-blooded Native American taken as a slave by another tribe and traded to white settlers for a quilt. Apparently, a quilt was then a valuable commodity. Or, rather, a young slave girl from a rival tribe wasn't.

In 1975, Mom was a shy elementary school teacher's aide, frustrated with the Utah dating scene. She was the daughter of a dressmaker and former school principal; Mom's grandfather had been a sheepherder in rural south-central Utah, tending his flocks against a stunning backdrop of dramatic red rock sandstone mountains.

Utah's legendary red rock national parks draw millions of visitors each year from around the globe, including to Capitol Reef National Park, near my family's small towns of Teasdale and Torrey. My mom's father, James Nephi Black, grew up in Richfield, Utah, and served in World War II as a member of the construction battalions of the Civil Engineer Corps of the US Navy (known as Seabees), building bases and harbors. He served thirty years as a blue-collar mill worker at Geneva Steel,[1] a factory created in Utah Valley in 1944 that's now defunct. (Fun fact: Grandpa Black's steel mill was used in the iconic dance scene in the cult classic 1984 film *Footloose* with Kevin Bacon.) Mom's parents had little money, but they always made sure their five daughters were fed and clothed, with a little extra money to spend on their beloved pet horses and dogs.

During an earlier stay with an older sister who lived in Hawaii, Mom began dating a handsome Catholic from Connecticut. She cut things off when it became clear they couldn't reconcile the religion question. So she moved back to Utah and prayed for her Mormon Prince Charming. Eventually, she got Ralph. But at first, no suitor materialized. Fed up again, she almost moved nearly three thousand miles away to accept a teaching post in Maine. I've wondered what would have happened in that alternative scenario—the Mormon pickings would have been slimmer. She may have either converted someone to LDS or become an old maid. But the Maine job was never meant to be.

"I went and talked to my bishop about it," I remember my mother telling me. "He said I could find someone here in Utah."

Mormon bishops occupy a revered place in the community, especially playing matchmaker for singles. Many of them relish the role. They act with such zeal it's almost like they get a bounty from God for each couple they forge, each new Mormon family built. After all, bishops are brokering heavenly entry for these lovebirds via a Mormon temple marriage.

Later, the story goes—both parents swear it—my mother and father each had separate revelations from God to attend a specific Mormon chapel in the Salt Lake City neighborhood of Federal Heights. It was the sign they both needed. They showed up there, met, and felt an instant spark. They were married several months later inside the Salt Lake City temple, the 253,000-square-foot crown jewel of Zion with its six meticulously sculpted gray granite spires, one adorned with the gold-plated angel Moroni sounding his trumpet, proclaiming the Restored Gospel. A small reception was held at my maternal grandparents' home forty-five minutes south in Provo.

My parents made up for lost time and did their part bringing Mormon spirits to earth. The ten of us were born within a span of thirteen years, along with a couple miscarriages and a stillbirth. Mom had nerves of steel, raising so many kids. But there were times she said she verged on a nervous breakdown—and with all those kids and so little support, I don't blame her. Having a big family can be a beautiful blessing, but you need the right community. My mom, Judy, is one of the most selfless people I know, though sadly Dad's influence made her an expert at negative self-talk.

Today, I cannot imagine being pregnant or recovering from miscarriages for a dozen years like my mother did. Growing up, however, I felt that having eight surviving children was not enough. My cousins had ten kids, and my competitive side wanted to beat them. I wanted eleven children to "multiply and fill the earth" as Adam and Eve were commanded in the Book of Genesis. As I grew older, slowly that figure dwindled, from eleven down to six or eight. Then it was five for some time. But as the years flew by without finding the right match—and sabotaging my healthy relationships—I suffered considerable anxiety about whether that would come to pass as my fertility window shrank.

With no health insurance and scant prenatal care, when my birth rolled around, Mom knew little about what was happening inside her womb, which previously worked like a well-oiled machine. Before me, Mom already produced six children. She would later produce a stillborn son and three more healthy children (including two born at home) without the need for a C-section—a dangerous feat, considering some physicians advise against vaginal birth after Cesarean (VBAC), which was especially true back then, particularly without medical supervision.

Ralph didn't believe in health insurance. To him, it was attached to plodding office jobs held by schmucks who worked from nine to five.

"My employer was Heavenly Father," Ralph explained, "so we knew He would protect us."

Who could argue with that? Why hedge your health bets when the Almighty Himself is on your side? We were big winners in God's lottery, so we chanced it growing up.

During the December just before I turned ten, I played soccer with a brother in the basement and my foot slipped on the partially deflated ball. I fell backward, bashing my head against the corner of the wall. Ralph laid a guilt trip on me almost as thick as the blood oozing from my head. If I chose to go to the ER like an average American and get stitches, Ralph would pay out-of-pocket expenses.

"That means no Christmas gifts for you and your brothers and sisters," he threatened.

Have seven angry siblings blame me as the Grinch because of my failed soccer skills? No thanks. That "selfish" decision would forever go down in the annals of family history. So I decided to be the anti-Grinch and save Christmas. I shook with fear and squeezed out tears as I made numerous silent prayers. Kneeling on our dolls' bench and grasping my teddy bear Pinky, I bowed my head and let Ralph play doctor, dousing the wound in dime-store rubbing alcohol. He sewed up the back of my head using Mom's needle and brown thread, the excruciating sound of the punctured weaving reverberating through my skull. He left the stitches in for about a week, with dry blood scabbing up in the meantime until he snipped the strings away. The scar on the left side of the back of my head— a smooth, white bald spot the size of a dime—is my permanent reminder of that harrowing night.

Ralph also regularly played orthodontist, using the broken stub of a Popsicle stick to move our teeth into what he considered alignment. When I was thirteen, my left incisor tooth stood at nearly a ninety-degree angle. My four older brothers mercilessly teased me, calling it my "snaggle tooth." Ralph's Popsicle-stick pressure felt like torture, and it backfired for me. Today, the root of my top left incisor is completely dead, requiring a root canal, and the top of the tooth is permanently discolored brown—despite attempted dentist whitening—because of his botched ortho work. My root canal is the manifestation of physical trauma from Dad, though it required a much cleaner, quicker treatment than the countless hours of therapy needed to treat the emotional trauma. My "soul-onoscopy" took decades to complete.

In all, Mom gave birth to ten babies and suffered three miscarriages. She followed the Mormon cultural standard of bearing as many children as possible to provide unborn spirits with mortal bodies that would be raised LDS. (One LDS family I knew in Missouri had twenty-one children from the same mother!) Two of my nine live-birth siblings didn't make it past infancy, and some of us who did survive at times wished we hadn't. Those feelings came as we grew older.

I'm not sure where all we lived during our family's early years, but our birthplaces dot the map. Six out of ten were born in scattered Utah towns, the rest in Massachusetts, Maryland, and Virginia.

My earliest memories are around age four, living in Hudson, Massachusetts, a small town about forty-five minutes west of Boston. Ralph told us he had been working as a temp for a Harvard professor who quickly realized Ralph's genius and wanted to give him more responsibility. Things were looking up in our real-life *Good Will Hunting*.

Mom forced me to wear my dark auburn-brown hair with bowl-cut bangs. I despised those bangs, not only for their uniform rigidity but because the girls at church had long, flowing hair and bangs they could sweep back in ponytails with enviable frilly bows and curls pressed by their moms. Mom kept the back part of my hair slightly longer but cropped just above my shoulders. She wouldn't let me grow it too long because sometimes we didn't have running water to wash it regularly; plus, it'd get too tangled with rat's nests.

Besides Scripture, the first book I remember reading was

Johanna Spyri's *Heidi*, a beautiful story about an orphaned five-year-old girl who lives in the Swiss Alps with her irritable grandfather. Through reading the Bible together, Heidi helps soften his heart away from anger against God for the tragic deaths of his son and daughter-in-law.

I also pounded out scales and études on our cheap, off-key secondhand piano.

"Do you love to sing and play, making music all the day? Curve your fingers nice and round, that will make a lovely sound." Those are lyrics from the first song I remember playing, a very simple melody requiring only the most basic motor skills because nearly each note was sequentially placed on the piano. Music gave me a happy escape. Playing the piano (and later, violin and oboe) is an immersive experience, and it gave me an outlet for my emotional angst as time went by. My dad said music did the same thing for him decades earlier as he reeled from childhood trauma.

When it was time to enter kindergarten, the teacher's aide told me to stop counting during my aptitude test because I could count ad infinitum thanks to drilling from Mom, who earned a college degree in elementary education and carefully taught us all how to read.

On paper, our family was strong. We had highbrow books and classical music. In academic studies, families are categorized by socioeconomic status, or SES. By this yardstick, we had the highest SES metric because my father has a master's degree and my mom a bachelor's degree and my grandpa owned considerable wealth. But SES doesn't capture how mental illness mixed with religious zealotry can completely unravel what nominally should be a stable home. The ravages of abuse and mental illness are great equalizers—they afflict billionaire and homeless families alike.

For my fifth birthday, I received a miniature broom-and-dustpan set made of shiny dark blue plastic with a black broom brush. It was the first of Mom's failed attempts at domesticating me into a clothes-sewing, apple-canning Mormon housewife. I hadn't asked for the set, but I do remember being excited about the fact that it belonged to me and me alone. It was also new. These were anomalies in my existence of thrift-store relics and hand-me-downs from cousins and church members. Such is communal life in large, poor families.

As much as I didn't love the miniature broom, I hated the full-size broom Mom used to prod and smack and punish us kids for myriad rebellions. Her techniques would rival the discipline described by hard-charging mother Amy Chua in her bestselling 2011 memoir, *Battle Hymn of the Tiger Mother*. Chua complains that most Western mothers, unlike Chinese and other Asian mothers, are lax and coddling. We called my Mormon momma bear "Dragon Lady"—that was her CB-radio name as we connected our motorhome/car caravan traveling cross-country. (My eventual CB radio name was Big Hornet, after my seventh-grade basketball team, the Hornets.)

Mom deployed an effective blend of spankings and guilt with the utmost skill. Using her teaching experience, she taught numbers and letters to her toddlers, because preschool was for selfish women's libbers who entrusted their most precious, vulnerable assets to complete strangers. This was a recipe for disaster and potential abuse. And better to keep abuse in the family than farm it out.

My mother was the manager that kept the family running while Ralph, a modern-day Don Quixote, chased windmills. As a good Mormon wife, she supported Ralph's priesthood wholeheartedly.

All Mormon males are ordained in the priesthood order, not just a select few as in most other faiths, which have professional, full-time clergy. Thoroughly convinced of his exceptional spiritual gifts and unique mission to save America, Mom could be hard as nails with us kids, but when Ralph came around, she bowed quietly to his spiritual authority.

Somewhere around that fifth birthday, social workers tried to rescue us in Hudson. These "buttinskies" (they butt in—get it?) as Ralph liked to call them, were concerned that our physical needs weren't being met and that Ralph was bellicose and abusive. I'm not sure who notified them or how they took notice, but they decided the six Sheffield children were prime candidates for foster care. Perhaps it was a neighbor or teacher worried about our ability to eat regular meals. Here's one example from an essay Ralph wrote about God providing, sometime around 1985, while he edited his religious pamphlets:

> One morning, during prayer, I was inspired, emphatically, to revise and enlarge the Bookmark of Quotations (into its present form), and that I must not leave the work—for any reason—until finished. This was a severe test of faith, because I feared we might run out of food, and that there wouldn't be enough money to buy more unless I worked the street project that day, as usual. Nevertheless, I understood that, having prayed for guidance, one must follow that guidance once it is given. So I quickly set to work on the Bookmark, trying not to panic.
>
> After several hours, the thing I dreaded—happened. My wife informed me that we didn't have enough food for the evening meal. "Thank you, Dear," I said, "I'll take care of it." Returning to my study area, I fell to my knees and pleaded with God to know

how I could keep both *the scriptural command to "provide for my own," and the directive He had given me to "not stop working on the Bookmark for any reason." The Lord responded that I should determine how much money we needed to get us by. Pondering briefly, I decided, "ten dollars would do it." (Our family was smaller at that time.) Immediately, I started to leave, intending to pawn my watch or ring in order to put a meal on the table, then resume work on the manuscript. But, as I reached for the door, I felt a terrible sense of rebuke, as if I were doing something very wrong. Again, I prayed, to know what it could be, since I was going to get the money, as I assumed I should. "No," the Lord reproved, "you were not told to get the money, but to decide how much you need. Now, return to your work." Almost trembling at this chastisement, I resumed editing the Bookmark—obedient, yet in galling suspense. But I was soon startled when our seven-year-old son came running into the room. "Daddy!... Here!" he said, handing me something. To my astonishment, it was a ten-dollar bill! Incredulous, I asked where it came from. "Behind the building in that pile of old boards," he answered. Instantly, I remembered Abraham, and how God had provided "behind him a ram caught in a thicket." Looking heavenward, I rejoiced, "Thank you, dear God! You can still do it, I see. Thank you!"* [2]

Beyond his tales of financial recklessness, Ralph also weaved fantastical street fighting stories as we kids gathered together for the obligatory morning and evening prayers or lay in bed at night. At bedtime, he had what he called his "story bag," tantalizing us by pulling out an imaginary script of a tale that he might first tease us with then later discard in favor of a different one for that evening. He loved to tell of his travels, of the street fights with bums and fellow buskers who tried to block him from playing his music and passing out religious pamphlets. With a solid build, Ralph often bragged he was an intramural wrestling champion in his college days, so his stories usually ended with the enemy bleeding in the gutter or apologizing for their encroachment. Sometimes there was a mysterious intervention, like the stranger with a black belt in karate who defended Ralph from a bully (kicking Ralph's attacker in the throat) who was an experienced boxer. Occasionally, Ralph ended up in jail but was usually able to bail himself out by, say, pawning his watch.

Ralph later said he told these stories with such ebullience because he needed a way to entertain us, since we were too poor to afford a television. But when the social workers called us kids in for interviews, somehow these fights came up, and the horrified social workers were determined to snatch us from the clutches of a violent street beggar.

Yet my father, a charismatic and domineering man, had a way of beguiling people, at least long enough for him to make an escape. He also programmed us to defend him in any circumstance, a result of twice-daily indoctrinations we got during morning and evening Family Prayer. This was him in rare form, a man with a rapt audience expounding on everything from religion to politics to why fraternities were nothing more than collections of lazy, horny, spoiled potheads. Ralph himself apparently drank beer while a member of a college fraternity. It was one of his deepest regrets. He swore he didn't have consensual sex until marriage (though, tragically, he was sexually abused by a babysitter). He also swore later, as a married man, that God instructed him to go to strip clubs, ostensibly to preach to women and try to save their souls. Eye roll, please.

I remember feeling overwhelmingly special that, out of five

billion people (and yes, we're at eight billion today), I was born into a household with such an elevated and essential mission. So when the social workers came around, snooping into our personal business, it was no wonder we defended Ralph with a ferocity these nosy government bureaucrats must've rarely encountered. They were meddling with God's messenger, and gosh darn it if we would let them take us away from him. When they came to our house, I was so worried they'd steal me that I hid under the couch. But I couldn't outwit their wiles forever. They brought my siblings and me to their office.

I don't know which social workers' office it was, Boston proper or somewhere in Hudson township. I do remember the waiting room was filled with toys we didn't have at home. But I refused to let myself be tempted by the allures of the stuffed animals and the wire maze with wooden block beads, its gleaming primary colors taunting me, daring me to touch. I was too loyal to sell out for a cheap thrill.

Somehow, we convinced the authorities we were properly fed and that violence wasn't commonplace in our home—a temporary reprieve for Ralph. Such is the fate of many children and women trapped in cycles of poverty and abuse, too afraid or incapable of asking for rescue.

Years later, with my Harvard master's diploma in hand, I still can't verify that Ralph worked for anyone at the university, let alone for someone who admired his brilliance. Regardless, Ralph fled Boston, determined to escape the meddling ways of buttinskies—secular New Englanders and their pesky child-welfare interventions. We fled to the Wild West: Utah. I felt a mixture of relief and dread: happy we were free from prying child-welfare authorities, nervous about moving near the grandparents, aunts, and uncles my parents felt were wayward and spiritually lax. Would they corrupt us? We'd keep our armor up.

Chapter 2

Man on a Mission

Veritas numquam perit.

—*Lucius Annaeus Seneca*

"Veritas numquam perit." Truth never perishes. Actor Johnny Depp quoted[3] those famous words of Seneca, an ancient Roman Stoic philosopher and statesman, at a key moment for Depp. In one of the most-watched court cases in history, Depp had just triumphed over actress Amber Heard, his ex-wife. A jury ordered Heard to pay Depp $10 million in compensatory damages and $5 million in punitive damages for alleging he was a domestic abuser.

The court listened to secretly recorded audio of Heard where she admitted she hit Depp and also mocked him, saying even though she committed violence against him, no court would believe him because he was a man and she a 115-pound woman.[4] For his part, Depp—caught on tape and text also saying awful things about Heard—was ordered to pay Heard $2 million, a ratio of 7.5 to 1 in damages—overwhelmingly against Heard. The case riveted America—it blew other news stories out of the water in spring 2022 and set record viewership figures for Court TV, which streamed it live for weeks.

The verdict was clear: Heard was an aggressor against Depp, who testified he stayed with Heard in part because he was emotionally paralyzed due to his violent mother and felt retraumatized by Heard. *People* magazine reported: "'The verbal abuse, the psychological abuse, was almost worse than the beatings,' Depp said in his testimony about his late mother... Some of the violence [his mother] inflicted, Depp alleged, included throwing an 'ashtray,' 'a high-heeled shoe' or 'a telephone.' He said she would hit her children in their heads, and 'had the ability to be as cruel as anyone can be.'"[5]

Depp's sister Christi Dembrowski affirmed their mother's abuse, which also included physically abusing their father, who never retaliated in kind. Whatever you think of this case, and some Heard supporters saw a system rigged against her, it certainly became a pivotal cultural moment. It shattered the narrative that men and boys cannot be abused. It showed that women's abuse of men shatters men's lives. Yes, it's true, statistically speaking, that men are *far* more physically abusive than women, but our culture hasn't honestly grappled with how female abuse can devastate men and boys.

My father, Ralph Alvin Sheffield Jr., endured sexual assault as a toddler, and that abuse reverberated into his children's lives. I believe his childhood abuse contributed deeply to his subsequent mental illness—likely elements of antisocial personality disorder, borderline personality disorder, narcissistic personality disorder, and psychopathy—that convinced him he needed to fulfill what

God told him was "The Mission" to save America from destruction and become US president someday.

Born and raised in Salt Lake City, Ralph Jr. was the son of Ralph Alvin Sheffield Sr., a wealthy real estate developer. While his father was land rich, both my father and his siblings say their family lived spartanly—a product of the Great Depression, which taught folks they must hoard to survive.

My dad's sexual abuse came at the hands of a horrid female babysitter named Ada when he was around four years old. His sister, Charlotte, a couple years older, said Ada locked her in the closet while she committed the heinous act. Charlotte said she could hear my dad cry out for help.

Ada tore off toddler Ralph's clothing and fondled him, kissing his body until he fainted. She left bite marks all over his body, which his parents later discovered.

"If you ever tell anyone, I'll kill you," Ada threatened afterward.

That night, a terrified Ralph Jr. tried to convey to his parents what happened. But he was born in 1938 Utah, a time and place when childhood sexual assault wasn't openly discussed, and both Ralph and Charlotte said their parents essentially dismissed his concerns. They didn't call the police against this vile woman to hold her accountable for her crime. They didn't schedule counseling or therapy. And they didn't call church leaders to pray for healing over the deep spiritual trauma this woman caused, which Ralph said later drove him to the brink of suicide.

Instead, Ralph said his parents temporarily cheered him up by purchasing a large mechanical toy steam shovel. He vividly described its brightly painted orange metallic carriage, black wheels, and functional derrick lifting device that made him a hit with the neighborhood kids in the sandbox, since it could actually carry sand or marbles.

This temporary distraction and glossing over of trauma later haunted him. There were also societal reasons for him to suppress the pain—his generation came of age among strong male archetypes, when father knew best and mother played the sweet bystander. From what my aunts told me, the curmudgeonly father portrayed in *A Christmas Story* nearly captures Grandpa Sheffield, and this prototype rubbed off on my dad, Ralph Jr. I'm all for masculine men, but there's deep harm in suppressing and ignoring ravaging physical, emotional, and psychological damage instead of adequately processing and healing from PTSD.

Ralph said shortly after the assault, a strange man in a car stopped outside their house and offered him candy, and later a female teacher kept him after class and did the same. In both cases he rejected their candy offers and fled because of a warning from his father about a young boy who'd been abducted and murdered. A witness saw the little boy lured into a car by a man with candy, and authorities later discovered the boy's dead body. The boy's photo and the tragic story appeared in the newspaper, which Grandpa Sheffield showed his young son, urging my dad to never take candy from a stranger. It's no wonder Ralph turned inward and self-isolated in many respects—the adults around him were unreliable and dangerous.

The family lived in the heart of Salt Lake City, in a middle-class, hilly neighborhood, again reminiscent of the movie *A Christmas Story*—all the more fitting because the protagonist of that film was also a blond boy named Ralphie.

Salt Lake City is a beautiful town, glistening during the winter because of the valley snowstorms below the stunning Wasatch

Mountains. This hilly neighborhood is sadly where Ralph lost his closest middle school friend, a boy named Richard, who suddenly died in a sledding accident on the Eighth South hill.

"This caused me to turn more earnestly to God in prayer, and to my own mind in contemplation," Dad later wrote in his memoir draft. "Thus, these two—God, and my own conscience—gradually became my actual and most trusted friends thereafter." This inward yardstick for his own morality no doubt contributed to my dad's isolating megalomania later on. His own conscience eventually became indistinguishable from what he claimed was God's will.

When I was a kid, Ralph loved the 1960 musical *Oliver!*, a heartwarming tale of the adorable orphaned protagonist in the *Oliver Twist* novel by Charles Dickens. Oliver is an unloved and abused young orphan boy who is exploited by caretakers, victimized, and abducted by thieves. After Oliver is sold to a harsh undertaker, he tussles with the undertaker's apprentice who insults Oliver's dead mother. As punishment, Oliver's locked in a cellar filled with empty coffins. It's in this engulfing dark place that Oliver sings a hopeful song, called "Where is Love?" one my father fell transfixed by each time our family watched this classic film (we watched it countless times). Oliver is singing about the love of a lost mother: *"Where is love? / Does it fall from skies above?/ Is it underneath the willow tree / That I've been dreaming of?"*

Ralph often told us he felt orphaned while growing up, which seems strange on paper, given that he was from a two-parent home with an older sister who adored him, along with three younger siblings who all grew into well-adjusted adults. But when you're struggling with unresolved pain and trauma from childhood sexual abuse—which your parents didn't fully comprehend, as Ralph's didn't—perhaps that's a natural response. Ralph said his parents forced him for several years to live in a dungeon-like basement, and that made him feel isolated, dejected, and depressed, away from the warmth and love upstairs. With the arrival of his third sister when Ralph was ten, and with his dad's law offices headquartered at home, there wasn't room upstairs. Ralph said it wasn't a proper basement apartment—nonfamily renters occupied the basement under the front part of the house and his area was a walled off, former storage room, next to the furnace room. His room didn't have a connection to the upstairs house; he stumbled outside (even in freezing snow and rain), up the wooden stairs from what he called a "shanty-like entrance" to use the bathroom or get a drink of water inside the house. Dejected by bullies at school and church, Ralph slipped further into depression in the near-solitary confinement of his bunker.

It breaks my heart that my grandparents didn't do more to help my dad heal from the trauma of his childhood sexual assault. Ralph said his assault led him to suicidal fantasies as an adult. Sexually abused kids are three times more likely to attempt suicide than other adults, according to a 2019 University of Manchester academic literature survey of sixty-eight different studies by psychologists.[6] That survey also found suicide attempts are two and a half times more likely for people who experienced emotional abuse or neglect as a child, something that manifested in my siblings' and my lives, as many of us contemplated suicide as adults.

Cambridge University research published in *Psychological Medicine* shows children who experienced multiple abuses (called "complex abuse," or repetitive incidents of different types of abuses) are as much as five times more likely to attempt suicide.[7] They say "time heals all wounds," but sometimes it doesn't. It's no wonder my dad felt despondent even as time passed, since research shows that when abused children grow up, the risk of suicide attempts increases. This is why Jesus said in Matthew 18:6, "If any of you cause one of these little ones who believe in me to stumble, it would be better for you if a great millstone were fastened around your neck and you were drowned in the depth of the sea."

In an eternal sense, God heals all wounds, but during this broken mortal existence, the scourge of childhood abuse compounds and often passes through generations. It takes enormous effort to break these chains of abuse and prevent the cycle from continuing.

Over the years, Dad would often say, "Jesus loves me, but He doesn't like me." There's no Christian scriptural basis for this interpretation. God's love is pure, unconditional, and all-encompassing. Sure, God might not like things that we do—He abhors sin, after all. But God doesn't single out people as unlikable—I defy anyone to give solid theological basis for that.

I can't help but think Ralph's false belief that Jesus didn't like him may have stemmed, in part, from the self-loathing (including suicidal ideation, self-starvation, and obsession with perfectionism he'd never attain) wrought by this brutal childhood assault. Perhaps the attack is part of why he later turned to wrestling. My dad, at his peak, was 6'2" and barrel-chested, an intramural collegiate wrestling champion for the University of Utah, the state's flagship university today with more than 34,000 students.

Grandpa Sheffield wanted Ralph Jr. to follow in his footsteps and become an attorney, but Jr. chose the musician's route, to my grandfather's disappointment. Just like the artist Salvador Dalí tangled with his father, my dad felt undervalued and misunderstood by his own dad. Ralph Sr. had a stable, reliable, business-like mind and ruthless negotiating skills. Ralph Jr. was a sensitive, volcanic, creative muse.

Ralph Jr.'s world-class musical talent likely was in part due to his genetic hypersensitivity. This gave him uncanny precision when plucking out a pulsating vibrato and other nuances of a complex classical guitar melody like "Malagueña" by Ernesto Lecuona or "El Noi de la Mare" by Miguel Llobet. But this innate hypersensitivity, which enabled him to teach himself classical guitar and reach the upper echelons of this field, has a dark underbelly: intense over-reaction to any slight or perceived slight. Psychologist Elizabeth Scott explains this condition of emotional hypersensitivity well: "A highly sensitive person (HSP) is a neurodivergent individual who is thought to have an increased or deeper central nervous system sensitivity to physical, emotional, or social stimuli . . . being an HSP does not mean that you have a mental illness. High sensitivity is a personality trait that involves increased responsiveness to both positive and negative influences. Some refer to this as having sensory processing sensitivity, or SPS for short."[8]

Is my dad an HSP? I firmly believe so. Am I an HSP? Without a doubt. I'm off the charts when I take the assessment test known as Aron's Highly Sensitive Persons Scale (HSPS),[9] and I suspect my siblings are, too. Ralph probably inherited this from his mother, who was an impressive musician in her own right. Grandma Sheffield composed dozens of songs and musicals, including "Come to Utah," for the 1947 Utah statehood centennial celebration. Her 1955 play, "The Gentle Witch," won a prize in the LDS all-church play-writing contest and was published and produced throughout the multimillion-member Mormon Church. Her son later wrote a song called "Hear Us, Heavenly Father," published in the official January 1970 red-covered hymnal for Mormon children called *Sing with*

Me. This hymnal was used by millions of LDS children around the globe until an updated version came out in December 1989, and my dad's song didn't make the cut.

As Dr. Scott notes, our family's SPS is not a disease or disorder, but when managed incorrectly, it heavily influences the onset of toxic personality disorders.

In my dad's youth, Grandpa Sheffield was a far stricter parent than Grandma Sheffield. Grandpa was also more rigid and controlling with his first two children than the younger three, born after a gap of about seven years. My dad and Aunt Charlotte were fourteen and sixteen years older than their youngest sibling. By that point, Grandpa Sheffield mellowed considerably and wasn't as demanding of the younger kids.

Throughout his life, Ralph Jr. fought constant inner warfare between his free-spirited tendencies and his conservative roots, intensified by pressure to follow after his businessman and attorney father. Later, I'll get more into how I discovered the roots and extent of Ralph Jr.'s radicalization, but it likely accelerated during his college years. He says he engaged in all sorts of worldly and rebellious pursuits, including drinking alcohol in a fraternity, consuming pornography, wearing frivolous (but stylish) haircuts, and even smoking weed. He claims he was never forced to read the Book of Mormon, but as he reached the age when young Mormon men are expected to complete a two-year proselytizing mission, he rebelled. Initially, he rejected a mission, saying he wanted to focus on guitar playing. But before finalizing his choice to sit out the mission, he decided to finally sit down and read the thing. What happened next was family legend. As he read, Dad said he received a vision. It was a fountain of light springing out of the pages of the Book of Mormon.

Now, I certainly wasn't there, so I have no idea what happened. And I know people have spiritual experiences. I respect that. What I find deeply troubling though, in the words of Susan B. Anthony, is that "I distrust those people who know so well what God wants them to do, because I notice it always coincides with their own desires."[10] Jesus said by their fruits you know them, and the fruits of Ralph's eventual steps, I believe, indicated a false prophet.

He went on that mission, fulfilling an official duty of the LDS Church. He served in London, England, and he had a jolly time doing it—I think that's why he didn't want to stop preaching. He recounts stories of miraculously converting people, including one woman who, in those days, required a husband's signature to get baptized. Hubby refused to do it, until Ralph and his fellow missionaries fasted and prayed mightily. Ralph says her husband showed up in a complete trance and signed the permission slip for his wife! When hubby snapped out of it, he remembered signing it, but was furious that he'd done it with no idea what overcame him. But it was too late; the baptismal deed was done. Many years later, in 2011, Ralph emailed me about an additional story from his official LDS mission to Great Britain. His proselytizing team met an elderly widower who promised his dying wife he'd forever remain faithful to their particular religious sect, Christadelphianism. Christadelphians are a small group of about 50,000 members (mostly in the UK) who reject the Trinity and the immortality of the soul.[11] My dad wrote:

> As the years passed, however, his conscience began troubling him that he had not yet found the true Christian church. The more he prayed about it, the clearer the admonition became: He must continue searching. He sought out and held discussions with

representatives of various denominations—Catholic, Methodist, Baptist, Jehovah's Witnesses, and others . . . Then, it occurred to him that he'd not spoken with "the Mormons." He contacted our church. . . . As we met with the gentleman, we were impressed, not only by his intelligence and knowledge of the Scriptures, but by the earnestness of his character. After prayerfully reading the Book of Mormon, he said that God had made it absolutely clear that it was true, but then told us of his quandary over the promise he'd made to his wife, not to leave their church.

We respected him for the great love he had for his wife, and also because his word meant so much to him—which is probably the reason that the Holy Spirit could reach him so profoundly, preparing him for the fullness of the Gospel, even before he encountered it. We urged him to pray about his dilemma, since he obviously needed God's help to resolve it.

When we met with him again, he surprised us with a joyous request to be baptized! He said that in answer to his fervent prayer, he'd received a vision, wherein his wife had appeared to him, telling him that "where she now was, the promise he'd made to her was no longer binding upon him." He was soon baptized and given the gift of the Holy Ghost.

Ralph had other stories like that from his official LDS mission. But when time drew to a close for that mission, which is typically two years, it became clear he didn't want to stop. I've heard of other Mormon men who experience this, like military veterans who want to remain deployed.

But all good things must end, and Ralph was honorably sent home to Utah—except he decided God hadn't stopped the missionary call on his life. So he embarked on a lifelong quest to continue proselytizing. Reviewing his letters to his family during that time and subsequent years, his mother was deeply concerned about this radicalization. He became very preachy to her, and judgmental, calling her and my grandpa to repentance. He told them they weren't devout enough, and that they'd draw down God's wrath for not raising their kids strictly enough and personally failing to study Scripture adequately.

As a classical guitarist who reached the highest levels of that field, he served as professor of guitar for Brigham Young University. He also spent two years in Spain, focused in the Catalan region, the cradle of classical guitar. But he mixed his guitar expertise with homespun preaching, reportedly sleeping in Mormon churches without authorization, serving as an itinerant pastor of sorts. This happened without any sort of formal call or paperwork from the LDS Church, which is very organized and centralized. It's one of the best-run organizations in the world in terms of order, synchronicity, and hierarchy, and its vast assets would rank as a Fortune 500 corporation as a for-profit institution. It's like the military with its intense discipline among the ranks.

So this wild-eyed musician preacher running around without proper authority posed a huge red flag. Ralph kept showing his promise as a brilliant musician. He won a nationwide contest for young composers and was a hand-selected master-class student of classical guitar legend Andrés Segovia. But he gave up trying to revive his flourishing secular music career when God called him—so he claimed—to be a street preacher unofficially, self-coronated to fulfill "The Mission."

Eventually, everything collided and Ralph was laid off from his Brigham Young University job. His mother tried to intervene and get it back. By that point, it became sour grapes for Ralph, and he decided to go solo. He'd take his mission directly to the streets, playing his beautiful classical music with a small electronic amplifier plugged in to the base of his wooden guitar. The music attracted listeners, admirers he'd lure in while passing out his religious brochures. Eventually, over time, he forced his eight children to join him there on the streets, playing as a family ensemble.

Ralph brainwashed us to believe that he was a prophet sent by God to save America from destruction and was destined for White House residency. Our family had a special mission to assist him by passing out his homemade religious brochures, calling his collection of quotes and scriptures *Ponderables*, to pedestrians while playing classical and Broadway music as a ten-member family orchestra. He was a solo artist, plucking dazzling flamenco rhythms or strumming jazz melodies like Erroll Garner's "Misty," before we joined him on the streets.

He later spelled out this genesis in a biographical essay he wrote around the time he came in fourth out of five candidates during a Missouri US congressional primary run:

> *I wasn't a busker by necessity, but from devotion to America, and obedient to the directive I received in answer to prayer about earning my living altruistically. . . . As a young man, I petitioned God to help me earn my living in a way that would make the world a better place, and not to seek money for its own sake. God's answer gradually unfolded into a challenging directive: I must cease university teaching, and (with the support of my dear wife) begin a humbling, even dangerous public awareness project in the streets — performing music and proclaiming, with brochures and posters the godly ideals that built America.*

My first humble edition of Ponderables (our brochure of quo-
tations about America's founding ideals of faith, freedom, fam-
ily, personal responsibility, etc.) was published under the name,
"Daniel Strong," as a reminder to myself to be fearless in facing
the dangers I frequently encountered in the streets.

Later, in the ensuing years, Ralph would half-heartedly attempt a real estate career, even earning his real estate license. When I was in fourth grade, I felt immensely proud of my dad's Coldwell Banker real estate agent business cards featuring his photograph, his graying mustache (thicker and longer than his dad's) adding a distinguished air, alongside a real office phone number. But those cards were quickly obsolete, as he'd never last long in any professional office environment, clashing with his dominant ego and departing in a huff. Eventually, he settled into living off rental income from properties bought with his father's inheritance, but the properties were managed by outside firms, since he didn't have the temperament to consistently manage something so boring—he was a creative genius, after all. Unfortunately, his poor money management cost him two of those properties to foreclosure.

Somehow, during his undergraduate or master's studies at the University of Utah or shortly thereafter, Ralph says he met a fellow male artist in that college's art scene who became infatuated with my dad and started a years-long lustful stalking obsession. My dad is known to make up wild fables, so he's not a terribly reliable witness. I don't know exactly what happened with this alleged stalker, but I do remember that in residences with phones, we would sometimes get repeated phone calls from an unspeaking caller who would sit silently—though occasionally we could hear breathing.

Not heavy breathing, just normal, but a presence sitting there and refusing to hang up until we did.

Ralph said part of why we moved so much was to avoid this unwanted paramour, and we splurged to get caller ID, an extravagant luxury in a mid-1990s Utah trailer park. As far as I know, Ralph never told the police, and he handled this stalker situation in pretty much the worst possible way: having his female children answer the phone. That's right. My father had my sister and me pick up phone calls from his gay stalker because we were girls, and this predator only wanted to hear a male's voice. There we were, nine and ten years old, defending our dad from the sexual advances of another adult male. The whole thing was exceedingly strange and terrified me, though a tiny part of me felt proud and powerful that I could protect my own father. I'm glad things never escalated further, and as the years passed, the calls stopped, and eventually this individual passed away. I'd already left home, so I don't know the full details, but I think the calls may gradually have stopped sooner with the advent of cell phones—harder to trace than a landline.

Ralph said he nearly starved himself as a young man because he was addicted to pornography and needed to purge himself from lusting after women. He planned to fast for forty days, just like Jesus had done. I'm not sure how far he got into those forty days, but he says God told him to go up into the mountains above Salt Lake City—the lofty, magnificent Wasatch Range (think *The Sound of Music* Alps but in the desert) running vertically across northern Utah—on a hot summer day. Utah is a desert and can easily get above the nineties, temperature-wise, and Ralph says he was completely dehydrated and saw buzzards starting to circle above him in the air. Because he moved so slowly, they thought he was dead.

He was talking to God and made a promise to follow the Holy Ghost for the rest of his life. As soon as he made that oath, he heard the sound of a faucet pressurizing or dripping nearby. There was a spigot installed to tap into the mountain streams—a miracle. Ralph refreshed himself with the water, his fast completed, his commitment to God solidified forever. This was just as Jesus had done in the desert after fasting for forty days, immediately before Jesus' public ministry began. Dad's Messiah complex was far from subtle.

Dad reached the masses through a self-published poetry book and thousands of homemade pamphlets. The pamphlets were printed on legal-size paper and folded up six times width-wise, accordion-style, and he stamped the word "bookmark" above his photo (which later became a photo of the whole family) on top of page one, in hopes of nudging readers to keep them around for a useful purpose. They contained hundreds of quotes in tiny, squint-eyed print: verses from the Bible, the Book of Mormon and other LDS Scripture, and wisdom from the Founding Fathers. Inter-spersed among all these were quotes from the big man himself—Ralph Sheffield Jr.—alongside thoughts from Gandhi, Martin Luther King Jr., Voltaire, and Mother Teresa. In the *Ponderables* bookmark, Ralph referred to her as "Teresa of Calcutta" because he eschewed the blasphemous Catholic tradition of calling anyone but God, God's wife, and one's earthly parents Mother and Father. Yes, even Mother Teresa wasn't good enough for my dad.

While I'm all for holding up shining examples as prototypes, and most of the bookmark's quotes are profound, I eventually thought it curious that my father would equate himself with men and women who were instrumental in improving the human condition, while he himself abused his children and completely butchered their emotional development.

Here's how he explained The Mission, in his own words, in an essay he posted on his website as an excerpt from his autobiography:

> *Though I held a masters [sic] degree (and had started a doctor-ate) I decided, with the support and faith of my dear wife, to devote several years of patriotic service to my country in music and word, as others have done so in arms. Performing a variety of music (from Bach to the Beatles) in streets, subways, parks, etc., I distributed tens of thousands of these Bookmark brochures, lift-ing people's spirits, discussing the priceless heritage of freedom and faith Americans enjoy, and how they must cherish these blessings—meeting the responsibilities and destiny they imply— or lose them. Some of the people dropped money into my guitar case, which provided a humble living for my family.*[12]

Ralph's music attracted listeners, to whom he would offer his free brochure bookmarks. Unfortunately for him, many times they'd get tossed into a nearby trash can or the would-be reader walked a few paces, pivoted, and returned the paper to Dad's music stand. That didn't faze Dad—it was just further evidence of the depravity of American culture and why he must keep pressing on with The Mission. He had gumption, I'll give him that.

Before he fully embraced his dad's inheritance money, Ralph relied on the money people threw into his open guitar case. After staking out his street corner (which wasn't always easy—he was jailed for turf battles), he'd toss a few dollars inside the case to get the ball rolling. A good day would net maybe $200–300, a bad day

$50 or less. I now have a personal rule against giving money to any street musician who looks over age thirty. If it's a starving student, I might help, but I get the heebie-jeebies thinking about what an older busker could be harboring back home. My father seemed to enjoy fighting in the streets, brawling with homeless people, panhandlers, and other musicians. He also physically abused us, causing my brothers serious physical injury and deep psychological damage to us all.

Clearly, he'd never get monetarily wealthy off his street performing, but my dad saw himself as a rich man because he had his morals. Now I think there's much truth in this idea. There are insanely rich people who are miserable because, to quote rapper T.I. in the song "Live Your Life," they're "piss poor morally."[13] But things get dicey when someone's moral theories cause intense suffering for others, despite their supposed best intentions.

Ralph's narcissism wasn't totally unfounded, as he'd taught himself how to play guitar and became a protégé of virtuoso classical guitarist Andrés Segovia. Before his death in 1987, Segovia received ten honorary doctorates, a Grammy Lifetime Achievement Award, and was knighted by the king of Spain. Scientists even named a main-belt asteroid after him, 3822 Segovia. Talk about a rockstar!

In 2009, a professional classical guitarist named Ramon Amira, on the Delcamp classical guitar forum, posted an inquiry about my dad's musical compositions and Dad's collaboration with Segovia. Amira wrote:

About twenty five years ago I read a review somewhere of a new classical guitar suite entitled "Conquistador." The review was very favorable, and quoted Segovia as having praised it. I have never been able to find this suite anywhere, not on recordings, not live, not on sheet music, etc. Has anyone ever heard or even heard of this music?

No one had ever heard of it, but [another writer] *pointed me to a Google reference that named the composer. His name is Ralph Sheffield. I'm trying again. Has anyone ever heard this, or heard of it, or seen sheet music?*[14]

Classical guitarist David Norton, who knew my dad and was versant in the works of the legendary Segovia, served on the board of the Guitar Foundation of America (GFA). Shortly later that same day, Norton replied:

Ralph was a religious extremist, a far-far-far right wing fundamentalist who opted to live out his time waiting for The Apocalypse in a van parked in the west Utah desert. A brilliant performer by all accounts, but in all other aspects a nutcase, who never wrote out anything AFAIK. In 1973, he drove from Salt Lake City to Santa Barbara CA to attend the very first meeting of what became the GFA, and was so upset that Segovia himself wasn't in attendance that he drove back that same night and was never seen by GFA people again.

I've mentioned to a few local people (who knew him back-in-the-day) that Ralph Sheffield seems to be alive and well. The unanimous consensus is a complete lack of interest in reviving communication with him. "Let sleeping dogs lie" was one of the nicer sentiments expressed. "Doesn't DC have ENOUGH problems without him living there?" ran a close second.

Nearly three years later, another forum poster named Grudnick replied, posting a photo of my dad sitting on a foldable step stool, playing guitar with his religious bookmarks set up on his left side, his brass bowl accepting donations in front:

> *I noticed this thread, I met Mr Sheffield very briefly, I was not aware of him prior. I will not be dismissive of anyone expressing their belief, I thought it tragic that a talent of his stature is acting as a busker / protester. Protesting against what? A culture that protects our freedom to be eccentric, and waste our gifts.*

In 2007, the *Washington Post* highlighted a social experiment that brought me to tears. It represented what happened in real life to my dad. Joshua Bell is a world-class violinist. But he decided to go undercover and take his extraordinary gifts—along with his $3.5 million Stradivarius violin—and grace a DC Metro station with strains of Bach and other angelic sounds:

> *Joshua Bell has arrived as an internationally acclaimed virtuoso. Three days before he appeared at the Metro station, Bell had filled the house at Boston's stately Symphony Hall, where merely pretty good seats went for $100. Two weeks later, at the Music Center at Strathmore, in North Bethesda, he would play to a standing-room-only audience so respectful of his artistry that they stifled their coughs until the silence between movements. But on that Friday in January, Joshua Bell was just another mendicant, competing for the attention of busy people on their way to work. . . .*
>
> *In the three-quarters of an hour that Joshua Bell played, seven people stopped what they were doing to hang around and take in the performance, at least for a minute. Twenty-seven gave money, most of them on the run—for a total of $32 and change.*

That leaves the 1,070 people who hurried by, oblivious, many only three feet away, few even turning to look.[15]

Reading this article made me weep. It was my father, but it was his entire life, not just forty-three minutes of squandered genius. My father had numerous gifts and a wonderful legacy from his parents, both in raw talent and finances. He thought he was doing God's work, but he could have been light-years more effective if he spent more time asking God what He wanted instead of recklessly following his own ego, harming his children in the process.

Chapter 3

The Family Business

Grief is the price we pay for love.

—Queen Elizabeth II

There's a fascinating book called *The Psychopath Test: A Journey through the Madness Industry*, written by Welsh journalist Jon Ronson. It dissects the rubric used to determine if someone is a psychopath—which is handy when meting out prison sentences or determining mental health treatment. Ronson also meets an expert psychologist who believes many politicians, CEOs, and other type A people who are high-functioning in society hide their psychopathy.

My sister Julie and I were living as roommates in Manhattan when we discovered this book as adults in 2013. We pored over the book and became convinced our father met many of the criteria for psychopathy, which is what experts published in Cambridge University's *Development and Psychopathology* journal say is "characterized by persistent antisocial behavior, impaired empathy and remorse, and bold, disinhibited, and egotistical traits." Check, check, and check.

Ralph often liked to quote the Scottish politician, activist, and writer Andrew Fletcher, who was convinced of the power of culture to shape a country's destiny and said, "Let me make the songs of a nation, and I care not who makes its laws."[16] Dad loved this thought because it meant his musical credentials vindicated him against pressure from his father, a powerful state legislator and real estate developer who served as a majority whip in the Utah House. But Dad had broader ambitions for his life—and so apparently, did Satan.

In his own words, an excerpt of a letter from Dad to my siblings and me:

Oct 14, 2008

Some years ago, I received a prompting from the Lord, the reason for which, I didn't fully grasp at the time. It was thus: "Satan, the adversary of all souls, has realigned his forces and re-assigned himself, personally, to you and your family, among certain others." I didn't think much about it then, because I was of the common naive notion that "devils are devils—kind of like bowling pins, all pretty much the same. (So what's the big deal?)" But what has resulted has been devastating to sacred family relationships, as the sinister interference from relatives (some of whose wickedness has been almost beyond belief) has brought backbiting, envying, conspiracy, betrayal, absconding, apostasy, immorality, lying, embezzlement, bullying, and even violence. Thus, there was something implied, more grave than I realized, in

that warning from God—that Satan's hosts (unembodied spirits)
are as diverse in their abilities to deceive, corrupt, and destroy
as are the varied talents and abilities of humankind to achieve,
create, and serve—from the drunkard loafing in the lounge to
the scientist creating in the laboratory. Yes, we have seen the dire
results of this "re-assignment of personnel" by the Evil One. But
we must now do everything in our power to repair those wicked
harms to our family, or we, and not just some nefarious relatives
will answer to the Eternal Judge.

I'm certainly no expert in the wiles and methodology of Satan, nor do I desire to be. But there seems something narcissistically grandiose about claiming you're such a threat to the Underworld that lesser demons can't handle you. You require the personal attention of the most elite demon, Satan himself.

Dad's obsession with following the Holy Ghost led him to coerce our family to swear a solemn oath before God that we'd follow the Holy Ghost with exactness for the rest of our lives "or be destroyed." I was twelve when I swore allegiance to a God who demanded strict adherence to His messenger, the Holy Ghost. Who could imagine higher stakes? When I later left home at age eighteen, my father would remind me of my covenant, saying I was in violation and thus unworthy to be in my family's presence.

We took the oath during a family visit on a windy spring day in 1995 to Adam-ondi-Ahman, the site where Mormons believe Adam and Eve went after their expulsion from the Garden of Eden. LDS founder Joseph Smith revealed the Bible's Garden of Eden was at modern-day Independence, Missouri, with Adam-ondi-Ahman some eighty miles north. Smith said Adam and Eve walked the earth not in the Middle East or southern Mesopotamia, as many biblical scholars believe, but in Jackson County, Missouri, near Kansas City, the western half of the Show-Me state. Sadly, today it's an area with heavy meth and opioid trafficking.

Mormons also believe Adam-ondi-Ahman in Missouri is where Jesus will return first, before heading to Jerusalem. That's why my parents live in Jackson County today, along with various other premillennialist Mormon offshoot groups and mainstream devout LDS people. That includes a sizable cohort of Samoans who converted to Mormonism in the 1960s and 1970s and moved to Jackson County.[17] During parts of middle school, I learned to greet people with "Talofa!" and enjoyed Samoan-style roasted whole pigs with pineapple and other luau fruit in the church gym.

That day at Adam-ondi-Ahman, I wore a white baseball cap, a dark pink pullover hoodie, and blue jeans as we scampered through the Midwest grasslands, which include some three thousand acres of undeveloped farmlands owned by the LDS Church. Ralph solemnly gathered us around and swore this exact spot was where Adam, the first man in the Bible, gathered his children, three years before his death, to bestow his last blessing. Waves of joy, awe, and slight fear rushed over me as we trod that windswept prairie grass.

In that spot all ten of us swore an oath to God that we would Follow the Spirit (FTS) and lead perfect lives or be destroyed. The oath made me uneasy, but I reasoned that even though Jesus was the only perfect person in the world, if I did my best to FTS, He would understand.

Little did I know, this type of rigid, black-or-white perfectionism would haunt me for decades as I struggled to understand the world is broken and God would never expect perfection from any mortal being. My false perfectionism also led me to verbally abuse others, blind to the hurt I was causing because of my self-righteousness.

Murderous gangster Al Capone was an expert at covering his tracks. On October 17, 1931, Al Capone was found guilty of tax evasion. As *Forbes* writes, "The gangster who had reportedly boasted, 'They can't collect legal taxes from illegal money' was sentenced to 11 years in prison for failing to file tax returns." Capone was a wealthy mobster, who grew his fortune above $100 million, or $1.5 billion in today's dollars. On May 16, 1927, the US Supreme Court ruled in *US v. Sullivan* that "[g]ains from illicit traffic in liquor are subject to the income tax would be taxable."[18] This ruling gave the feds enough ammo to lock Scarface up.

My flighty dad was far from a bootlegging mobster, and there was no Saint Valentine's Day Massacre body count like Capone committed. But like Capone, for many years, my dad didn't pay his taxes. And he was good at covering his trail—he'd tangle with the local Mormon authority but then bob and weave away.

Ralph, Mom, and my brother Benjamin were all excommunicated in 2013. They were thrown out because Ralph insisted that a regional LDS authority confessed to my dad that he was addicted to pornography.

"No I'm not, and if you don't take that back, I'm kicking you out," the authority basically responded. My dad claims the guy confessed after my dad confronted him with a "revelation" about this man's illicit hobby. To me, it seemed another case of Ralph making up "revelations," like the one where he falsely claimed I'd had an abortion while I was studying abroad in London during college. I was a virgin. And there's no such thing as an Immaculate Abortion. If there was any doubt about his prophetic calling, I knew then he was a liar. Dad also falsely claimed my uncle installed a hidden camera to spy on my sister Sophie while she undressed in her room.

Mom backed up Ralph's pornography allegation. Benjamin did, too. This wasn't their first pornography accusation rodeo. Ralph accused multiple other LDS stake presidents, bishops, or their counselors of pornography addiction. It was one of Ralph's go-to charges. And apparently in one instance, an authority confessed that he actually *was* a pornography addict! So he stepped down from the role. That emboldened Ralph to continue his claims.

But this time, the pornography accusation didn't stick. Ralph, Mom, and Benjamin were removed from LDS Church membership through the standardized process of a vote by a disciplinary council.

Ralph was thrown out at age seventy-five, well after all eight of his kids reached adulthood. I think my dad should've been excommunicated far earlier for child abuse and doctrinal heresy, but like gangster Capone, he was nabbed for a much less serious charge. I wish the LDS Church did far more to protect us from abuse, but we live in a broken world. Through God's healing, I've forgiven the LDS Church. I still have many friends and family who are LDS, so I know there are wonderful people in that faith.

The Lafferty family, the murderous polygamist offshoot Mormons profiled in the book and TV miniseries *Under the Banner of Heaven*, didn't pay taxes either. For them, God's law was higher than man's law. Ralph felt the same. We saw this similar sense of religious entitlement from suicide cult Heaven's Gate founder Marshall Applewhite (a fellow musician like my dad), who was arrested in Texas for failing to return a Missouri rental car. Applewhite was extradited to St. Louis and jailed for six months, all the while claiming God authorized him to keep the car.[19]

Applewhite and his cult cofounder Bonnie Nettles, like my dad, couldn't stay still. Early in their cult planning, the *New York Times* reports they "hit the road, this time driving more than 8,000 miles in one summer month: a rudderless zigzag between California, Utah, Montana, and Idaho. They went up to Canada and down to New York. Their money ran out. They slept in a tent. They often ate only rolls and butter. All the while, a close review of their letters shows, they talked and talked about their mission, almost exclusively to each other—God's truth undergoing rewrites, with this earthshaking hypothesis and that biblical proof, ideas exploding in them like percussion bombs."[20]

One of my dad's favorite Scriptures justifying his maverick ministry is from the Old Testament in the book of Numbers, chapter 11, verse 29. It's when the Children of Israel are wandering in the desert after their exodus from Egypt and informants tell their leader, Moses, that two random, regular guys from the desert encampment, Eldad and Medad, were prophesying outside of the official priesthood channels. Ralph loved Moses' response, telling everyone to chill out: "Are you jealous for my sake?" Moses asks. "Would that all the LORD's people were prophets and that the LORD would put his spirit on them!"

While I admire Ralph's idealism and his sincere desire to repair what he saw as creeping moral decay, his tactics and approach were appalling. To accomplish his amorphous goal, he sacrificed the health and stability of his family by keeping us in a constant state of poverty and transience. As we got older, Ralph blew inheritance money from his father on expensive ad placements in national newspapers. We're talking upward of sixty thousand dollars a pop to pay *USA Today* or the *Washington Post* to run his treatises—clearly marked as ads, not real journalism.

In an age when dwindling ad revenues threatened the viability of a shrinking print news market, publishers were happy to snap up dough from a man wrapped in delusions of grandeur. It's a pity; newspapers should require that people submitting these types of ads have enough personal wealth to ensure their eight children are not eating broth made from municipal park grass and living without running water in a shed in rural Missouri. Eventually, some outlets stopped accepting Ralph's ads because his messages became too extreme. Ironically, years later, *I would get paid* by these same outlets printing my journalistic writing. While our family starved, my father wasted his birthright trying to purchase influence, and tragically, there's not much to show for it. He claims otherwise.

When he penned a paid ad for the *Washington Post* in the late 1990s urging the continuation of Democrat Bill Clinton's impeachment trial, he claimed shortly after that Republican Newt Gingrich appeared boosted and invigorated in his zeal to prosecute Clinton, resulting in Clinton's impeachment two days after Ralph's essay ran. Of course, there's no evidence Newt read the paid-advertising musings of a self-made Utah soothsayer. Newt never made any mention of the ad or my father.

Ralph also claims his writing inspired Ronald Reagan to designate Martin Luther King Jr. Day, because a man who Ralph swore was a Secret Service officer picked up Ralph's bookmark brochure highlighting the reverend's work. He says the man was dressed in the standard dark suit costume with an official-looking earpiece and got his hands on the bookmark while Ralph played guitar at Lafayette Square across the street from the White House. I have yet to hear any historian give credence to this generous self-assessment from Ralph.

Ralph's daily indoctrination sessions—twice a day, at morning and night—could stretch on for hours at a time. He called them "family prayer" sessions, but the actual praying part usually lasted a few minutes. The rest of the time meant Ralph recounting stories from his British mission or his US street mission. Family prayer in the evenings often started out with one of us kids reciting a joke, an inspirational quote, and a word of the day—a job to which we were assigned in turns. This is the part I still agree with today—the part where we looked at the outside world with inquisitiveness and humor. Dad collected voluminous joke books from thrift stores (filled with eye-rolling "dad jokes" and puns), along with LDS quote books and other resources for us to use.

During college, Ralph took a course in Latin, which he endlessly referred to when teaching his kids the root words behind the building blocks of the English language. I found this occasionally fascinating, though sometimes boring. Looking back now, I love this about my dad—his intellectual curiosity and love of words.

That normal, positive activity was overshadowed—through a daunting ratio—by toxic, self-righteous sermons, punctured by his screams at anyone dozing off.

"Wake up, Carrie!" he'd snarl, his nostrils flaring above his thick, graying, '70s-style mustache. "You need to save your soul. Your body's weakness is controlling your mind. This is why you dress like a slut. You are a slave to your carnal flesh."

Besides yelling, he might also try to physically intimidate me by moving his face within inches of mine. Rattled, I'd sit up.

Maybe he'd start by reading a passage of Mormon Scripture, let's say from the Doctrine and Covenants, section 95, verses 5–6 and 10:

But behold, verily I say unto you, that there are many who have
been ordained among you, whom I have called but few of them
are chosen. They who are not chosen have sinned a very griev-
ous sin, in that they are walking in darkness at noon-day....
my servants sinned a very grievous sin; and contentions arose
in the school of the prophets; which was very grievous unto me,
saith your Lord; therefore I sent them forth to be chastened.

"The Lord prompted me to open my book to this passage," he'd start. "I'm prompted that each of us have sinned grievously against the Lord and The Mission. I want each of us to confess and repent *now*. Otherwise, The Mission will be taken from us."

This meant all ten of us must identify something wrong we'd done and contritely beg forgiveness. I'd rack my brain about what to confess in front of nine other people that was sufficiently sinful but not frightfully embarrassing enough for my siblings to mock me about.

Ralph's "sin" was usually that he hadn't been controlling enough of his kids. "Mother, what are we raising?" he'd ask Mom in disgust while shaking his head and putting his face in his hands after I had supposedly committed some sin—like wearing my black-and-white plaid jumper slightly above the knee.

During family prayer, Ralph made fire-and-brimstone pronouncements about what would happen if any of us kids left home to pursue our own dreams.

"Heavenly Father chose every member of this family and requires each of us to fulfill this Mission *with all our might*," he'd forcefully preach, his brow furrowed over his piercing blue eyes, ever the charismatic politician's son. "If not, God will smite each of us down for running away from our assignment."

Family prayer also meant Ralph and Mom endlessly repeated how we must Follow the Spirit (FTS) rather than the world or even the human-run LDS Church. They'd often say mainstream Mormonism was "Churchianity" rather than "Christianity." FTS was our secret family code, something above and beyond regular Mormonism, which my parents considered too handbook-driven and sanitized. The LDS Church did not FTS anymore.

Occasional fasting (abstaining from food to cleanse yourself) is embraced in both secular and spiritual settings. The LDS Church asked members to fast once a month; that was child's play for my dad, who made us fast once a week. Fasting more frequently helped us FTS better.

"Did you FTS today?" they'd ask.

"Were you FTSing when you made that choice?"

"Why didn't you FTS when you put on that slutty dress?"

"You didn't FTS when you ate that extra cookie."

Wite-Out is supposed to blot out typos in printed or written words. But in the '90s, it was the tool of choice for schoolkids to graffiti on our Trapper Keeper binders. I was proud of my dark purple Trapper Keeper, something I owned new, rather than from a secondhand thrift store.

The acronym FTS was *so* engrained in us that I felt a rush of spiritual euphoria when, in seventh-grade biology class, my classmate—a shorter guy with brown eyes and a long, curly brown mullet who wore Mario Bros. T-shirts and pulled his white gym socks up too high—showed up with his Mead Five Star Trapper Keeper with the letters "F.T.S." carefully scrawled across the width of the Keeper in large, Wite-Out lettering.

Was this my future husband? I started to quiver with excitement at finally meeting someone who understood my entire foundational worldview! This classmate was a sleeper soulmate; I'd had no idea he was so spiritually sophisticated. I barely mustered up the courage to stammer something like:

"F.T.S.—that's cool," throat seizing up, palms sweating.

"Thanks," he said. "It means Fuck This Shit."

My jaw internally dropped to the floor. Clearly, this was not my Romeo after all.

Family prayer was also when Ralph would needle out of us what sort of dreams we'd had the night before. He wanted to interpret them. Mom the secretary dutifully listened and recorded Ralph's Freudianisms in a spiral-bound notebook we called "the Dream Book." At first, I thought this novelty was cool, our very own in-house Zoltar. But it got old pretty quickly because, invariably, our dreams were metaphorical messages from God telling us that while Ralph was holy and righteous, we kids were helplessly wicked, and that our family had a vital mission to save America from destruction by helping our father assume the US presidency. The dreams also confirmed how evil not only his own kids were, but also my parents' families of origin.

One epic dream came from my younger sister, who dreamed about Grandma Sheffield's third husband, Ernie, the bane of my father's existence. Ralph thought his mother was disloyal to her dead first husband, Ralph Sr., the father of her kids. Ralph said Ernie beguiled his mother, who married Ernie (and her second husband, Wayne) against God's will.

"My mother prayed to ask Heavenly Father about these marriages, but instead of listening, she just did what she wanted," he'd often say.

He thought his mom should live in lonely isolation (associated with premature death) rather than happily remarrying companions, as she did twice after outliving two of three husbands. Dad also claimed that Ernie illegally influenced Grandma Sheffield to write her son, my dad, out of a portion of her will.

That morning, Ernie, then in his late eighties or early nineties, made a cameo in my sister's nightmare.

"Ernie had his pants down," my sister said while describing the dream. I don't remember anything else except this shocking image.

Ralph seized on this.

"Ernie is evil," he cried. "He's exposing himself as the satanic man he is. He's pulling his pants down in the dream in front of you because he has no respect for decency or our family. God is revealing to us how perverted he is."

Ralph's hours-long family prayer rants about his kids' evilness and failures no doubt contributed to my self-destructive feelings, paralysis, rigid perfectionism, and suicidal ideation later in life. I was set up for failure, and fail I did, big time.

Chapter 4

Mormon Mind Meld

We'll find the place which God for us prepared
Far away in the West
Where none shall come to hurt or make afraid
There the Saints will be blessed
　　　　　　—William Clayton, "Come, Come, Ye Saints"

Our motorhome crossed thousands of miles on Dwight D. Eisenhower's freeways as we drove across America's heartland during family orchestra tours. I especially loved I-70, its gray ribbons cutting through green cornfields and yellow wheat. I loved the warm summer nights at freeway rest stops, where tall prairie grass housed the glow of winking fireflies at dusk. Life was simple, and I felt proud to live in this beautiful, free country.

We made some enchanting stops in our motorhomes—full credit to my dad—setting up a lifelong love affair with America's people and scenery. We drank in the inspiring, luminous granite sculptures of Mount Rushmore, which we unknowingly stumbled upon during Sturgis—the world's largest motorcycle rally. At least half a million bikers from around the world happened to gather during our jaunt to South Dakota—we were fascinated by the leather chaps, ponytails, and Harley-Davidsons. Another time, we tasted spicy jambalaya while visiting the French Quarter and other parts of New Orleans—including a bayou swamp tour led by a family whose daughter could put marshmallows on an alligator's head! We also traipsed the acreage around the cozy stone Vermont home where poet Robert Frost wrote "Stopping by Woods on a Snowy Evening."

I loved tracking our path in our jumbo-size Rand McNally paperback atlases of the United States. No Google Maps, no Map-Quest, no Garmin or TomTom GPS. I prided myself in my navigational skills, telling my dad how far it was until the next rest area or gas station. As we approached a state line—say leaving Kansas and entering Colorado on I-70—I loved playing the game of who entered the new state first, pushing my fingertips to the very edge against the windshield or trying to roll down the passenger's window and stretch beyond that. I kept eagle eyes to warn Ralph of cops and notify him of speed limits.

Sleeping ten people in a motorhome is a feat of physics. We accomplished this by squeezing the three girls into the overhang above the driver's cockpit. Mom and Ralph slept on the fold-out couch bed. The four older boys stacked two and two in double bunks on either side of the window, while the youngest, John, nested on a daybed cushion against the back window.

We sisters fought over bedding territory, though we tried to keep it fair through a rotating schedule. As we grew taller, all three bed slots involved sleeping with our heads partially inside the sideways-tilted plastic milk crates holding our secondhand and Walmart-bought clothing.

Each slot had its seasonal downfalls, though the prime spot edged closest to the main living area. This gave the best mobility for a bathroom trip, leg stretching, and proximity to space heaters providing warmth during the cold months. The privacy curtain blocked out most of the light, though usually a sliver peeked through the Velcro fastenings. The biggest problem was noise; faucet taps if we were hooked up to water, conversations, and various nesting sounds.

The middle spot provided cozy body heat warmth on either side during winters, but like a middle plane seat, this was the overall worst spot, because you were hemmed in, especially during suffocating summer months. The slot closest to the horizontal overhang window stretching the width of the cockpit meant spying powers on the outside world—like a crow's nest on a pirate ship. It meant a cool windowpane to rest your forehead on during sticky summers or fog up with your breath and play tic-tac-toe, write your name, or draw hearts. But the windowpane's glass proved unbearably chilly during wintertime, and sometimes we'd stuff a sleeping bag, blanket, or clothing as a buffer. You were also stuck crawling over two sleepy, sharp-elbowed girls en route to the john.

Life in a motorhome had its charms, but also pitfalls. A big one: toilets. One small toilet for ten people, an inhospitable arrangement when sewer hookups froze or the septic tank brimmed to capacity with urine and feces and needed an RV site dumping. It was also tough when my oldest schizophrenic brother locked himself inside the tiny—roughly two-by-four feet—bathroom for hours, meticulously wiping every body crevice and doing God knows what else. The stench of fresh sewage was commonplace enough that my nostrils quickly grew accustomed. Ralph also tried to mitigate the putrid scent with bright blue–colored chemical treatments, both liquid and powder—the kind you'd see in an outhouse. We basically lived adjacent to a permanent outhouse for untold gallons of ten people's waste.

If a bathroom emergency became too great, this could mean an impromptu stop at a state-run rest stop, wild woodsy or field area (bring your own TP), or gas station. Flying Js were hands down our favorites—yes, they catered to the eighteen-wheel semitruck professional drivers, but we "four-wheelers" felt welcome, too. These truck stops were wonderlands of kitschy figurines, candy, Slurpees, and forbidden coffee (Mormonism bans coffee and tea). I felt palpable excitement around these truckers, modern-day cowboys swapping salty tales of the road as they moved billions of dollars in consumer goods inventory, keeping our economy humming.

Occasionally, Ralph said the Holy Ghost wanted him to hightail it somewhere at breakneck speed, which could mean a bathroom break didn't fit the schedule. He kept a bottle—usually an empty plastic sixteen-ounce Ocean Spray or generic brand grapefruit juice bottle (grapefruit is his favorite fruit by far) or an empty jumbo glass pickle jar—near the driver's seat for such urinal emergencies. He'd tell his daughters to look away if he needed to do some business and someone would help pull the privacy curtains on either side across the width of the motorhome cockpit. Occasionally if my brothers were allowed to drive, they'd relieve themselves this way, too.

One time, Ralph wet his whistle on what he thought was grapefruit juice. His grapefruit juice came in both pink and yellowish coloring. You guessed it: That yellow "grapefruit juice" in his cockpit bottle came from a human bladder. A gush of droplets spewed from his mouth as he spit the yellow liquid out the window, some sprinkling on the steering wheel.

"Who did this?" he thundered. But he couldn't prove it wasn't his own self-sabotage.

Life on the freeway posed safety risks to our bevy of young children, especially the girls, who could get kidnapped and trafficked in a heartbeat before anyone even realized a kid was missing. Every pit stop meant constant vigilance and a slight knot in my stomach. We had no illusions about the depravity of people who didn't follow the Holy Ghost.

Since COVID hit hard in 2020, living in an RV somehow found a new cachet in American culture. This is one trend I personally can't fathom. We're a First World country. There's no need to subject yourself to Third World travails. Though in fairness, motorhome life is far more glamorous without nine prying roommates, including a toxic Nostradamus prophesying doom and gloom over you and the entire world.

I don't recount these stories to complain or knock anyone struggling with homelessness or poverty. Some of the happiest, most fulfilled, and generous people are the poorest. We've all heard stories of families living in abject poverty living lives of deep fulfillment because they are wealthy in unconditional love. But our family suffered immense physical instability combined with the spiritual and physical abuse that I believe led to debilitating mental illness for myself and my siblings.

Growing up, our Mormon faith was our primary identity, but too often, Ralph's interpretation of this faith—far from mainstream—kept us isolated, and the motorhome enabled his destructive narcissism by yanking us away from any helpers. The motorhome was Ralph's escape hatch from accountability for his abuse.

And in 1988, we needed an escape hatch. We had six kids at the time (one more came later that year, born at home and sleeping in a cardboard box for her crib; the other in 1989)—a small army for any parent. We made the cross-country trek to Utah, fleeing the East Coast child-custody buttinskies trying to take us away. From when I was about five through age eleven, our family lived mainly in Utah (except for a motorhome sojourn at a campground in 1990 in Liberty, Missouri—an important town in Mormon history). These years were important in solidifying my Mormon identity. Despite our transient lifestyle, I loved Utah—its trailer parks, RV campgrounds, and houses. I loved being surrounded by people who thought like I did. They understood my fear of burning if I touched the holy water in the Catholic church in downtown Salt Lake City, which we visited during a kindergarten field trip. They under-stood the moral dilemma of whether I should attend the sleepover of the lone Catholic in our fourth-grade class. They too might feel apprehensive about attending a rummage sale at a rare local non-denominational Christian church in Sandy, Utah (incidentally, the hometown of the polygamous family in the HBO series *Big Love*) for fear of contributing money toward a questionable cause. But these are feelings children in any dominant religious group experience against any other religious minority.

I loved Utah's clean mountain air, wide blue skies, fiery sunsets, and stunning views along the snowcapped Wasatch Front of the Rocky Mountains. While we were too poor to afford skiing (and when my elementary class visited one of the local resorts on a field trip, my mother refused to sign the school waiver to let me take a lesson, afraid the ski lift cable car would collapse), as an adult I later loved the exhilarating feeling of fresh powder on my face as I zoomed down the same slopes that Olympians competed on during the 2002 Winter Games.

I loved Utah's big families, with pets and trampolines (we didn't have our own for financial and safety reasons) and the arcade down the street. I loved that I could ride my secondhand bike in the neighborhood without fear of abduction—though my brothers enjoyed a wider radius than me since I was a girl—to see our neighbor's pet goats and pick grapes from their grapevine. I loved the Mormon congregations we lived in, known as "wards," organized geographically. In our wards, the boys went on overnight scout camp trips and ladies of the Relief Society organized casserole brigades for families with new babies. One neighbor at church in our Sandy ward joked about an episode with her young child, who'd misunderstood the words of the famous Mormon hymn "Come, Come Ye Saints," a motivational song about suffering and hope along the Mormon trail westward to Utah. Instead of understanding the first line, "Come, come, ye saints, no toil nor labor fear," he thought the song was talking about finding relief on the john: "Come, come, ye saints, no toilet paper here," he sang one day. This story had our congregational family in stitches!

It was an admittedly funny slipup, one that we as Mormons alone could truly relish. The song was written by William Clayton, a former clerk for Mormon founder Joseph Smith. It became the unofficial anthem of the Mormon pioneers who braved the Midwest plains to settle and create a new life, free from religious persecution among desert lands. They were driven westward from settlements in New York, Ohio, Illinois, Missouri, and Nebraska. People are shocked to learn that Missouri legalized killing Mormons, by executive order of the governor, from 1838 until 1976, under Missouri Executive Order 44, commonly known as the "Mormon Extermination Order." The Extermination Order came after voter suppression by non-Mormons terrified of the growing power of Mormons at the ballot box. My ancestors were betrayed by governments claiming to offer the pursuit of happiness for all, regardless of religious persuasion. But they took the persecution as a badge of honor, similar to the early Christians in the Bible's New Testament.

Misery loves company, and so the Mormon suffering bound its followers even more tightly together. The flame of spiritual unity warmed their souls as they trudged through harsh trails and bitter winters to virgin desert soil out West. Utah, at that time, was not even part of the United States—my people were expelled from America! They sang "Come, Come, Ye Saints" around campfires along the trail to Utah and in pioneer settlements spread throughout Idaho, Nevada, and California.

Today, the song is a favorite for people celebrating pioneer heritage, a tradition so revered that countless Mormons around the world don felt hats, suspenders, bonnets, and prairie dresses; ride in covered wagons; and pull makeshift handcarts to commemorate those religious refugees. My family took part in these festivities whenever we could (or the Holy Ghost allowed).

The date of July 24, 1847, when Brigham Young led the Mormon pioneers to Salt Lake Valley, is a state holiday commemorated by fireworks, parades, and rodeos. There's even a Days of '47 beauty pageant open only to contestants who can prove their ancestors migrated to the region during those early Mormon days. My aunt won that pageant in 1955, two years before she was crowned Miss Utah USA and later Miss USA. She traveled the world with her crown, proud of her Mormon heritage and making certain to fill her goblets with milk so everyone knew she did not drink alcohol, which Mormonism bans. I felt extremely proud of Aunt Charlotte, who left us too early in 2016 at age seventy-nine from Legionnaires' disease. She was the loving mother of eight grown children and served for ten years as a coloratura soprano in the famed Tabernacle Choir.

For our family, Utah Church leaders in our local congregation organized a twelve days of Christmas surprise, leaving presents and decorations on our family's doorstep during the twelve nights leading up to Christmas. It meant we had a real Christmas, with toys and treats galore. We were that poor family that your family might select as your pet project. I saw no shame in this, just pure gratitude. As an adult now, I try to pay it forward through sponsoring secret Santas and angel trees in my local community.

To my delight, and later agony, one year our secret Santas gave me a Barbie, which my mother made me return to Fred Meyer and exchange for a pink plastic comb and brush set.

It's ironic that many nonreligious feminists take issue with the original Barbie because they say her body dimensions were fantastically curvaceous and created unrealistic body images for girls. They said if she had been a real person her spine would warp or snap due to the impossible ratio of boobs, waist, and hips.

These feminists, who abhor the patriarchal structure of Mormonism, came to the same conclusion as my mother: no Barbies allowed. But my mother held modesty concerns: Barbie dresses like a two-dollar hooker. Her miniskirts and tank tops would corrupt me, lead me to become an exhibitionist burlesque dancer. Barbie was verboten in our house.

"Carrie, don't you want to be modest?" Mom would ask if I complained. "That doll dresses like a slut. Heavenly Father wants you to be worthy to be married in the temple. If you dress like that, no good man will want to marry you. Only bad men like girls who dress like that."

On the few occasions I could play at a friend's house, I felt secretly indulgent holding the plastic whores, which my naive friend toted around in innocent bliss. But I knew better.

———

Following the Mormon custom of writing your family history for future generations, I've fairly consistently kept a journal since age eight, the traditional age of Mormon baptism. It's a marker known as the "age of accountability," when the LDS Church teaches that mortals can first knowingly choose right from wrong—and be tempted by Satan.

Journaling's a cultural practice in Mormonism that I heartily endorse. It's therapeutic, enlightening, and helps organize chaotic, racing thoughts. I highly recommend journaling to everyone. It's never too early, and it's never too late to start.

Leading up to my eighth birthday, I pondered what sort of evil deeds I would commit once Satan could beguile me. I felt afraid I'd murder someone just because I was legally susceptible to Old Scratch under God's law. A couple of weeks after I blew out the candles, I realized that, somehow, I managed to avoid slitting someone's throat.

To celebrate, I joined maybe a couple of dozen other eight-year-olds dressed in all-white, Church-issued, reusable jumpsuits (or white dresses for girls whose parents were rich enough to buy their own—mine weren't) at a modest tan-brick chapel in Sandy, a suburb just outside Salt Lake City. It was in the Hillcrest First Ward (congregation) in the Hillcrest Stake (Mormons use the word "stake" as in the "stakes of Zion," i.e., a biblical throwback to describing God's people as being in a big tent with stakes in the wilderness). In areas outside Mormon-dominated regions, a baptism is an individual affair, so the ceremony is curated for the child or the adult convert, who often picks their own music and speakers. But in the heart of Mormon country at that time, the masses necessitated assembly-line-style baptisms. I took part in a group devotional and hymns followed by an individual dunking by Ralph.

I recently found a transcript of my dad's confirmation blessing, which he immediately gave me after the baptism. Confirmation is when Mormons believe the Holy Ghost is conferred upon you because you've taken the step of baptism. My mom saved the blessing transcription in a box of files she kept—it's a handy system she created, a file for each school year for each child. I plan to do that for my kids someday, God willing. We'd changed out of the white jumpsuits into regular church clothes, but my hair was still wet from the immersion. The priesthood-holding men in my family (including my maternal grandfather, who we later found out solicited gay prostitutes), along with the bishop and his two counselors (a trifecta called the "bishopric" in Mormonism), pressed their hands on my head to confer the Holy Ghost.

The blessing's actually quite kind and loving. I don't think it's a coincidence that those three years of my life attending the same school—East Sandy Elementary during kindergarten, second, and third grades—was the most stable time of my entire childhood. It was when I felt the most secure. Here's what my dad said:

Carrie, you are loved by your family and especially by God more than you can realize. Through your baptism, you are welcomed into the Kingdom of God and given the sacred and mighty Gift of the Holy Spirit, which will protect, and enlighten, and guide you even unto eternal life. Obtaining eternal life is not easy but nothing else a human being can achieve can compare to its preciousness.

We bless you socially that you might choose your friends and be a loving and gracious sister. We bless your parents to be tender and caring while firm in guiding you along the path of truth and righteousness. We bless you in your schooling, that you might be diligent and wise to prepare yourself to reach those attainments, and develop and perfect your talents in those ways most pleasing to God and the needs of your fellow beings as your own.

We bless you in the days of courtship that you might choose wisely and prayerfully those whom you should associate with. Select your future husband with the greatest possible care and obtain the distinct confirmation of your Father in Heaven. Heavenly Father misses you and awaits earnestly the day of your return.

It's jarring how that baptismal blessing stood in sharp contrast to the curse that Ralph pronounced upon my head ten years later when I told him I wanted to leave for college instead of staying under his roof and helping his ministry. Raising his hand to the square, as they say in Mormonism—that is, holding your right hand directly outward, elbow bent at a ninety-degree angle, tips of fingers pointing heavenward—Ralph swore in the name of Jesus that if I left home, I'd be raped and murdered.

But on my baptism day, I never imagined my father would speak such a curse over me. My baptism was an uplifting day overall—one of the rare family events that my dad didn't sabotage. (For example, my dad challenged my uncle to a fight at my Harvard graduation. Ralph was furious with his belief that he'd been ripped off in family inheritance. "Meet me under the clock at 3:00 p.m.," he snarled to Uncle Ivan. Ivan never showed. Dad also refused to take any photos with me that day, saying I didn't deserve any. I still snuck one shot from below, unfortunately showing a bit too much nostril.)

I got a little party to celebrate my baptism, held at my parents' small tan-brick Sandy house and attended by cousins, aunts, and uncles. It was a rare family occasion when Ralph didn't make a scene. Perhaps he felt proud that he'd ushered his daughter's soul into Mormondom.

At Utah family gatherings, Aunt Judy and her husband brought all or some of their ten children, including six daughters. They sometimes brought black garbage bags full of their used clothing for us kids. They were cornucopias of delight for my sisters and me. Frilly, puffy '80s sleeves, pastel bows, and sashes everywhere! Mom wanted her daughters to fulfill their gender roles as stay-at-home mothers, but she didn't subscribe much to the latest feminine fashions—too worldly, shallow, and expensive. I idolized these cousins with their big blonde perms and stable home where they dominated local sports and theater. They lived the life I dreamed of.

At the party, Ralph's sister, my aunt Susan—a sweet, devout soul with wispy blonde hair and rosy cheeks who lived in the windswept farmland countryside of Midway, Utah—gave me my first journal. I didn't know it until after her death, but years later, Susan tried to engineer some type of rescue of my siblings and me from Ralph, but her attempts were unsuccessful.

This journal she gave me was a volume with dark purple cloth binding and a blue, pink, and white floral pattern scattered on the linen cover. I didn't know Aunt Susan very well, and I didn't have a particular fondness for burgundy, but I was hooked. These pages would harbor my private hopes and fears.

My first journal entry in the book from Susan was on March 2, 1991, my baptismal date—a rather uninspired three sentences about how the water was warm at first but cold after the dunking, and how my neck hurt because all those male relatives and church leaders' hands pressing on my head hunched it during confirmation.

My second journal entry is from the next day and gives a run-down on our family dinner menu: "beans, patatoe [sic] salad, and cookies." The closing sentence: "I think BYU is #1."

Even at that young age, I was already steeped in the culture of revering Brigham Young University, crown jewel of the Mormon education system. Mormon babies are dressed in BYU jerseys, and, when they're older, their mothers sing the school's fight song to wake them for school: "Rise and shout, the Cougars are out, along the trail to fame and glory!" Fathers take their kids to "family day" during BYU football spring training and buy them fresh desserts from Creamery on Ninth, the university's very own ice cream mecca. Mormon parents get doe-eyed talking about how they met while studying at BYU, coyly known as "Breed 'Em Young University."

For all its shortcomings, Mormon culture does revere education (to a point—heretical books are verboten) and self-improvement. And it makes sense, because Mormon doctrine teaches that if members live righteously, they will become gods and goddesses someday with their own planets to rule, to be "joint heirs" with Jesus Christ. The god of Earth lives on his planet named Kolob, where he spends all day copulating with his wives who create "spirit children," i.e., you and me. And whatever knowledge we acquire here on earth will transfer with us to the afterlife, so we must constantly strive for excellence and knowledge, both temporal and spiritual. All that knowledge no doubt comes in handy when managing the affairs of a planet.

Talking with non-Mormon friends on this concept, I realized many people—especially Protestant and Catholic Christians—see this idea of deity-in-embryo as shockingly profane and narcissistic. I never saw it that way; I found it inspiring and empowering. What better way to motivate a kid who's a social reject to eschew booze, pot, and broads than to tell him someday he'll be master of an entire planet if he keeps his nose clean? It sounds awfully like the concept of seventy-two busty virgins feeding grapes to the devout Muslim martyr in paradise. Not too shabby a reward; even a salivating Casanova might convert.

The problem with this high-reward modeling is that it can create reckless devotion here on earth—for example, a suicide bomber, or Ron and Dan Lafferty, the fundamentalist Mormons profiled in *Under the Banner of Heaven* who murdered their younger brother's wife because she wouldn't let her husband marry another wife. These cases are incredibly rare and don't illustrate life for the average Mormon or Muslim, but as various writers have documented, demanding religions harbor dark underbellies that nurture extremism by creating unrealistic demands of perfection or devotion. It also engenders a smug "holier than thou" mentality that often creates friction with neighbors and sometimes the law.

As a school kid, our family bounced around various parts of Utah, from houses in Sandy and Orem to trailer parks in American Fork and Provo. This was because Ralph was guided by the Holy Ghost to uproot us to wherever he felt Heavenly Father told him to go. The Holy Ghost's orders also coincided with fears that

government workers were on our tail—either child custody med-
dlers or Democrats angry at Ralph's essays.

Those three years at East Sandy Elementary in Jordan School District in the suburbs of Salt Lake City gave me inklings of confidence.
I dominated our school's 5K foot races for girls in my entire grade
level, winning blue first-place ribbons two years and a red second-
place ribbon one year. That gave me an extra boost because my dad
said a couple brothers and I walked pigeon-toed, and he sometimes
made us sleep with our feet inside light brown shoes attached to
metallic foot braces. He'd picked up the secondhand contraption
from Deseret Industries, the Mormon version of Salvation Army
thrift stores. Whether he was correct or not—no pediatrician diagnosed us—I appreciated he cared, but it added to my insecurities.

At East Sandy, my report cards show a girl starting to emerge
from her shell. On an initial second-grade report card in 1990 (preserved thanks to Mom's archiving) from East Sandy Elementary,
Mrs. Crocheron wrote, "Carrie has excellent academic skills. She
is quite shy in class but enjoys participation." My tormenting older
brothers found this and underlined the word "shy" to mock me.
But in a later report card, Mrs. Crocheron said, "Carrie seems to be
progressing and enjoying school more each day. She is much more
outgoing and confident."

Whatever wellspring of confidence I built at East Sandy, it ran
dry with each successive move, including leaving Sandy for Orem,
Utah, about thirty-five miles south. I dreamed how our lives would
be infinitely better if those social workers in Massachusetts successfully took us away. Or I imagined that all eight of us kids would run
away and live together like the orphaned siblings in The Boxcar

Children book series. At least then we'd avoid living with non-Mormon alcoholics and drug-addicted foster parents.

I began to yearn for my parents' divorce. Mom almost left Ralph when I was in fourth grade, the only time I recall her asserting herself so forcefully. It happened while we lived in a small, rectangular split-level house with light brown siding and a dark brown shingled roof in Orem, near Mom's sisters and mother. Mom had four sisters, including one with Down syndrome. The other three married and had kids, and all were fiercely strong, independent characters—by no means domestic chattel. Years later, they told me Mom was the shy, sweet one, but after marrying Ralph he took her thousands of miles away and brainwashed her to view the rest of the family as vile sinners. As an adult, Mom refused to attend her sister's funeral after she died at age sixty-five of sudden heart failure, clinging to decades-old perceived grievances committed by this teenage younger sister.

Mom got active in my fourth-grade school's PTA at Vineyard Elementary, even leading planning for a school carnival, complete with cotton candy, a clown, and popcorn. I was so thrilled to be her daughter, I felt like I would burst. At the Orem house, Mom also taught nursery school children during Sunday School, pulling on her university art school training to give them lovingly hand-colored drawings from famous nursery rhymes. She also convinced her sisters to pool enough money to print and bind at Kinko's a thin, black hardcover book she compiled of family genealogy filled with pedigree charts, interviews with her parents and siblings, old family photos, and historical records about the Black (her dad's family name) and King (her mom's maiden name) family histories. It's a beautiful collection that I cherish today.

Mom garnered strength from living near her parents and

sisters, including the aunt who saved both our lives at my birth. That aunt gave our family our very first nice glassware dinner set, a collection of thick glass plates with a grape pattern etched inside and tall, clear, formal glass cups. They were the fanciest things I'd ever seen in our home. For the first time, I saw Mom starting to find her voice.

I was young, so I don't remember all the details, but around that time, Mom—tired of Ralph's lies about a special prophetic "Mission" to save America and put himself above the LDS Church leadership—tried to get Ralph to stay at a hotel while she considered moving us in with a sister. Ralph layered on the pressure. She ultimately caved, and by fifth grade, we moved from a house to a trailer park with a less friendly school environment and less family contact. No more carnivals. Eventually, Mom rejected her own family, and later also refused to attend her mother's funeral, saying her mother sinned by having a baby out of wedlock. Mom forgot that part of the Bible where Jesus says only the sinless can cast stones. By the time I finished fifth grade, I'd attended seven schools scattered throughout Salt Lake and Utah counties, and another while living in our motorhome in Missouri. Before graduating high school, I attended ten more, plus home school. This meant that despite my mom's best efforts to scrape together a decent education, my little world careened in disruption and chaos. It was a far cry from the pampered private school education many of my Harvard peers received. Yet one constant each morning: Mom made sure our brown lunch bags waited for us in the kitchen, our initials in black Sharpie on top.

Though we sometimes participated in free school meals programs because we lived below the poverty line, we tried to avoid government handouts (and often we didn't file our income taxes—Ralph said God told him not to as an Abrahamic test). That went against the principles of self-reliance and government suspicion ingrained in the Mormon psyche, thanks to government persecution at all levels. I'm convinced that's part of why Utah is one of the reddest of the red states politically—Mormons want as little government as possible. So instead of living off government dole, our family made do with half-piece bologna sandwiches and hot dogs sliced into thirds, lengthwise. During those early years, we also received plenty of Mormon welfare from what's known as the "Bishops' storehouse," basically a food bank for poor LDS families.

The Bishops' storehouse is funded by tithes and "fast offerings" (the money people save on the two meals they would otherwise eat on the first Sunday of each month), and it's typically generic, Mormon-branded bulk dry goods, everything from lentils and fruit to cereal and canned tuna. I'll never forget the putrid, squirming weevil larvae in our Bishops' storehouse cracked-wheat cereal. They blended in with the cereal while dry, so it was tough to spot them until they writhed in the milk on your spoon.

On a blistering summer day just after first grade, our motorhome meandering came to a rumbling halt as we ran out of food, somewhere in small-town western Missouri. While Ralph tried to rustle up money on the streets, Mom and the kids ate broth made from city park grass and chicken bouillon cubes. The cubes came in gold foil packaging, and I felt dazzled by their shine. Little did I know they were a poor mom's way of lining stomachs to ease hunger pains when we lacked access to the Bishops' storehouse.

What bothers me most about that memory is that my dad seemed more upset at the thought of someone finding out about his children eating grass than the fact that his kids were eating grass because he'd failed to provide enough food fit for human stomachs.

"Judy, we've got to be careful," he chastised my mom. "People who don't follow the Holy Ghost will hold this against me if we run for office."

He was keeping an eye on the future, contemplating following his dad's political footsteps. And indeed, decades later, he did run for Congress in that same state.

So much constant moving left me shy and tongue-tied. My four older brothers weren't any help, seeking ways to mortify me, as big brothers do. They stole my purple, flowered journal, in which I'd write in pencil, and erased key letters of certain words to change their meaning. For example, I'd written, "today at school we colored a part of a picture." They changed it to "fart of a picture." Hilarious stuff. That experience mortified me, along with fear of my classmates discovering how I lived, not to mention my brainwashing that any non-Mormon I met was scary and sinful.

In seventh grade, our teacher assigned writing to Santa Claus with our Christmas wish. At age twelve, I asked Santa's help with my shyness:

12/21/95

Dear Santa Claus,

I know you're really busy, but I just wanted to ask you if you'll give me a louder voice. I know it sounds kind of funny, but more than half of the time I say anything, people ask me to repeat what I just said. If I try shouting, then people think I'm mad at them or being mean, even though I'm only trying to be audible. If you could give it to me for Christmas, it would be one of the best present [sic] I would ever receive.

Love,

Carrie

The median age in Utah is so low (about thirty-one versus thirty-eight nationally) because of the early marriages and jumbo-size families. Utah boasts America's highest birth rate and largest household size, and it leads the nation in the percentage of stay-at-home moms. But Utah is increasing its marriage age, and its average family size is shrinking.

"That's because we are more connected to the outside world now. Utah used to be an isolated, tiny place," Pam Perlich, a University of Utah research economist, told the *Salt Lake Tribune*, a Utah newspaper, in 2010. "As we become more connected to the outside world, we tend to resemble it more over time... Utah lags national trends by about two or 2.5 generations."[21]

As a child growing up in Utah, I didn't want us to copy the rest of the country. I felt dismayed when Salt Lake City became majority non-Mormon, an urban pocket within a rural, Mormon state. I wanted my Mormon Brothers and Sisters (that's what Mormons call each other, Brother Smith, Sister Johnson, etc.) to feel safe and united in our respite from a toxic world. I didn't want outsiders corrupting our pure, simple joys. Instead, I wanted to export my ideology outside Utah and convert the world.

My mother is rightly obsessed with one of our ancestors, Jane Johnston Black. She came from Northern Ireland, the daughter of a Methodist lay leader father who died when Jane was just sixteen. Her father's congregation cherished his memory so much they demanded she stay on and minister to them to carry on his name, which she did for three years. I think of her oratorical skills, the charisma and power she conjured at such a young age to keep her audience enthralled.

There is a nascent movement among some within the Mormon Church to give women the priesthood. But phenomenally strong women like Jane showed you don't need a formal priesthood to bless many lives, to heal, and to build heaven on earth. A pioneer in the truest sense, after leaving her European homeland she sailed to Louisiana and traveled up the mighty Mississippi River to join her fellow believers. She then crossed the fruited plains, eventually landing in Utah. She and her fellow converts preceded the Ellis Island migration crush. And she came for a religion in its infancy.

Jane and her compatriots believed in utopia, a shared vision of success and humanity. The early Mormons tried a form of communism (which failed, unsurprisingly, given what we know about communist experiments in China and the Soviet Union), in hopes of manifesting their most altruistic impulses. Still, Mormonism's founding is violent, dramatic, and thoroughly American, gritty, and inspiring.

When Mormon founder Joseph Smith and his brother were brutally assassinated in 1844 while held captive at Carthage Jail in Illinois, their companion John Taylor (later to become the church's third president, aka prophet) also got shot. He refused treatment from anyone else, demanding to see my grandma Jane because he trusted her skill.

Jane was a midwife who delivered three thousand babies along the Mormon trail. Historical records say she received a priesthood blessing from Brigham Young that she would never lose a child. She was a true badass in every sense of the word. She brandished her gun, a pistol tucked into her bosom, when threatened by an anti-Mormon mob in Illinois. She did the same against hostile Native Americans who threatened her family in Utah. She personally chopped off a man's leg with an ordinary butcher knife and a carpenter's saw while he lay unconscious in a whiskey-induced slumber. He needed an amputation from a farming accident and could have died from gangrene infection. She saved his life.

A point of pride I had growing up in the Church is that nearly all its clergymen are unpaid volunteers, meaning they aren't corrupted by mammon like so many televangelists. The average bishop is a man with a wife and kids and a day job, many times a businessman, lawyer, or doctor. The reward for his service is intangible, and a good portion of his volunteer time is spent helping the needy.

Since Mormonism is run by this lay ministry—which I thought democratic and egalitarian—every average Joe can be bishop or stake president, meaning he can run an entire congregation or collection of wards known as a stake. It's a reference to expanding the stakes of Zion's tent, and is not to be confused with the hunk of meat—many a Mormon joke has been cracked about the phonetic similarity between a Mormon "stake center" and a restaurant or "steak center."

This lay-leadership structure creates a catch-22. Salt Lake wants its members to shoulder the burden of leadership to maintain the spirit of self-reliance and grassroots equality that animated the early Church. On the other hand, they also want to keep order and prevent doctrinal catfights. The brilliance of the setup is that it weeds out the weak-sauce people who aren't fully committed to the cause. It is a self-perpetuating system, because it demands millions of volunteer hours from its members—men and women, boys and girls—who feel invested and devoted to the System. That makes it tremendously difficult to tear oneself away, and it was that way for me. I held plenty of leadership positions within the LDS Church from age twelve to when I left at age twenty-two.

My leadership positions, known as "callings," ran the gamut: secretary in the Young Women organization, pianist, Sunday School teacher for elementary school–age children, second counselor in the Relief Society. Despite my crappy home life and my nonexistent school social life, these callings made me feel special and wanted. You aren't supposed to reject a calling because it's a direct request from God. So usually people don't, unless they have a personal worthiness reason (i.e., they may drink coffee or worse) that the bishop doesn't know about. I grew up with my neighbors teaching me stories and songs about Joseph Smith, Nephi, and Moses. At the time, I thought this was utopia, Zion on earth. Neighbor serving neighbor, commoners leading other commoners.

There are many reasons why Mormonism has historically been so insular, many of them understandable, given the illegal, violent anti-Mormon pressures they faced for their theology. But despite the Church's efforts to paint its members as happy-go-lucky, normal people, many Americans—to the detriment of GOP presidential candidates Mitt Romney and Jon Huntsman Jr.—are suspicious because they view the faith as secretive and closed-minded. But it needn't stay that way, and the good thing is, it's not. Mormonism evolved greatly since its founding, and my hope is it will continue to evolve, to come clean about its history and its doctrines, bring transparency to its finances, and increase its tolerance for others.

For the record, the Bible says there is no marriage in heaven. In Matthew 22:30, Jesus says, "For in the resurrection people neither marry nor be given in marriage, but are like angels of God in heaven." Mormons say they believe the Bible, "as far as it is translated correctly." That means they selectively pick out doctrines they don't want to follow and say that LDS founder Joseph Smith restored the true Gospel, away from man-made perversions or simple oversight.

I left Mormonism as an unmarried professional woman at age twenty-two, well before I hit thirty. I don't think I could have handled the Mormon gossip about whether I was satanic, a lesbian, divorcée, damaged goods, you name it. Choose your poison. Ostracizing aging, unmarried women seems to be a universal practice around the globe. In Mormon culture, it's tough for men, too. Legendary San Francisco 49ers quarterback Steve Young, a descendant of Mormon prophet Brigham Young, once discussed the almost crippling premarital pressures being a single Mormon man at thirty-four. In 1996, he appeared on *60 Minutes* with Mike Wallace and quoted his great-great-great-grandfather: "Brigham Young once said, right here on these grounds, that anyone over twenty-seven years of age that's not married is a menace to society. So here's my grandfather telling me to get with it. You don't think that I feel the pressure? I guarantee it."[22]

Brother Brigham would have given Ralph Jr. an earful. But then, perhaps he wouldn't like the competition. Ralph cut a handsome figure with his muscular 6'2" frame, blond hair, and blue eyes. But as both Utah governor and Mormon prophet, Brigham had power, that natural aphrodisiac. He collected wives the way some men of means collect rare wine or vintage cars. Though no one knows for sure, it's believed Brigham Young had fifty-five or maybe fifty-six wives. The LDS Church's official website says, "He was sealed to over 50 women, many but not all of whom lived with him."[23]

Brigham built a huge mansion for his harem in the heart of Salt Lake called Lion House. Hugh Hefner's shtick was a pathetic knockoff of the original pioneer playboy. Brigham reportedly greeted newly arrived covered wagons of immigrants and took his pick of the fresh meat. He didn't tap into my family's gene pool, as far as we know.

We know family details because Mormons are aggressive genealogists and maintain the world's largest collection of family history records. This data helps Mormons trace their lineage so they can perform religious rites, including marriage sealing and temple initiations called "endowments," on behalf of their dead ancestors who died without accepting Mormonism and still need a baptismal dunking and initiation ceremony.

The idea is that even non-Mormons baptized in the afterlife will receive the chance to accept Mormon doctrine, despite not embracing it on earth. The LDS Church posthumously baptized thousands of people without their families' knowledge, getting in hot water more than once for performing this rite for Holocaust victims—their Jewish descendants were understandably furious at the presumption that victims of horrific antisemitism would convert to a Christian sect. Dead celebrities and public figures also got this baptismal treatment, from Elvis Presley to Adolf Hitler.

I did my share of baptisms on behalf of dead people until I quit Mormonism. As a believer, I thought this doctrine was beautiful. It answered atheists' concerns that many religions hoard salvation, only offering it to specific people. Baptism for the dead was a phenomenal equalizer that meant anyone, regardless of geography and time, could accept Jesus Christ. It's like the baptismal font was a cosmic vortex time portal connecting the dead and living.

Mormonism's founder, Joseph Smith, was a dreamer, and I suspect that if he lived today, he'd be quite the sci-fi geek. Mormons love *Star Trek* and Star Wars. It's no surprise that the creator of sci-fi TV hit *Battlestar Galactica*, Glen Larson, is Mormon.

I once had a boyfriend who worked in the tech space, a field brimming with many other pioneers, including those working on private space exploration. A startup investor, he schemed various ways to expand our knowledge of the universe and the survival of our species (and ended up being a narcissistic jerk—cheating on me the entire year we dated). He became enthralled when I told him about the Mormon notion of Kolob, the home of Earth's god who was once a man, and the idea that we could one day be gods and goddesses of our own planets. Mormonism's founding came long before the days of Neil Armstrong and astronautical space exploration, but, like the ancients, early Mormons obsessed over the heavens and what lay beyond the confines of our universe.

The Mormon hymn "If You Could Hie to Kolob" (in case you're wondering, as I did for a long time, *hie* is old English for traveling rapidly) explores these themes:

If you could hie to Kolob
In the twinkling of an eye,
And then continue onward
With that same speed to fly,
Do you think that you could ever,
Through all eternity,
Find out the generation
Where Gods began to be?

Or see the grand beginning,
Where space did not extend?
Or view the last creation,
Where Gods and matter end?
Methinks the Spirit whispers,

"No man has found 'pure space,'
Nor seen the outside curtains,
Where nothing has a place."

In my studies of world religions during travels around the globe, Mormonism stands out within the Christian diaspora as far more immersive and demanding than nearly every other sect. It provides deep-rooted identity, community, and purpose. While practicing, I took pride in this—the 24-7 nature of Mormonism meant my faith wasn't just a cute little Sunday morning club. The positive side of this extraordinary commitment is why many non-Mormons often tell me that Mormons are some of the most kind and decent people they know. Volunteerism, charitable giving, and community engagement are off the charts among the nearly seventeen million people in global Mormonism. The LDS Church says it gives $1 billion in aid annually and is often among the first to respond with medical aid globally to natural and man-made disasters. It provides millions of pounds of food each year, even to non-Mormon food pantries.

Perhaps to outsiders, this extreme devotion sounds too intense and far-fetched or unknowable. But the incredible sense of belonging is real, and scientific evidence showing the euphoric brain patterns of religiously practicing Mormons are the same brain patterns as crack, gambling, or sex addicts. According to research published in the journal *Social Neuroscience* in 2016, Mormonism is like a drug in its effects on your brain.[24] This makes it incredibly difficult to withdraw if you've totally bought in. Faith and religion can provide an unexplainable euphoria that's safer and cleaner than debilitating, addictive drugs.

This phenomenon is found in general spiritual or religious

experiences, not just Mormonism. For example, 2019 peer-reviewed research published by the Public Library of Science found similarities between non-drug-induced spiritual experiences and psychedelic drug euphoria.[25] *Psychiatric Times* in 2008 explored the discipline of neurotheology, or how the structure and function of the human brain predisposes us to believe in God.[26]

It was excruciatingly painful for me when I left Mormonism as an adult, and I felt suicidal for the first time. I was reeling from the chemical withdrawal in my brain.

Chapter 5

Inner-City Black and White

*I have a dream that my four little children will one day
live in a nation where they will not be judged by the color
of their skin, but by the content of their character.*

—*Martin Luther King Jr.*[27]

"Why do you always sit with the white girl?" the black boy sneered at my black female friend, Ounjanise. I was about eleven years old, in sixth grade.

I don't remember Ounjanise's reply. But I remember she didn't run away. She stayed with me.

That type of hazing was fairly common for me and my friends during my middle school years. During sixth and eighth grades, I attended two very well-funded inner-city schools in Kansas City, Missouri (during seventh grade, we took a detour into a majority-white suburb).

After playing his guitar and passing out his Mormon brochures on the streets of Salt Lake City, particularly in the high-traffic area of Temple Square downtown, Ralph decided it was time to leave Mormondom and return to the land of the heathens to preach the Gospel.

He first chose Jackson County, Missouri, because that's where Mormons believe the Garden of Eden grew and where Jesus will first return to Earth before He goes to Jerusalem. Even though the state is overwhelmingly non-Mormon, there's a big pocket of Mormon diaspora waiting there for Him to come back, though they mainly wait in the suburbs in a town called Independence (hometown of former US President Harry S. Truman, who was Episcopalian, not Mormon). Dad decided that, since Jesus would be coming there anyway, he might as well help do some advance groundwork for Him, kind of like a political operative hopping onto a campaign early to curry favor, and hopefully snag a job once her boss secures sweet victory.

But there was another reason Ralph chose Missouri, specifically. He was grateful to the Missouri judicial system. Several years earlier, in June 1990, it dismissed charges against him after police threw him in jail for assaulting a fellow street performer.

He said God "prompted" him to make the first shove during his Missouri street brawl. In our family, a "prompting" was a revelation from God: an epiphany of knowledge or to induce some action. Often during Family Prayer, our dad would pause and assign us to get, say, five or ten "promptings" from God.

Dad said God even warned him earlier that day that he'd be imprisoned. Later, my dad compared himself in this scenario "to those who passionately serve truth and justice [and] are arrested—from Jeremiah to Jesus, St. Paul, Hus, Knox, Galileo, Bunyan, Thoreau, Joseph Smith, Martin Luther King Jr. and others. With a gulp, I assented."

In an essay he wrote, "A Missourian by the Hand of God," Ralph shared the details of the fight:

I put my guitar in its case atop my brief earnings, praying in my heart to "do it right." I was prompted [by God] to respond to his aggression with a shove, not so hard that he might fall and injure himself or break his instrument, and well-timed lest he be struck by a car—none of which would he likely have considered for me. His devilish grin at my momentary pause (for his safety, waiting for a car to pass behind him) showed he'd misjudged me again. But when the traffic was clear, I shoved him. He staggered back a step or two into the street, then jerked back, unslung his guitar, laying it in its case (again unaware that I was allowing it), then charged like a grunting bull. I dodged his lunge, punched him, then wrestled him to the ground into a 'cradle-hold.'

Out of a small crowd gathering to watch the fight, a clever African-American fellow stepped forward and knelt beside us, referee-like, counting the ruffian out: "One, two, three, you're pinned!" The crowd laughed, but the rowdy kept hassling. So I wrestled him flat on his back and sat atop him, swinging my fist above his face, threatening a fierce final blow. "Are you going to grow up?" I shouted! "Okay! Okay!" he said, "Good fight!" . . .

The judge, rightfully, dismissed the case, and I was a free man. What a relief! By obeying God's counsel (to appear alone) I had avoided both an expensive legal fee, and considerable inconvenience for my intended witnesses . . . By its just verdict, the Missouri court system, too had gained my respect. My wife and I were much cheered by the fairness of the court's decision. "Someday," I said, "when the time is right, I feel like we're coming back

here to live. What do you think?" She said she would pray about
it. Later, after doing so, she told me the Lord confirmed it to her.

Dad uprooted us from Utah to Kansas City, Missouri, when I was eleven, when puberty started to hit, emotions were in overdrive, and math and science classes actually started to matter. It was an awkward time to drop a shy white girl from the trailer parks of Utah into an urban inner-city school that was around 90 percent black, where students threw chairs at each other, smoked pot (and God knows what else) on campus, and where sixth-grade homework seemed at a first-grade level.

At that time, our family of ten lived in a modest, white two-story house on Holmes Street, about equidistant between Troost Avenue (where things start to get sketchy/dangerous)[28] and Oak Street (where houses start to get real nice). It was a fitting metaphor for how our lives often careened from stability and calm into chaos and violence.

That first day walking on campus with Mom felt like I was entering prison or a juvenile detention facility. I tried to keep my eyes on the floor ahead of me. Sunlight streamed through the hallway while the armed guard inspected us, eying us with a combined look of curiosity and annoyance.

In this district, students waited in long lines to enter through metal detectors each morning, had regular bomb scares, and weren't allowed to wear certain color schemes (blue pants/blue shirt for the Crips gang or red pants/red shirt for the Bloods gang) to school, since they symbolized various gangs and could trigger violence.

I was the odd girl out who didn't speak Ebonics, an African

American dialect. Our Utah dialect was so foreign that people thought our family was from Ireland. With time, I eventually grew accustomed to the ribbings of the black kids who called me "Snow White" and were fascinated by my hair, constantly asking to touch it. The 2001 blockbuster movie *Save the Last Dance* starring Julia Stiles gives a flavor of my struggles, except she was older, and I wasn't nearly as cool as the lily-white protagonist Sara, who flounders at first as the new girl in the South Side of Chicago. Though we were both classically trained artists—she in ballet, me in violin and piano—my awkward shyness and Mormon fundamentalism would never attract a Georgetown-bound, pre-med suave heartthrob black classmate like she did.

Now why on earth would my father choose to put his kids in these perilous school environments? He said it was the Holy Ghost. It was our equivalent of his street preaching ministry, The Mission.

"The Lord tells me that if he wants me in harm's way, he needs you kids there, too," he'd tell us. "But don't worry, He says He'll be with us in every time of trouble."

"Stay as for years," he'd also say, urging us to pretend as though we'd stay there for the rest of our lives. This meant getting involved with as many arts, sports, and after-school programs as possible— more opportunities for missionary work. A silver lining of moving around so much (by that point, starting sixth grade meant my eighth public school) was if I hated the place, there'd be a good chance we'd uproot elsewhere before long.

Ralph said he wanted us to be examples of good Mormons and convert people to our faith. Of course, I did none of that. I kept my head down and tried to survive. I was a terrible daughter of a prophet. I wanted to fit in rather than save souls, because I had no idea how to interact in such an environment—so different and dangerous to me. The experience made me afraid to stand up for my values, terrified to preach the principles that I believed were true. I became a passive observer rather than a proactive leader. Paralyzed, I tried to be sweet and nonthreatening to avoid a beat-down. I became a people pleaser.

I couldn't save fellow kids who didn't understand my dialect and saw me as the ultimate outsider. I was sheltered and immature, with absolutely no street smarts. I became silent, tongue-tied, and depressed. I began to binge eat to dull my pain, secretly eating a whole jar of peanut butter over a couple days, slathering marshmallows and graham crackers with the peanutty goodness. Drugs, sex, and alcohol were out. Food seemed the one outlet that God wouldn't punish me for if I overindulged. The problem was, we didn't have too much of it around, and since I wasn't allowed babysitting or lawn mowing–type odd jobs, I couldn't afford my own fast-food runs to binge eat like I did later in college. Ralph hoped that enrolling in the inner-city schools would harden us up, but instead it gave me a squishy spare tire. He said our experience was like what Jesus went through, ministering to the least among us in society.

But in truth, we mere mortals cannot fully help others until we ourselves are rooted and strong. I was far from that and consequently became more codependent on Ralph and our family, since I struggled to make friends and my teachers weren't interested in helping. I sensed their annoyance at the white girl who knew all the answers and strove for extra credit. They rebuffed my attempts at becoming a teacher's pet, a title I desperately sought, since there was no way in hell I'd ever win any popularity contests among my peers.

I began to see our family "Mission" as my outlet from the insanity at school, and I practiced my violin for hours to help save our country from utter depravity. By the time we finished our inner-city schooling, our roving family orchestra played our musical ensemble on the streets of Kansas City in the downtown Plaza area during the school year, and during school breaks we drove our 1991 Winnebago Warrior motorhome to play various street festivals, campgrounds, and LDS churches from Portsmouth, Ohio, to Stevensville, Maryland. Our repertoire eventually included classical greats like selections from Bach's Brandenburg Concertos and Handel's *Messiah* and "Water Music," Mozart's Symphony no. 40 in G Minor, Edvard Grieg's "The Last Spring" along with "Somewhere" from the musical *West Side Story*, and even "The Pink Panther Theme" by Henry Mancini, just for fun. I didn't tell my classmates about my preaching musical escapades. I was mortified they'd label me a religious nutjob and beat me up.

Years later, on my college entrance standardized test, I scored in the ninety-ninth percentile for English among college-bound seniors (which meant I'd score even higher including non-college-bound kids). I later earned a full-tuition Harvard journalism scholarship for my staff writing work at major national media outlets. And until sixth grade, I never received anything but an A in my English classes. I was a perfectionist who was insecure in many other areas, except academics. They were my Broadway, my stage, my chance to shine. I landed on honor rolls and earned certificates and later a letterman academic letter (too poor to buy the jacket) and ribbons for my scholarship. I was shy, nerdy, picked on, and near rock bottom in the social pecking order, but academics were my refuge. So it was a kick to my gut when in sixth grade, at Southeast Middle School, Mrs. Martin gave me a B in English. I started crying. I couldn't understand, and I begged her to explain why. I never got a straight answer. I stayed after class and picked up trash in her classroom. I pleaded with her to give me extra credit projects, though nothing stirred her heart. Every other English teacher until Mrs. Martin saw me as her prized pupil. But now I felt like a pariah. I couldn't comprehend why she wouldn't see what the others saw in me. Eventually, I wondered if it was because I was white and she was black, and there were so few other white kids like me. I wondered if she thought that, by giving me an A, somehow she would validate what she believed was institutional white supremacy.

One day in sixth grade, we made shoebox dioramas. If you're not familiar with this concept, you get an old shoebox and cut a small peephole on one of the narrow sides for the viewer to peek in and see what scene you've erected. Mine was about dinosaurs, and I felt excited. The 1993 blockbuster movie *Jurassic Park* recently smashed records, and I grew fascinated. Our family owned some cheap, tiny brown and green plastic dinosaurs (excruciatingly painful to accidentally step on without shoes!), and I planned to glue a couple to the shoebox floor and glue leaves to the shoebox walls. I even got clever and brought a bag of dirt to glue to the base for the most natural look. But when I got to school that day, the lunch baggie filled with dirt set off alarm bells for one of the security officers. He pulled me out of line and inspected the suspicious packet. He thought it might be drugs colored brown with some type of dye.

"This dirt?" he asked, peering up at the baggie in his hand, moving it toward the light.

"Yes," I said, trembling and panicking, heart pounding. I showed him the other parts of my soon-to-be masterpiece. Though I struggle with my own addictions—like ego, social media, and insecurity—I don't believe in using drugs. I've never done them or been around them except secondhand pot wafting on the sidewalk

as I'm passing by. The guy eventually deduced my baggie was innocent and sent me on my way. I felt deflated and shaken.

One day in eighth grade, some kids on the bus after school
hurled insults at me, yelling out to each other and snickering that I
was gay. They were obviously playing some juvenile game poking
fun at the white girl, the different one. I shrugged it off and didn't
say a word and slumped, sitting stone-faced, head hunched down
and silent, praying their attention would turn elsewhere because
I didn't engage. Thank God things didn't escalate from there. I
wasn't exactly sure what "gay" meant, but I was glad they weren't
waving a Glock 19 in my face.

One shining moment suspended in my memory came during
an all-school music assembly inside the gym. There was no traditional stringed orchestra at Southeast Middle School, so I couldn't
play violin. From the sidelines, I heard our school dulcimer band,
woodwind/brass band, and trio ensemble, where my brother
Jonah played flute alongside a student clarinetist and their teacher,
a trumpeter. Jonah's photo with the band and trio made the yearbook from that day, the only white student visible in the group.
He wore blue jeans and a preppy long-sleeve shirt with horizontal
brown-and-black stripes and a white collar.

Jonah shone brightly, alone before the entire student body—
more than six hundred students—as a flute soloist with his teacher
accompanying on piano, playing "Sicilienne." Written in a minor
key, which means it is inherently more melancholy, dark, and mysterious than most songs (most are in a major key), this short piece
is sweetly piercing, reflective, and contemplative. It's written by
Gabriel Fauré, a generationally talented, quasi-Impressionistic and
Romantic French composer born in 1845. The piano bassline sets a
foundation like a stream of running water rippling below while the

vibrato flute melody flutters and soars like a bird above. Listening to Jonah's solo, I felt waves of pride for his talent. Jonah was two years older than me, deeply shy, and autistic. He wet the bed until seventh grade—a common trait among children with autism. Even when we weren't in violent, crime-ridden schools, he clammed up and struggled to make friends. But with his flute in hand, Jonah dominated. His teacher said he could make it to Juilliard, one of America's most elite performing-arts universities. Jonah displayed the musical genes of our dad and grandmother, but sadly, as happens with many artists, this talent came at the price of mental fragility. He later developed schizophrenia in his early twenties, though I'm convinced this wasn't a fait accompli if he hadn't been screamed at almost daily and occasionally punched and wrestled to the ground by a fanatical father. Just as the chaotic swirl of schizophrenia unraveled him and he became furious at Ralph's abuse, Jonah hurled his flute into a river, trashing it forever, his talent squandered.

But that day as an eighth grader, Jonah's sweet, melodious aural river flowed breezily through the gymnasium. This silver sound contrasted jarringly with the typical shouts, screams, and slaps puncturing the air and reverberating against the wooden bleachers of that same room. The gym was our morning holding pen; before school each day, while students lined up to get screened through metal detectors and bag searches, security ushered those who passed vetting to the gym until everyone got through. No gradual trickle of students infiltrated classrooms and caused mischief until teachers arrived.

We were all released at once to our classrooms, and in the meantime, as we sat in the gym, students frequently got into scratching, screaming, hair-pulling, and punching brawls. Usually, the fights started with someone accusing the other party of disrespecting or falsely judging them. Two or three per morning was normal; five or six was pushing it. In one morning, I witnessed more violence than in all my previous seven schools combined.

I'd seen violence at home from our dad against my brothers— Ralph constantly desired to prove himself the alpha male of the home—but school was typically my respite. Now that was gone, too.

One of my survival tactics in this environment was developing sharp insults and zingers. I didn't use them on anybody, but I was adept at giving lines to other people so they could insult foes during "yo mamma" confrontations and duels. That way, I earned allies who saw my value and wouldn't go after me. They used my material the way a late-night comedian relies on a stable of writers.

If you're not familiar with these verbal duels I'm talking about, here's how Encyclopedia Britannica describes it:

the dozens, in African American culture, [is] a game of verbal combat typically played by young men. The participants match wits by exchanging humourous insults, usually before an audience. Some versions of the dozens incorporate rhyme; in the 1960s those were important to the development of rap. The dozens received considerable attention from scholars during the 1960s as the Black Power movement and a black urban culture developed, and these ritual insults persisted into the 21st century. The topics available for criticism in the dozens include family, dress, appearance, economic status, and physical characteristics. The most common topic of insult in the dozens, though, is a person's mother. The phrase "Your mama..." serves to let the other participants know that the dozens has begun. The insults often take the form of puns and exaggerated comparisons.[29]

Commentary in the dozens can involve sexual issues, and this version of the game is called the "dirty dozens" according to Amuzie Chimezie, one of the first faculty members in the Department of Africana Studies at the University of Cincinnati.[30]

Sociologist Harry Lefever notes that the dozens is almost exclusively played by African Americans, with other ethnic groups often failing to comprehend the rules of the game and taking the dozens jokes seriously.[31]

It was a weird situation, but now as a grown-up, I get paid to deliver zingers in front of millions of people during live television news programs, so there was some talent level there, in terms of my ability to sass off. I was naive in anything sexual (thankfully), so I didn't do dirty dozens stuff, but I was good at making puns and trading barbs based on what someone said or did previously, quietly feeding punch lines to others calling out the weakness of rivals' jokes or insulting their athletic or academic prowess. I didn't get in trouble with my own mouth per se; I kept my head down enough to avoid that. In my own way, by helping fight dozens duels, I found a place in the Wild West that is inner-city middle school.

This was my first daily exposure with majority-black culture. In eighth grade, I tried to fit in by dressing like what's known in the vernacular as a "wigger," a "white n*****," in the mold of rapper Eminem. This was Mormon-adapted wigger, which meant needed adjustments after arriving at school, away from prying parental eyes, dressing in baggy pants with tight shirts (tight from wash shrinkage, not because of a sanctioned purchase) or overalls with my homemade boxer shorts peeking out on the sides, pulling my hair in a skintight ponytail at a ninety-degree angle on the very top of my head, and wearing cheap knockoff Nike-looking black sneakers (we couldn't afford the real thing). I wore a silver CTR ring, a popular jewelry piece worn by Mormons that stands for Choose the Right. It's got the three letters in the center of a shield (think the Warner Bros. logo), a phrase taken from the LDS hymn called "Choose the Right" by nineteenth- and early twentieth-century LDS songwriters Joseph L. Townsend and Henry A. Tuckett. The CTR shield first caught fire with LDS kids in Sunday School manuals during the 1970s, but CTR rings have promulgated for Mormons of all ages today. Every now and then, a curious black classmate asked me what it stood for, but I'd never divulge. I felt too afraid they'd think me a preachy, self-righteous, prissy white girl. This air of intrigue led them to hypothesize about a secret boyfriend's initials (i.e., Carrie and a mysterious T.R.) or that I belonged to some secret gang or clique—way more hardcore than the squeaky-clean truth. (Many years later, my brother would spin off his own ring with a shield and letters, an FTS ring, reminding wearers to "Follow the Spirit," the way our parents always reminded us to FTS when leaving the house.)

I also learned how to speak Ebonics. Eventually, when I returned to majority-white environments and would sometimes bust into the dialect, people called that racist. I didn't understand why, because to me, Ebonics was just another way to connect and communicate with people around me—how I could be understood by my inner-city classmates. You won't find me talking that way as an adult, because I don't live in that environment anymore, but also because I don't want to disrespect anyone. And I'm not cowering in fear of bullies, so I don't need coping mechanisms to be something I'm not.

I loved playing with a bunch of accents, from *Gone With the Wind*–style upper-class Southern and trailer-park Southern to French, British (upper- and lower-class), and Spanish. When I lived in the American South—my first exposure to the region—as a journalism intern for a local newspaper forty-five miles west of Charlotte, North Carolina, I gradually, simply through subconscious osmosis, began speaking with a soft Southern accent. I think my ear is finely tuned because I'm the daughter of a musician and a classically trained violinist and pianist; accents are audible inflections, similar to the subtle musical notation of a sharp or flat, major or minor key. I love learning dialects because they are rich and colorful. Of course, the way you use a dialect—the spirit and tone—tells you about someone's intent. With good intent, the more we learn about the people around us, the more we connect, and the less scared we are of each other.

Many years later as an adult, comedian Bill Maher's show on HBO invited me as an on-air guest. They gave me the list of my fellow guests, and among them was the name "Nas." I had no idea who or what Nas was. If I'd more fully delved into black culture, I would've known he's a multiplatinum, black rap artist from New York City who's revolutionary in his lyrics and musicality. I educated myself on Nas's repertoire and became duly impressed. I laughed inside after our show, an enjoyable episode, because during the after-party, I told Nas I came from a family of musicians. I asked him if he'd ever heard of the Mormon Tabernacle Choir, which various family members of mine belonged to (at that time and for many years, its name was Mormon Tabernacle Choir, but since 2018, it's just Tabernacle Choir). He said no. I chuckled because the Tabernacle Choir is similarly a global, platinum-selling phenomenon, albeit in a different genre and totally different cultural context. It's a bunch of lily-white suburban Utah Mormons singing religious hymns, who've performed for presidential inaugurations and royalty and created the longest-running radio and television broadcast in human history, *Music & the Spoken Word*. I love both the Tabernacle Choir and Nas, and I believe cross-cultural exchanges are good for the world!

To supplement what I saw as growing gaps in my education, I spent numerous hours at the Kansas City Public Library. To their credit, my parents loved public libraries and frequently brought us there; they became a quiet, fistfight-free, stabilizing constant, despite the perpetual transience. In eighth grade, I devoured as many Shakespeare books as possible, immersing myself in modern English translations alongside the Elizabethan English, which seemed indecipherable in many cases. Did I fully comprehend the texts? Definitely not, but they engrained in me a deep love for the Bard and his insights into human nature. I only wish I'd done the same with trigonometry or computer science books!

Another regret as an inner-city school student was how I treated my classmate Ruth. A fellow white girl, Ruth was also picked on and marginalized. We both existed on the bottom rung of the totem pole. The difference: she was slightly lower than me because she was overweight, her hair greasy, and her clothes were, hard to believe, less stylish than mine. At least, that's the sense I got witnessing other students bully her more ferociously than me.

"Ruth smell like dookie!" some bully might yell at her, using the slang word for human feces. "Ay, Ruth, you *stank*! Why you don't wipe your ass? Didn't your momma teach you how to clean your butt?"

Ruth would stare blankly in silence, then eventually hang her head and avert her sad, brown eyes.

Ruth didn't have the sassy mouth to fight back or at least deflect through sharing the dozens material. I regret that I didn't say anything. I didn't stand up for Ruth. I felt so bad that by the time my parents announced another move during the school year, I wrote a letter to Ruth and stuck it in her locker. I told her I was sorry. I never saw or heard from her again. I don't even know if she got the note.

I fulfill this imperfectly, but the story of Ruth—and my entire time in the inner city—taught me to stand up against bullies. It's a lesson I will learn for the rest of my life.

Don't ever let anyone tell you money is the magic wand to fix public education. For two decades, Utah ranked dead last in funding per student (Mormon-heavy Idaho finally claimed the title in 2021, leaving Utah second from last), in part because of the huge Mormon families, yet it's scored in the top ten among the fifty US states in student outcomes by *U.S. News & World Report.*[32]

Kansas City Public Schools are legendarily incompetent, despite huge per-capita spending boosts. Even with these generous resources granted by taxpayers, they were so rotten that in 2000, Kansas City Public Schools became *the first district in the United States of America* to lose accreditation. My eighth-grade school, Kansas City Middle School of the Arts, shut down permanently in 2011. The percentage of students achieving proficiency in math during the 2009–10 school year was reportedly 12 percent, far lower than the Missouri state average of 53 percent, and 14 percent proficiency in reading/language arts, compared to the Missouri state average of 54 percent.[33]

During exposure to these terrible schools, I witnessed firsthand the violence, drug abuse, and shoddy education that many black students endure here in modern-day America. We spent almost as much time dealing with students yelling at teachers or getting in fights as actually learning. Classmates threw chairs at teachers, who kept school security officers on speed dial.

This harrowing experience taught me how much, from a racial justice standpoint, we must improve in the realms of school choice and educator accountability. It showed me how children in majority-black environments are neglected by systems created and maintained by self-serving teachers unions, who offer hollow lip service for "racial justice," which keeps black children trapped in toxic public schools. Sadly, Kansas City is far from alone in this type of education stranglehold. Nationwide, these union bosses fight to stop the flow of taxpayer dollars to more worthy educators at public charter and private schools. This is one of the pivotal battlefronts in the fight for civil rights and social justice. A child's impoverished zip code—which correlates most often with black and brown races— should not trap him or her in a failing school. There are innovative funding models piloted now—Arizona, Wisconsin, and Florida, for example—where money follows the child, not the failing school.

I will get off my school-reform soapbox, but it is a deeply systemic injustice that children in our inner cities are subjected to daily violence and subpar instruction. I pray we as a country will repent and right this wrong. The good news is, there are millions of people working to do just that.

Chapter 6

Dangerous Crossroads

Even though I walk through the valley of the shadow of death, I fear no evil, for you are with me; your rod and your staff, they comfort me.

—*Psalm 23:4*

It was around the time of my inner-city trials that our lives changed forever through catastrophic illness.

Peter is the oldest of my seven siblings and seven years older than me. I idolized him. Peter drew biting political cartoons and told snarky jokes. He rode his own delivery route for the local Utah newspaper the *Green Sheet* (which he and my wiseacre brothers termed the *Green Sh*t*), where future Pulitzer Prize–winning journalist Jack Anderson covered local affairs as a teenager. Peter used his newspaper money to buy a coveted stonewashed pair of Marithé et François Girbaud jeans, featuring its stylish identifying white zipper tag. To his siblings' supreme jealousy, he even got to spend some time in Hawaii at a pineapple-picking camp owned by the Mormon Church. (Sadly, the Hawaiian camps weren't idyllic for all the young men. Some later sued, alleging sexual abuse.)

In 1992, when I was nine and Peter sixteen, Mom published her 130-page homemade collection of family history and genealogy. She wrote biographical sketches about family members from both her parents' sides, dating back to the early 1800s. Here's how she boasted about Peter, just a few years before this promising young man lost his grip on reality:

> *Peter Mark Sheffield . . . is an 11th grader. He was called to be president of his teacher's quorum. He won the Academic Fitness Award for achieving outstanding grades. . . . He was a winner in the Reflections Talent Contest Literature Division. . . . Peter is on the school wrestling team and enjoys playing basketball, baseball and video games. He has a natural gift for writing, drawing clever cartoons and making up funny jokes. He is a Boy Scout.*

As the firstborn of an alpha-male "prophet" who claimed Satan directly targeted him, it's difficult to imagine the pressure Peter labored under. Peter felt the gravity of his supposed sins (like listening to music by rock band R.E.M.—he buried those tapes in the backyard) and decided, like his father and like Jesus, to fast for forty days to cleanse himself before beginning a public ministry. He stopped eating. Not long after he commenced his fasting regimen, Peter's community college in the Kansas City area called my parents and told them to collect their son—he was punching the air and yelling at invisible foes. His diagnosis hit us hard: paranoid schizophrenia.

Peter eventually told us a bit about the imaginary beings who became his companions, like "Mrs. Bags." He couldn't or wouldn't answer our questions about Mrs. Bags or any other figments of his mind. If you spoke to him, he'd stare back blankly, with no recognition. He spent hours in the bathroom, shaving, cleaning his nose, and doing God knows what else.

Jesus healed poor souls tormented by demons. In stark contrast, my dad physically, spiritually, and emotionally brutalized us, making my brothers susceptible to the unknowably demonic suffering of schizophrenia. If you want true terror, forget Stephen King or any horror movie. Search for recordings of what schizophrenia patients say their auditory hallucinations (voices in their head) sound like. If you're really daring, like some loved ones of schizophrenics are, try wearing headphones for twenty-four hours with these sounds playing. This isn't cheap entertainment bought for the price of a movie ticket. It's human lives trapped inside their own skulls. The sounds are utter hell. Banshees. Screeching. Yelling. Gibberish. Hissing. And you can never. Shut. It. Off.

"Go kill yourself!"
"You're garbage. You're a piece of shit! Nobody wants you!"
"God's not real. He doesn't care."
"Do you think you matter? Fuck no. You should have been murdered."

Medication might alleviate symptoms, and patients' demonic voices display varying intensity. But it's no wonder the suicide rate for people with schizophrenia is a shocking more than twenty times higher than the general population.[34]

Peter obsessed over monitoring time and walked around carrying a small wooden table clock. He'd set multiple white plastic handheld timer alarms throughout the day. I think they helped snap him out of his stupors, when he'd sit or stand in place for hours on end, rocking, babbling, and muttering nonsense under his breath.

In a way, my dad almost seemed thrilled by Peter's diagnosis. He used his son's illness to drag us all into Dad's own delusional ministry.

———

Every young Mormon man is expected to perform a two-year, full-time volunteer period as a proselytizing missionary. For many years, the minimum age was nineteen, so typically a young man would either attend college or work for a year, serve his mission, return home, and then get married. A mission is a rite of passage into Mormon male adulthood, and, similar to military service, it very often begins with a boy and ends with a man, due to the grueling hours and the discipline.

When Peter hit that age, our family raised local eyebrows and got tongues wagging because "that Sheffield boy" hadn't put in his mission paperwork. Ralph, radicalized and shunning his own parents and siblings as deviants, felt anxious to recruit more converts to the LDS faith. And he appeared determined to do that with his wife and kids as the vehicle.

When Peter got sick around 1995, Ralph announced that we'd all rally around him, serving together in a permanent musical ministry. Every single one of our ten family members played piano in addition to at least one Ralph-assigned instrument. Peter played cello. I eventually played two: violin and oboe. Ralph promised if we were devout enough, then Peter would be healed.

In truth, Ralph did not want to send Peter—or any of his sons—on an official two-year mission because he believed the LDS Church had fallen into spiritual decay. He reached this conclusion after his own mission in England from 1959–1961. Our family would serve together and save both Church and country. Ralph said that, because he followed the Holy Ghost more stringently than Gordon B. Hinckley (the official prophet and president of the LDS Church), we would more effectively influence the "unwashed masses" through our informal channel.

For Ralph, that meant pushing us to rehearse individually and with our family musical ensemble, a chamber symphony group called the "Sheffield Family Consort," for hours nearly every day. Ralph, naturally, played conductor. Mom played piano, percussion, and sang. Thomas played French horn, Benjamin first violin, Jonah flute and piccolo, Sophie viola, Julie and me both second violins, and John rounded us out with clarinet and trumpet. It became clear that Ralph plotted this family orchestra years earlier through careful assignment of our instruments. We had no say in which instrument we'd play—Ralph told us God carefully selected each one. He assigned me to play violin when I was in fifth grade. My brother Thomas wanted to play saxophone, but Ralph kiboshed that idea quickly. No respectable chamber symphony group contained such a thing!

Thus, the Sheffield Family Consort officially began. As a middle schooler, I already had a few years of violin playing under my belt. During middle school summer breaks, we played a combination of streets and inside Mormon churches in Portsmouth, Ohio; Falls Church, Virginia; Fredericksburg, Virginia; Stevensville, Maryland; and a campground called Little Bennett in Clarksburg, Maryland. We also played at the LDS temple visitors center outside Washington, DC. The temple isn't open to non-Mormons, but its *Wizard of Oz*–like palatial design is a Beltway icon, with its six towering spires above 160,000 square feet, encased in sparkling white Alabama marble. I marked the milestone in my journal:

August 5, 1996

Today we gave a family home evening at the Washington Vis-itors Center. We played the Little Fuge [sic] by J.S. Bach the first time in public. I don't think we played that song very well. When we were rehearsing, we played it great. The Washington Temple is so beautiful on the outside! I hope I will be worthy to go inside it or other temples when I'm old enough. I hope that when we get home, I can travel to some temple and do baptisms for the dead.

Coming back off the road, after two years of inner-city trauma during my sixth and eighth grades, the Holy Ghost guided Ralph to enroll us in rural and suburban public schools, though we later tried homeschooling.

After a lovely freshman year in Kansas City's suburbs at Lee's Summit High School—the pinnacle of my K–12 schooling career—we packed up again and moved halfway across the country for Maryland. LSHS had been heaven on earth, and I immersed myself there as fully as possible. Spending time outside the house distanced me from the screams of my schizophrenic brother and Ralph yelling back at Peter that he deserved his accursed illness.

LSHS, home of the Tigers, boasts a nationally ranked symphony orchestra, where I climbed through auditions to principal second violinist. Our music teacher, Kirt Mosier, an internationally acclaimed composer and conductor, brought positivity and an ego-free passion to classical music—a refreshing joy to witness. I was still dreadfully shy and tongue-tied, but Mr. Mosier coaxed my violin skills to their peak. I also played point guard on the girls' basketball team (albeit second string on the freshman B team, but still, it was a spot!) and acted in the chorus and as understudy for Aggie Wainwright in our school production of *The Grapes of Wrath*.

I thrived in Lee's Summit—the hardest place for me to leave. Both hellish and heavenly schools never lasted long for us Sheffields. After that blissful freshman year, Ralph announced we'd head to the East Coast, where I'd start my fifteenth school—my sophomore year of high school at Gaithersburg High School in suburban Maryland, outside Washington, DC. This was a foreign environment, departing Jackson County, home of Mormonism's Garden of Eden, in a much more religious and conservative state, to plunge into the secular liberalism of Montgomery County, Maryland. It was a new mission field to help convert our peers to Mormonism.

These were uncharted waters, and I knew I'd drop in the social pecking order. I was right. The music program was decent, but nothing like LSHS. I played oboe in concert band and clarinet in marching band, wearing a gold Spartan helmet crowned with a mohawk-like blue broom. Our mascot was the Trojan. A nerdy, bookish band geek, I tried my hardest to be a good ambassador for the LDS faith. I failed.

Young Mormons aren't allowed to date until they're age sixteen. As an adult now, I think this policy makes sense, though as a kid I found it embarrassing and authoritarian. In my most rebellious action of childhood, I decided to flout the rules at age fifteen in Gaithersburg, and I illegally said yes to a homecoming date invitation. It came from a soft-spoken boy a year older with light brown hair who said he dreamed of going to Penn State. I hemmed and hawed when my mom confronted me after I told her I needed a dress for the dance.

"Carrie, these are types of dances where you need a date," she said sternly. "Are you *sure* you don't have a date? You know what the Lord says."

"I'm going with a group of friends, Mom," I replied. This was technically true. A group of six or eight of us, all his friends, were going as a group paired as couples. "We're going to dinner as a group before the dance and we'll all just dance together."

Mom wasn't buying it. After intense guilting, she eventually pried it out of me that I indeed accepted a date and promptly grounded me. I lied and told my date my parents grounded me for a bad math grade. I didn't want him to hate Mormons. The guy showed up at school on Monday with my corsage. I felt terrible about hurting him and for my rebellion against God.

After one semester in Gaithersburg, Ralph announced a horror: homeschooling. I'm surprised it took him that long—this setup meant we could supercharge The Mission. The motorhome could become his permanent itinerant ministry headquarters, rather than an occasional vessel for jaunting during summers and other school breaks. I partially blamed myself because of my failed homecoming cloak-and-dagger intrigue. I was the oldest daughter with four older brothers, and Ralph couldn't handle strong-willed daughters. He thought my sister, a year younger than me, and I were becoming too worldly. Our high school curriculum accreditation, eventually used for the second semester of my sophomore year and my entire junior year, came through Brigham Young University's correspondence program, today called BYU Online High School. We studied before widespread internet adoption, so everything arrived through the mail via the US Postal Service. My two elementary-age siblings used another correspondence program called Calvert Homeschool. Aside from the complete peer isolation, I did enjoy interacting with the BYU professors, albeit in short handwritten notes via snail mail. I even earned some BYU college credit for my university-level Old Testament course.

As we absorbed this homeschooling change, Ralph told us we'd uproot to a new homebase—Branson, Missouri. In Branson, Ralph turned on the charm and convinced a local Christian farmer named John Johannes (who later rued the day he met Ralph Sheffield when the deal eventually went sour) to create an installment lease, sans bank, allowing Ralph to gradually pay down ownership of a plot of land with an abandoned country church, complete with rows of wooden pews.

Ralph beguiled the devout John with tales of spiritual prowess and revelation. Dad cultivated an uncanny knack for connecting with evangelical Protestants by criticizing LDS Church theology. He also promised John a thriving Sheffield Family Consort music scene in what Ralph named the American Heritage Theater, an entertainment outpost nine miles north of the famed Branson, Missouri, country music mecca strip. This "Nashville for families," over the past six decades, has drawn millions of visitors annually for acts as disparate as Andy Williams and the Osmond Brothers to Ozzy Osbourne and Dolly Parton's Stampede. As a world-class musical talent, Ralph brought looks, charisma, and stage presence. Like other big Mormon families on the Branson music scene— the Osmonds (Jimmy Osmond was my Sunday School teacher! Nice, humble guy), the Hughes, the Duttons, the Bretts, and more, we boasted high potential. But we lacked a more business-savvy manager, because Ralph refused to let anyone try; he felt paranoid they would screw us over. So, instead, we floundered.

Behind the church stood a red-brick shed with a white metallic roof made of corrugated tin siding. The property also included a small, 941-square foot blue house and a mobile home on the far north end. All told, it was a decent 1.36-acre parcel of land, and to maintain my sanity and get some natural endorphins, I'd jog the perimeter.

Of course, rather than stay in the blue house or mobile home, which we did briefly, Ralph's preferred living setup became the red shed. Perhaps it made him feel more righteous by putting everyone in physical misery. Show business masks deep pain, but we reached next level. If we complained, Mom and Dad called us "the summer soldier and the sunshine patriot," condemned by Founding Father Thomas Paine.

From my journal on February 29, 2000: "We're moving from our motor home into our red apartment/shed. It's very dull & dingy & depressing & cold, but if the Lord wants us to, I hope I'll do it with a willing heart."

Inside the shed, there were no doors, just makeshift curtains, so you heard *everything* in each of the partitioned "rooms"—one for the parents, one for the five boys, and one for the three girls. In the winter, we had no furnace, so we relied on anemic space heaters plugged into a makeshift electrical system running from an external generator. With no running water inside, we either hooked up a green PVC hose or hauled buckets of water from a ground pump outside to the shed's kitchen area (just a sink, basically, and the microwave powered by the outside electricity hookup).

Here's my journal entry from March 17, 2000, age seventeen:

I feel like I'm rotting & wasting away, like I'm miserable when these teenage years are supposed to be some of your happiest. I would like to go to college in Utah; this question is looming over my mind constantly. If I go, Dad will say I'm a worldly rebel, evil, and will end up being destroyed. You know, the only reason I'm feeling so bad is because I have no friends, am a nerd, and getting fatter because I feel depressed and then go eat. If Dad would let up a little, I wouldn't want to leave home, but I'm afraid if I don't, even for a little while, I'll end up an obese, ugly, dumb loser with no self-confidence. Men are that they might have joy [here I was directly quoting the Book of Mormon, 2 Nephi 2:25], *and I don't have much. Listen to me whining away. The devil loves to put sad thoughts in people's hearts.*

Oh, how I fantasized about Mom's failed divorce attempt as I drifted asleep in the creaky triple bunk bed, nearly scraping the ceiling of the shed, or as I elbowed for space in the cramped motorhome overhang, three sisters fighting to avoid being the one forced to sleep against the cold glass.

Mom, I imagined, would remarry a normal Mormon man with a steady job, a real estate agent or a doctor, and we'd live in a suburban Utah cul-de-sac. He would get us a trampoline. He might let me play with Barbies. He wouldn't make us live in a tent or uproot us from school every few months or make us wither in homeschool. He would get us health insurance instead of stitching up the back of my head by hand. He would buy braces for my crooked teeth instead of using a snapped Popsicle stick to push my teeth around and deaden my root nerves. I told myself that if only Mom were stronger, Peter wouldn't have gotten sick with schizophrenia and morphed into a human zombie.

In the midst of this squalor, Ralph believed he was destined for greatness. Here's another passage from March 17, 2000: "Dad says our mission is to save this country. He has had several promptings [from the Holy Ghost] that he should be President of the United States . . . I want to save [sic] country, but I don't have enough faith. I mean, here we are, out in the middle of nowhere, living in a shack & motor home, don't have any friends, no connections, don't go to church, and I feel like a social cast out. But I know that through God, all things are possible. Maybe He's purging out all our lusts and bad character traits."

Our lovely puppy, Maestro, a stray who'd wandered into our Branson yard—nobody responded to "Found Dog" signs we'd posted with his photo; I secretly hoped they wouldn't—proved the saving grace of that era.

We named him Maestro. "Maestro" is Italian for master, so we technically called the dog our master. Clever, no? The name also has a musician tie—you call an orchestra conductor "maestro" and what we'd call Ralph as conductor of our family orchestra. An adorable beagle-mix mutt with brown ears; black, white, and brown patches; an incredible sense of smell; chocolate-brown eyes; and an ebullient temperament, he licked human faces incessantly. Before Maestro, we'd sporadically owned cats. Maestro forever opened our hearts to the canine realm. His fur captured waves of tears from my numerous teenage weeping sessions.

There's definitely a right way to homeschool and properly socialize, but as usual, we flamed out spectacularly. Here's my journal entry about homeschool from February 24, 2000, age seventeen:

> Peter has been getting worse lately, threatening to fight & call the police or social workers. I really hope he can get better...I wonder if we're ever going to St. Louis and when we'll go back to church. I haven't spoken with anyone who knows my name (outside of the family) for about 2 months. It's enough to make you feel pretty isolated. But even if we did go to church, I probably

wouldn't have anything to talk about with other people my age, even though there are some homeschoolers.

February 28, 2000:

I'm starting to get so chubby, I have no friends, I never go any-where, practically, and I feel miserable sometimes. I kicked the wall of our shed a few times and said a prayer, and it made me feel better.

And another, July 2, 2000, during a summer trip to Utah, where our motorhome sojourned in a trailer park:

No matter how hard I try & pray to force myself to enjoy it, or at least tolerate it, I end up wishing it were over even more. Sometimes I yearn for a normal childhood, but I can't erase the past. Besides, if I were 'normal,' I would probably end up shal-low, empty-minded, a worldly person, maybe even a sensualist. It's kind of like those people in India who try to purge themselves of all desires, even to the point of subjecting themselves to abuse through the caste system. So here I sit, gabbing to paper under the shade of a tree in a mobile home park.

Finally, after a whiplashing fall semester enrollment at Ozark High School my junior year that Dad aborted after two weeks, the clouds broke just before my senior year, and Ralph said we could reenter public schools. My three semesters of homeschool were agoniz-ing, and I felt thrilled to rejoin other students, this time in my seventeenth public school. I'm not sure what made the Holy Ghost change His mind about homeschooling (could be partially that the Calvert curriculum required more hands-on care, and my younger siblings were stubborn as oxen), but I wasn't asking questions lest this precarious joy crumble. God works in mysterious ways.

My senior year started as a blank slate at Parkview High School in Springfield, Missouri, a college town about forty miles north of our Branson homestead, yet still deep in the Bible Belt. Ralph chose Springfield because he said God told him to finish up his doctorate in music composition, which he'd started decades earlier at the University of Utah. Springfield is home to what's now called Missouri State University, a massive state school with more than twenty thousand students. Springfield, Missouri, is the birthplace of dystopian novelist Daniel Woodrell. His work *Winter's Bone* crafts a haunting portrait of this high-poverty, drug-infested Ozarks region. Playing the protagonist in the movie adaptation proved Jennifer Lawrence's breakout role, qualifying her for the Hunger Games franchise. It's filled with people who might be dismissed by Coastal elites as "White trash."

We moved into a modest white 1,100 square-foot, two-story rental on East Normal Street, right next to MSU's campus. We stayed there for one semester before Ralph decided to move us back to Maryland and homeschool, but by that point I'd earned enough credits to graduate a semester early from high school.

I didn't know my eventual fate; I felt ecstatic simply to enter a public school again. I knew nobody at Parkview, but resolved to try my best. With no orchestra, I sang in the chamber choir and took district honors from my solo audition. We enrolled too late, so I missed joining fall sports. I took an on-campus MSU course in political science, where I earned three credit hours and an A grade.

I felt proud and sophisticated, a high school girl competing with college students. Outside the classroom, Springfield held the key to unlocking what became my passion and calling: journalism.

I loved poring over newspapers whenever I could get my hands on them at school or the library. A portal to the outside world, they spoke about matters of politics and war that impacted our lives. Our local daily newspaper, the *Springfield News-Leader*, invited area high school students and other young people to contribute to a regular guest column called Young Voices.

I'd spent many hours growing up jogging in cross-country and others sports, so I felt fairly health conscious. Exercising was my natural antidepressant. It angered me to learn that Parkview High School's parent district, Springfield Public Schools, sold out and allowed vending machines on campuses in exchange for a $5 million payment over five years from junk food companies.

This encouraged unhealthy eating and increased the sugar on campus, something we didn't need with rising obesity and ADD. They put a price tag on children's health and sold it to the highest bidder. I felt so incensed by this that I wrote into Young Voices, and they ran the piece! That meant more than thirty thousand subscribers and other readers could access my thoughts. The essay ran with my photo and its tagline identified me as a Parkview senior.

I didn't sit on the school board and couldn't directly vote on this initiative, but the piece contributed to the debate as one of many voices (and a rare student voice) arguing against the action. I engaged in discussion about things that mattered and affected our community. I even received a few fan-mail letters sent to my high school, including from a woman who congratulated me on being a young woman in a male-dominated space sharing my voice, and encouraged me not to stop. She gave me a boost of confidence to continue. A social misfit among my peers, in this media arena, I shone.

I wrote other essays about stem cell research, global warming, and even teenage dating culture ("the principles of introspection, self-control, citizenship and civility are severely lacking in many of today's teenagers," I wrote. "If we were better taught to control our characters, we could then learn how to control our passions and bodies.").

While this triumph in news pages brought excitement and cultivated my writing skills, this time frame brought sorrow from a harrowing assault by my oldest brother, Peter.

I was seventeen, and it was getting late in the evening. I'd tried to help clean up the house. *Why of all ironies did we live on Normal Street?*

That week saw a terrible snowstorm—thirteen inches, uncharacteristic for Springfield, so far south. School closed for three days. I hated that. I never understood why my classmates complained about their weekends ending. I couldn't wait to escape home.

The damn snow and school cancellations that ensued meant I missed outside social interaction, including my beloved Christmas choir concert. Maybe my oldest brother, Peter, caught terrible cabin fever, causing pent-up aggression. A couple months before, in October, he shocked our family when he threw paint all over our neighbor's porch for no apparent reason. He also kicked the beloved family dog, Maestro, and afterward our darling pup would growl and snarl whenever Peter tried to touch him.

That snow day, December 14, happened to be Mom's birthday, and we celebrated with cake and ice cream. My brother Benjamin left his shoes strewn across the living room, so I picked them up and walked down the hallway toward the boys' room. (During the times we lived in houses, the five boys usually shared a room, and the three girls shared another.) I bent over to put the shoes down inside the dark room. A shock ran up my spine as a dark, monstrous hulk lunged at me. I screamed. Then I screamed again when the light from the hallway revealed Peter's contorted face.

"That's not funny, Peter!" my voice cracked with fear.

"Yes, it is!" Peter cackled as he lunged toward me, trying to grab my chest, and instead tightly squeezing my armpit. "I wanna have sex!" he roared.

I ripped free and raced out down the hall toward the living room. He followed in hot pursuit, managing to grab my left breast. Mom heard me screaming. She ran and tried to pull us apart. Peter grabbed at her, too.

"Peter, stop!" Mom yelled. "You're letting yourself spiral again," being sure to add, though fruitlessly, "Say a prayer!"

I screamed again and fled into the girls' bedroom. My heart pounded, and my entire body trembled as I slammed my back against the door and slid down to the floor to keep it shut. My legs locked and braced against our triple bunk bed for support. I looked down at my chest, buried beneath a baggy Lee's Summit High School speech and debate sweatshirt Mom had bought at a local thrift store. LSHS gave me my blissful freshman year, the best year of my life, and the sweatshirt served as a memento of my speech triumphs (first place in "Humorous Interpretation"!). Because it was now sullied as a vestige of pain and fear, I later trashed it.

That's usually how my childhood went—something to cherish followed by something harrowing that shattered any foundation of beauty or grace.

Tears streamed down my face as I struggled to keep Peter out. *Thuds. Rattles. Screams.*

With no door lock, I tried to slide our tall pine dresser in front of the door to block it.

Cheaply priced thrift-store furniture can be surprisingly hefty, but that's how Ralph liked it. He viewed thrift-store furniture shopping as a master class for learning to follow the Holy Ghost. Sure, the Spirit would help Ralph find the best deal, but along the way, he developed his rogue Mormon Jedi skills. Ralph endlessly beamed about the high-quality pieces he discovered. For some still undetermined reason, the Holy Ghost is fascinated with hutches.

The heavy dresser barely moved. *Is it possible I angered the Holy Ghost, and this is His retribution?*

My little sister, Julie, woke up startled. She'd fallen asleep with the lights on. At twelve and the youngest girl, she always snagged the bottom spot in our triple bunk bed.

"What's happening!?" she asked, her normally placid blue eyes filled with distress.

"Peter's trying to get me!" I whispered anxiously. I didn't think Julie knew about rape. We didn't talk about sex in our family, except to condemn it as Satan's domain.

I again straightened my legs, locking my knees once more as I pressed my feet against the edge of the bed's headboard. Waves of fear washed over my shaking body.

The door handle rattled and rattled. I heard commotion, other brothers yelling and tussling. Then silence. My brothers successfully pulled Peter away.

As I carefully peeked through a crack between the door and the frame to make sure the danger passed, a million thoughts shot through my mind: *Why had Peter grabbed me? What would he do if he caught me? What if no one could help me? Will he do this again?*

Peter was massive. He inherited my dad's genes, tall and

barrel-chested. With brown hair, and a round, freckled face, Peter wore near coke-bottle glasses. He stood about six feet, but obese and built like a football linebacker. He could easily crush me into submission, especially when amped up on a combo of meds, testosterone, and adrenaline. By comparison, I'm a small woman, 5'2"— an inch under even Mom's petite height.

That senior year, my high school demanded a school nurse's note proving I weighed the minimum 110 pounds required to donate blood. I felt thrilled to donate—like I was giving immortality! Mom needed multiple blood transfusions during my birth because of the emergency Cesarean section, so almost decades later, it only seemed fair to return the favor.

My school nurse, however, seemed begrudging about it. I understood—she was simply doing her job and didn't want the liability if something went awry. In the days leading to the weigh-in, I stuffed my face with scrambled and hard-boiled eggs (eggs are a staple for poor families—cheap and full of protein). I made the grade, a respectable 113 pounds. Soon after donating—and feeling on cloud nine—I got terribly sick with a cold and flu, leveling me for weeks. Plus, they told me I hit elevated cholesterol of 217, thanks to all those eggs I'd been wolfing down. After that, I decided I'd find other ways to give back moving forward.

It's still disgusting for me to think about it. When Peter assaulted me, he was twenty-four, near the age of peak testosterone and male sex drive. His illness also peaked. The cocktail of medications his doctors cycled him through might as well have been Skittles for all the good they did. Perhaps the drugs were actually worse for his brain than candy. During the nearly six years since he'd been diagnosed with schizophrenia, Peter flared up in numerous violent episodes. Yes, he kicked our beloved family beagle, Maestro, but

more often he lashed out in violent brawls with my dad. Ralph handled the physical barrage, and he seemed to relish the fights.

During one rehearsal, on February 29, 2000, Peter fell into a fit
of rage. I wrote about it in my journal:

*Peter said the opening prayer, and then he started ranting & rav-
ing. He hit Jonah from the side and threw his cello & broke it.
Dad took it to the repair shop. Mom & Dad both had promptings
that Peter is out of the mission; he's crossed the line. He's going
to keep living with us unless he gets violent, but he's not going to
play music with us anymore.*

Then later, on March 14, 2000:

*Around 4:00 A.M., Dad took Peter to a mental hospital in Spring-
field [MO]. Mom & Dad went to visit him today, they just got
back. (It's 10:47 P.M.) Peter has been getting into so many fights
& arguments, with Dad & other family members. Late last
night, he said some more horrible, evil things, and Dad said he'd
crossed the line. He called several hospitals, and took him to the
one called Cox Medical Center. It was the night shift, but dad
said he felt a really good spirit there. It took a long time for the
attendants to get Peter to sign in. Dad had to write an affida-
vid [sic] about Peter's behavior. Luckily, most patients only stay
there for about 2 weeks, until they are deemed mentally stable to
leave, because they are given medication & treatments. Dad got
home around 10:30 A.M. & he slept all afternoon. Peter called
while he was asleep, and Mom talked to him on speaker phone,
while I & others were listening. He said they were torturing him
there, forcing him & giving him shots, and that he wanted to*

come home. That was the first time I'd heard him cry for years. He
was given medicine, and slept most of the day, that's what Dad
said. If he keeps taking medication & is deinstitutionalized, the
medicine will only mask his symptoms and if he forgets to take it,
he might do something terrible like what is on the news. He won't
be as evil & rude, but he will become dependent on a substance
which influences his brain. I have prayed & fasted for Peter, but
not nearly as much as I should have. I must admit that I'm even
embarrassed in public with him sometimes. I know it's not Chris-
tian, and I need to love Peter, no matter what, because God loves
me even though I'm sinful, rebellious, and idle.

However, Peter's banishment didn't last long, and he soon
rejoined playing with us, subdued by medication. In one especially
bizarre rehearsal, Peter seemed extra neurotic, which caused Ralph
to claim Satan was attacking Peter. To expel the demon, Ralph
ordered us to kneel and pray. We were playing Beethoven's famed
Fifth Symphony in C Minor, the exhilarating first movement that
would have induced the Romantic Period's version of a mosh pit—
what a thunderous resonance of musical power!

The first four notes are recognizable to almost any human in
the Western world (and much of the Eastern, too). The first three
notes are pounded out like bullets in rapid succession—three G
eighth notes in resounding unison for the whole group—followed
by the E-flat half note with a fermata, or brief hold.

"Ta-ta-ta tah!"

Then the same piercing pattern happens again, but the second
time with three F eighth notes and an extended two-bar D note
with fermata.

"Ta-ta-ta tah!"

Ralph said Peter cast out demons each time Peter played those notes, that he preached a nonverbal Mormon musical message that, if set to words, proclaimed: "The Church is true! The Church is true!" We broke Peter free from Satan's grasp that night, thanks to Beethoven's genius. Peter calmed down.

Sometimes the rehearsals grew fraught when Peter thrashed into a violent episode. Ralph wasn't shy to wrestle Peter, or any of us kids, to the ground. The juxtaposition of the transcendent classical music with the chaotic physical rampage felt searing. But since that was all I knew, I acquiesced. I wholeheartedly believed in the cause of using music to attract people to hear the word of God.

Ralph enthusiastically told us that if we faithfully served alongside Peter, God would heal our brother's schizophrenia. But about ten months after that Beethoven-infused exorcism, Peter assaulted me. My left breast and armpit still throbbed as I sat on the bedroom floor, barricading the door, gasping for air, and choking down sobs. *Our musical mission wasn't doing much healing.*

Here's my journal entry from December 17, 2000, three days after Peter's assault, when I described what happened the day after the assault:

Peter's a derranged [sic] insane person, and not safe to live around. On Friday he left the house w/no coat in the snow & tried to throw himself in front of a bus. The bus stopped & called the police, who arrested him & took him to the mental hospital. It's so sad that a human life has been destroyed so bad; that his mind is completely twisted. He yields to Satan's temptations and his countenance becomes wicked.

Perhaps Peter felt guilty for his assault and knew he'd done something very wrong. We didn't get full details about his suicide attempt, but I do remember us all feverishly praying for his safe return. While this wasn't his first hospitalization, it was his first attempt to take his own life.

The ambulance rushed Peter to Cox North Hospital, part of a medical system in Springfield, where I'd been volunteering as a "Medical Explorer." My mom felt inspired that I'd become a nurse or something in the medical profession (because of our famous Mormon midwife/nurse/surgeon ancestor, Jane Johnston Black), so I donned the coed program's white coat—making me feel like a budding superhero—and shadowed doctors. Yet again, an item that brought me pride felt tarnished. The white coat, and its glory, became eclipsed by sorrow for its association with my brother's tribulations.

Peter came home only to get continually hospitalized thereafter. I knew he wasn't well, so I didn't blame him for attacking me. If anything, I blamed Ralph for pushing him over the edge. But I also couldn't shake the fear that next time, Peter might succeed. Several months later, near my eighteenth birthday, I wrote in my journal:

The other night, I had a scary nightmare about Peter assaulting me. I woke in a start, quivering and crying. Peter left his note-book in our room and I looked at it (I was cleaning and packing) to see what it said. Peter had written down some thoughts, and they were disgusting, about "mating," "people can get married at age 18," "the body clock instinct is to mate" and crap like that. It was so nasty; I don't even want to write or think about it, but I'm really scared sometimes in Peter's presence. He's an insane creep. On my birthday (a sad day), the family (as is our tradition

on any B-day) was saying nice things about me. Peter said "Car-
rie's pretty." That's the first time I ever remember anyone saying
a compliment or anything about a family member's appearance.
He also says that, "Carrie can be a model." I don't think I'm over-
reacting when I remember what Peter did last December and said
to both me and Mom. I cannot live in a house where I don't feel
safe. Sometimes I feel like either Peter goes or I go.

Repeatedly during our early-morning and evening indoctrination sessions, known as Family Prayer, Ralph said Peter's schizophrenia was God's punishment for being "rebellious." Basically, he
thought Peter deserved it because he was a punk who toilet-papered
our neighbors' homes and pulled other normal teenage hijinks. I
began to grow angry at Ralph for his self-righteousness. It became
increasingly apparent that our brother could never lead a normal
life, one marked by college, marriage, and children. Part of me
started to think that's exactly how Ralph wanted us: permanently
broken and helpless so he could control us forever.

Doctors say that schizophrenia is usually triggered by both nature
and nurture. I'm 100 percent convinced our traumatic upbringing
contributed to our family's sickness of mind and spirit. After Peter
was hospitalized again, he emerged sedated under a regime of drugs
that temporarily stabilized him away from violent outbursts, so I
didn't feel as physically unsafe. But his spirit seemed broken; there
was no hint of the boy he used to be. My brother Jonah received a
schizophrenia diagnosis in his midtwenties, later in life than Peter
and without recurring hallucination characters.

We suffer chemical-imbalance tendencies on Ralph's side, but just how much they would manifest in a more stable environment is a burning unanswerable question.

As the years passed, I'd feel guilt for prized moments in my budding career. After I earned my Harvard graduate degree, occasionally I thought, *I would gladly trade in my master's degree if Peter and Jonah could become well again.*

Of course, there's no magical process for making that happen, and instead I would cry about how my sweet brothers became broken shells of the promising boys I'd known and loved.

It proved a long, winding path, but Peter's assault eventually catalyzed me to scrutinize my faith, to pray for God's protection and guidance, and, eventually, to reject Ralph's false prophecies and run away from home. I'm the fifth oldest sibling, but the first to escape the clutches of The Mission.

That harrowing night back in 2000 taught me a lesson reinforced time and again: life's most wrenching crucibles can propel us to our greatest moments of growth and freedom.

⌒

Chapter 7

Finding the Motorhome Prophecies

No legacy is so rich as honesty.

—William Shakespeare[35]

The moment I realized Ralph was a false prophet, my entire world fell away. It was a nuclear shock wave. Sorting through Ralph's private boxes, I squatted in the white fiberglass trailer hitched behind our motorhome. It was the dead of winter, and a small space heater purred softly, emitting rays of welcome warmth.

The trailer, along with the motorhome, plugged into the power line for our nineteenth-century farmhouse in idyllic Laytonsville, Maryland. Despite the chipped white paint, the farmhouse appeared elegant with its wraparound pillared porch. But that was outside. Inside, the house was rotten and decaying—like what we hid behind our smiling family photos with our musical instruments and matching star-spangled outfits.

Why did the ten of us live cramped together in the motorhome instead of the relatively spacious farmhouse? Because getting the heating and plumbing fixed in the farmhouse required overhauling the well water mechanics and oil-tank system—too expensive for us. Plus, Ralph relished the spartan life—suffering strengthens character.

It was 2001, just after I turned eighteen. It was a horrible birthday meal; my father got into a screaming match with my youngest sister, Julie, because he said she wolfed down her food too fast. To retaliate and teach her a lesson, he picked up his red-sauced spaghetti with his hands and stuffed pasta noodles into his face, all while making yelling, horrid noises.

Disgusting table manners aside, my father previously decided it was time to write his autobiography, believing it would become a monumental treatise that would automatically convert anyone who read it. He compared himself to the Book of Mormon prophet Mahonri Moriancumer, whose power with words was so great that anyone who read his writing would feel completely and immediately consumed with belief.

Instead of letting me get a job as a camp counselor, a receptionist at a local optometrist, or a cashier at the local 7-Eleven to earn money for clothes and college application fees, Ralph offered to pay me a nominal salary (we're talking maybe three-to-five dollars a week) to electronically transcribe and summarize documents from his past using our clunky, pixelated word processor.

After previous months of tortured arguments with Ralph— and prayers and pondering about whether I truly believed in his prophetic mission—I decided these documents would unlock my future. Until that time, I accepted Ralph's claims at face value, believing and wanting them to be true. Now in physical danger from Peter, I needed to discern once and for all whether Ralph was indeed prophetic. These documents would either reveal Ralph's greatness or demonstrate a creative yet deeply troubled mind. I would either be fully converted to the family mission, or I could separate with a clear conscience.

Through our years of travels and constant moves, we lost most of our possessions, from Mom's beautiful paintings created during her time as an art student to my treasured petrified buffalo tooth given to me by a rare family friend. Yet, somehow, Ralph held on to boxes of his own possessions: photographs from his childhood, prized books, poetry, and letters from his time as a missionary in England.

I'm now convinced that for Ralph and many other offshoot extremists like him, Mormonism can create a type of savior mentality, where they see themselves as the secret weapon for rescuing all of mankind (it makes sense, given LDS doctrine teaches that every Mormon man can become a god of his own planet, co-ruled with his multiple wives), and Ralph fully bought this narrative. Mainstream Mormons, the official LDS Church in Salt Lake City, banned polygamy in 1890—in part to obtain Utah's statehood—but they continue to perform temple ceremonies that "seal" one man to multiple women in the hereafter. For me, heaven does not involve a husband whose love is shared with many wives. Ralph never tried polygamy on earth—though some homespun prophets leading Mormon offshoot cults do—so, thankfully, we didn't have to deal with that additional dysfunction.

Mormons like Ralph likely trace this savior mentality back

to the Church's founder, Joseph Smith, who was born into a poor farming family in upstate New York. With almost no formal education, through his wits, charisma, and social entrepreneurship, Smith founded a religion, raised his own militia, known as the Mormon Battalion, and won the mayorship of Nauvoo, an Illinois town then rivaling the size of Chicago. Smith preached that God of earth is a former mortal who achieved perfection through righteous acts and that we earthlings could emulate this example.

Smith later ran for the US presidency in 1844, and, as any good theocrat would, destroyed the printing press of the *Nauvoo Expositor*, a local newspaper critical of his polygamous acts and dictatorial tendencies. This landed Smith in jail, where a murderous mob assassinated him by gunshots. The year before his death, Smith gave the Saints what later became known as the White Horse Prophecy. Now, it's important to note this "White Horse Prophecy" is based on unsubstantiated accounts and is not embraced as official LDS Church doctrine. But it circulated widely throughout Church membership, including during my Mormon childhood, and I later wrote about it for the *Wall Street Journal* in 2006, when Mitt Romney considered running for president the first time.

According to his followers, Smith predicted American citizens' basic rights would come under threat, and the US Constitution would "hang like a thread as fine as a silk fiber."

"A terrible revolution will take place in the land of America," he reportedly said, "such as has never been seen before; for the land will be left without a Supreme Government, and every specie of wickedness will be practiced rampantly in the land." It would require the Mormon people, symbolized by a white horse, to ride in and save the republic from collapse. "I love the Constitution," Smith continued, "it was made by the inspiration of God; and it will be preserved and saved by the efforts of the White Horse."[36] Smith borrowed the white horse imagery from the apostle John in the Book of Revelation.

The prophecy, in various forms, was recounted in contemporaneous personal journals and spread by word-of-mouth among Saints in early settlements in Illinois and then Utah. Later tellings of the story escalated its drama, painting pictures of a single Mormon man rushing in like a White knight in shining armor during a constitutional crisis.

Church prophets after Smith toned down the prophecy, rejecting the white horse imagery but embracing the concept of the Constitution as a divinely inspired document that will face malicious attacks from unspecified enemies. Growing up, LDS Sunday School teachers across the country commonly discussed the idea that the Constitution is under attack.

Awestruck by this prophecy, I hoped my father was *the* White Horse. When Ralph got into arguments with several Mormon bishops who questioned his megalomaniac behavior, he quickly moved to a new ward and said the Church was the problem. They were the ones who didn't follow the Holy Ghost as closely as Ralph. They were craven, spiritually weak, and unholy. These fights were fairly common, no matter where we lived or visited. But even if he did mesh with the local bishop, we never stayed long; Ralph didn't want us getting too comfortable.

To paraphrase Ronald Reagan, Ralph didn't leave the Mormon Church; the Mormon Church left him. Yet, he still clung to his belief in the prophetic mission of Joseph Smith, his belief in the divine translation of the Book of Mormon. There were times Ralph teetered on the verge of creating his own sect of Mormonism (there are dozens and dozens of them in the Midwest and Utah, including the all-too-honestly titled Fundamentalist Church of Jesus Christ of Latter-Day Saints led by polygamist and convicted pedophile Warren Jeffs). Instead he became more hard-line and isolated inside the mainstream church. This saddened me because I loved the LDS Church; it was a bedrock of my identity. I felt dual loyalties to my church and my father. I didn't know that soon I'd have to choose between them.

According to Ralph, God—known as Heavenly Father to the LDS Church—said my dad receives personal guidance from the Holy Ghost more directly and correctly than pretty much anyone on earth, including the Mormon prophet living in Salt Lake City. The idea of personal revelation is a mainstream Mormon concept— but when misapplied, it's dangerous.

I'm sure most people of any stripe, religious or otherwise, will tell you now and then they have intuition or gut feelings that they try to live by. Stuff like, *Did I really turn off that curling iron? Should I really keep the extra change from the cashier?* But red flags fly when a man tells you he's Raphael, the archangel messenger mentioned in apocrypha Bible books and the Mormon scripture book Doctrine and Covenants (can you blame him? His given name is Ralph, after all). Warning bells also sound when someone tells you he had premonitions about the terrorist attacks of September 11—though of course, after the fact. I wondered, if he knew about the attacks, why didn't he say something?

During one conflict with local leaders, my dad stood up, "bearing his testimony" during the monthly fast and testimony meeting, which occurs the first Sunday of each month. Members skip two meals and give the food money to the Bishops' storehouse for needy families. And the Sunday sacrament service is basically an open mic for the congregation to share their spiritual experiences, their testimonies, in front of the whole crowd, which might average up to two hundred people. A natural performer and charismatic extravert, Ralph *loved* open mic days.

He would often take the occasion to criticize the LDS Church for what he believes is a neo-Catholic theology he calls the LDS version of papal infallibility. Catholic dogma on papal infallibility teaches that when the Pope speaks with the full authority of his role, called *ex cathedra*, there is no possibility of doctrinal error. This doesn't mean the pope cannot sin when he's off the clock, acting in his personal capacity.

My dad says the Mormon Church adopted its own version of this, an "our prophet can never lead the church astray" theology.

President Wilford Woodruff, the fourth LDS prophet and church president, gave an 1890 address canonized in Doctrine and Covenants, i.e., official scripture, where he introduced this idea.

"The Lord will never permit me or any other man who stands as President of this Church to lead you astray," Woodruff said. "It is not in the programme. It is not in the mind of God. If I were to attempt that, the Lord would remove me out of my place, and so He will any other man who attempts to lead the children of men astray from the oracles of God and from their duty."[37]

In our itinerant life, dropping in on various LDS Churches, Ralph often brought up why he found this deeply problematic—he thought it put the official LDS prophet on a pedestal, creating false perfectionism when only Jesus is perfect.

In this ward, he started giving his spiel during open mic and felt a tap on his shoe, behind his heel. Apparently, the bishop or one of his advisers was kicking him, urging him to stop! Ralph was incensed! He didn't let the move cut him short, and he said his piece. But we hightailed it out of there as quickly as possible!

Growing up, I thought my father was generous, strong, and always right—like most kids do. Today, in some areas, I still think he is. But it took me years to comprehend the double-edged sword that is religious devotion, how it can motivate and unify but also isolate and harden. The unmasking of my father, the faux prophet, took careful study, buckets of tears, and pleading with a God who seemed silent.

Our family grew $60,000 in credit card debt, in part to pay for publishing Dad's essays as advertisements in national newspapers. I grew restless as I contemplated whether to stay under Dad's roof. From my journal on January 1, 2000:

> *I think he's afraid of me leaving the house. He told me he wants me to be like Jesus & live w/my parents like He did until he was 30. This is completely hypocritical of my parents, who both moved out during college. I hope I'm not being rebellious, but at the same time, I hope my parents are reasonable . . . am I being manipulated? Dad said he had a prompting that our family can save our country from being destroyed b/c of wickedness. And if we don't save them, we will be eternally sorrowful & damned. What if this is true? It's a scary thought.*

For weeks prior to that decisive moment in the trailer, I dutifully entered Ralph's thoughts into the word processor. I spent hours riffling through letters from his mother, and carbon copies of his responses, that contained heightened concern about her increasingly radical, preachy son who thought she was worldly and shallow.

And then, I found something else, penned in Ralph's own hand. My heart pounded as I knelt in the trailer, horrified as I read the yellowing, handwritten manuscripts, ink blots coalescing to spell out his thoughts.

Mormons consider four books of scripture canonical, or official doctrine. One is the Bible (King James Version, both Old and New Testament, in case you're wondering), the Book of Mormon, the Pearl of Great Price, and Doctrine and Covenants, which I mentioned earlier. Each of these books is written in old-school, Elizabethan-style English. That means "thee" and "thine" instead of "you" and "yours," plenty of "thou shalt" instead of "you will." While the first three scripture books I mentioned are supposedly of ancient origin, Doctrine and Covenants is a collection of revelations from God given to LDS founder Joseph Smith during his life in nineteenth-century America.

In his handwritten pages, Ralph used his spiritual name, "Daniel Strong," which he claimed God gave him. He'd talked about this name before, along with God's supposed name for my mom, Joan Strong, which might have referenced Joan of Arc. What I discovered in the trailer were Ralph's "prophetic" divine dictations, similar to the ones that Joseph Smith received and memorialized in the Doctrine and Covenants. "The D&C" in Mormon-speak were Smith's orders from God on managing the mechanics of founding a religion—what Smith called the Restoration of the original Christian Church, which he claimed fell away under Protestantism, Catholicism, and various denominations.

It's not in the D&C, but to give you an idea of the timbre of Smith's revelations, he told his followers that an angel visited him three times, the last time with a drawn sword, and threatened his life if he didn't start practicing polygamy. It reminded me of when Ralph said, as a married man with young children living in the

Boston area, that God had told him He wanted to test his mettle by sending him to a strip club. This test would illustrate whether Dad possessed the moral fiber to withstand carnal temptations. Dad happily reported he passed with flying colors because instead of getting a lap dance, he taught a stripper how to pray using the Four Steps of Prayer, Mormon style. Dad pointed out that Jesus hung out with prostitutes and thieves, since they most deeply needed salvation. Yet somehow, I think Jesus would raise a brow at invoking His name to justify sexually charged voyeurism. In Dad's mind, his strip-club foray was not an act of brazen hypocrisy; it was a man obedient to his God.

Mormon scripture uses formal Elizabethan English, the type of language you read in the King James Version of the Bible. The style and tone of the "revelations" of "Daniel Strong" were almost identical to those of Smith's D&C, which is largely the quotidian trappings of where and when to move people, how to discipline, and logistical pitfalls to avoid.

I felt so horrified by Ralph's dozens of pages worth of expositions that I didn't tell a soul. I didn't even record them in my journal. But I do remember reading something close to this:

And thus I say unto my servant Daniel, thou shalt take thy wife, Joan and shalt travel to the land called Boston, where thou shalt tarry until I shall direct thee. Fear not, for thou shalt be imprisoned for sharing my Gospel. Thou shalt be spat upon and persecuted in every manner. Thou wilt be tempted to lean on carnal security, to seek financial gain to provide for thy family. But do not be deceived. Do not lean on thine own will, instead follow my Spirit and, just as with my servant Abraham, I shall provide thee with the ram in the thicket to preserve and provide. Thou hast suffered grave tribulation for my sake, but thou shalt be rewarded in eternity for saving souls in Zion.

In that fiberglass trailer, as the sun was setting, I quivered as I knelt down to God. I was in shock and feared Ralph was living an ungodly and blasphemous life. I'd seen this playbook before. Since its founding, Mormonism had been constantly plagued by rogue soothsayers who claimed they either outshone Smith or were his true prophetic heir. Ralph even copied Smith's ambitions for the White House, similar to Smith's failed 1844 independent presidential campaign. Dad repeatedly told us over the years that he planned to run for office someday, and he finally did make a failed run for Congress in 2010 (he came in fourth out of five in the Missouri GOP primary[38]—thrilled he wasn't last).

Seeing such an egregiously cheap knockoff of Smith, there in black and white, made Ralph's heresy that much more unmistakable. As a devout LDS Church member, I knew that if Ralph were the White Horse, these revelations would come through proper, official channels.

I told God that unless I was mistaken and Ralph truly was a prophet, I would leave home, even if that meant I'd get disowned. I asked Him to show me otherwise, and until He did, I would follow that course. I immediately felt flooded with an unexpected peace.

Chapter 8

Escape

I am no bird; and no net ensnares me; I am a free human being with an independent will.

—Charlotte Brontë[39]

I knew Ralph wouldn't take news of my desire to leave for college well. I'd been dreaming about leaving for college, perusing the BYU admissions website, looking at entrance essay questions as a homeschool student my junior year of high school. But those were casual pipe dreams until I found Ralph's handwritten prophecies. That made me pull the trigger, because my devotion to the official LDS Church superseded my devotion to an errant prophet, even if he was my father.

Shortly after finding his handwritten prophecies, I told my dad that I wanted to go away to college. In response, he pronounced a curse upon me if I chose that route. In Mormonism, there is a phrase called "raising your hand to the square." Here is more from retired LDS Church instructor Craig R. Frogley about what exactly that means and why it was so meaningful:

> *Elder Loren C. Dunn explains the significance of this physical action: "To sustain is to make the action binding on ourselves and to commit ourselves to support those people whom we have sustained. When a person goes through the sacred act of raising his arm to the square, he should remember, with soberness, that which he has done and commence to act in harmony with his sustaining vote both in public and in private." One legal historian notes: "Now, bringing an arm to the square has a meaning. A square is a four equal sided geometric figure. If you raise an arm 'to the square' then your arm has to represent two sides of the square. That means it will be at a 90-degree angle. The right arm will be held straight up. This indicates truthfulness, honesty, candor and frankness. That is the meaning of holding your arm to the square."*
>
> *Raising our arm to the square becomes, then, a form of commitment whereby we show that our behavior, our works will "square up" to the standard from heaven as established by our foundation stone, Jesus Christ. It is a sign of our oath of integrity we give before God, as measured against the divine standard to which we bind ourselves.*[40]

Up until that date, Ralph controlled his seven other children, including my four older brothers. Peter's schizophrenia left him mentally incapacitated. The other three, for various reasons, chose to stay at home and support Ralph's "prophetic calling," aka "The Mission." I was the first girl and first to defy my father by demanding freedom.

I posed a menace to his system of control. When he raised his hand to the square, sitting on his stool during family prayer in the motorhome, he raised his hand against what he deemed a satanic threat to the power he held over his family of ten people. His steely blue eyes bore daggers into mine:

"Carrie, you are full of Satan. I prophesy, in the name of Jesus Christ, that if you leave The Mission, you will have your virtue stolen, and you will be destroyed. Your life will be stolen also."

Having your "virtue stolen" means getting raped. I knew my father would be angry if I told him I wanted to leave. But I didn't expect him to say this. He raised his hand to the square other times with other siblings, including Peter. Peter got into fights periodically with my dad. It was almost like Ralph developed a sick schadenfreude when the child who caused him inconvenience got smitten with a permanent, debilitating psychiatric illness.

Mom also got into terrorizing prophecies. Hers came more through dreams, though, instead of Dad's "revelations" or "promptings." She told me she'd dreamt that I left home and landed in a gutter in a body bag. She later told me God told her I'd develop schizophrenia if I didn't repent.

An ex-Mormon friend of mine says a cult is something you can't leave with your dignity intact. It's an interesting idea. I think it has merit, though it's more complicated. Whenever we put anything ahead of God and His unconditional love, then everything unravels. As I saw later in life, you can build your own cult with yourself as the only member. Our self-centered culture too often encourages us to worship ourselves or the adoration of others. My family was absolutely a cult environment aimed at terrifying a young woman to keep her paralyzed so her parents could control her life. It was the same for my siblings.

It was 5:00 a.m. and I was eighteen, sitting on the back stoop of Normal Street waiting for my best friend Summer to pick me up. I first met Summer the fall of our senior year at Parkview. We quickly became friends in our speech and debate and English classes. We were about the same petite height—she maybe an inch shorter—but next to me, she was light-years more worldly. With large, expressive hazel-green eyes, Summer wore her brunette hair in a pixie bob cut. Because of her full cheeks, people said her doppelgänger was Christina Ricci. I idolized Summer, who starred in school plays, picked up trophies at state and national debating competitions, and later beat me out to place as a top runner-up during our competition in the 2002 Northeast Missouri (NEMO) Fair Queen Pageant. She had, and still has, chic style and taste.

Summer owned a beat-up maroon Volkswagen Cabriolet with an ill-fitting black convertible top. But the car was *hers*. So I didn't care about its pitiful condition, because it provided us with freedom—to party, to blare '80s music, to cruise around and try to meet boys. In hindsight, fortunately, I didn't have much luck in that last area. There was no way I'd risk getting pregnant, since that would immediately happen, I believed, if I spent time alone with a non-Mormon male. Summer drew my parents' anger when she took an interest in my brother Benjamin and hoped to bring him as her date to our homecoming dance. Unfortunately, at twenty-one, he was over the age limit her mom set for dates (nineteen), and Summer urged him to fudge his age. Benjamin refused and instead ratted her out to my parents, who warned me to keep away from her.

I didn't agree with Summer's actions on the homecoming front, but I knew she still had a good heart. Summer is an empathetic and beautiful woman, inside and out, and I think that's why she risked rescuing me from Ralph's "Mission." She has a special love for the downtrodden. In college, she worked as a case manager for mentally ill and troubled young people. Later, she lived a fairy-tale life— at age twenty-six, she married a Frenchman, and she lives happily with her husband and two sons (including one cutie adopted from China) in the tropical paradise of Costa Rica. For years, they lived in the rolling hills and red Basque stucco roofs of southwestern France, near the world-class beaches of Biarritz.

Spending time with Summer was like magic. She was my only high-school friend who took a deep interest in my well-being and my future. Summer assured me I had unique skills and talents, that I wasn't just another nameless, forgotten Sheffield kid—an appendage of Ralph's desires. She understood I needed help, that I lived in constant fear of my father's wrath. Little did she know that for her act of kindness, she'd go down in Sheffield family lore as a villainess whore.

A few days earlier, I'd graduated from Parkview High, my seventeenth public school. It was an awkward day. I borrowed my sister Sophie's white dress printed with pink roses that she'd bought at a thrift store five years before. Excited to finally get my diploma, I tried not to mind that almost nobody remembered me, since I'd only attended for that fall semester and returned only for the graduation ceremony—because God told Ralph to move us to Gaithersburg, Maryland, and live in a motorhome set up in the backyard of a dilapidated farmhouse. A couple months later that senior year, we moved seventy miles south, to Fredericksburg, Virginia, where Dad dreamed of opening yet another "theater" to promote Mormonism and classical music. Our family of ten lived in cramped, two-bedroom quarters attached to a commercial building that Dad bought with inheritance from his father. The five boys lived in the musty, unfinished attic filled with raw plywood beams. My brother Jonah crashed through the roof while climbing down the ladder, landing heavily bruised below.

Just before my high school graduation, all ten of us caravanned more than one thousand miles in our blue Chevrolet Astro van (which broke down and we temporarily abandoned) and Chevy Blazer SUV—from Fredericksburg to Springfield, Missouri, where we'd be for the graduation, and to check on their property forty miles south in Branson. I'd already resolved to leave home, so I secretly packed extra clothes and a few books with my violin in the back of the Blazer. I felt slightly guilty for my secret, but I felt peace in my plan.

Often at pivotal moments in my life, songs pop into my head—a soundtrack for my emotions. Perhaps it's a genetic feature as the daughter of a former music professor whose mother also composed music. For example, years later, Debussy's "Clair de Lune" rang inside my head the day in 2012 when my essay describing my estrangement from the Mormon Church was accepted by the *Washington Post* (an essay, I was told by an insider, that was read by members of the LDS Twelve Apostles). It's a lucid, peaceful lullaby, and the title literally means "moonlight" in French. It sounds like you're floating in the air above a still, placid lake.

The day of high school graduation, in popped the Beatles' "Eleanor Rigby," a song about "all the lonely people" and how Eleanor

Rigby wore a fake smile and "died in the church and was buried along with her name / Nobody came."⁴¹ That was my life, where I'd end up at my current trajectory—scared, abused, and alone.

The next day, I told my dad I wanted to spend the summer with my friend Summer and asked his permission. He said he'd check with the Lord. A little while later, Ralph came back and said God said no, that He needed me with the Consort to keep playing on street corners and passing out the brochures. He said if I left, I'd ruin The Mission and be like Judas in the Bible, who betrayed Christ. It's funny how Ralph's desires so perfectly aligned with God's supposed will. He said his skill came from years of listening to the Holy Ghost. I say it was Ralph's ego and unhealed trauma festering behind what philosopher Friedrich Nietzsche calls the universal "will to power." Regardless, I decided since I'd turned eighteen a few months before, I didn't need his permission anymore; it was time to go. It wasn't a secret; in my goodbye note, I told them where I was going and included Summer's address.

That early May morning, Summer and I whispered in hushed tones as we loaded my violin and clothes into her Cabriolet, my hands trembling. The muffler sounded like it had indigestion, and I worried my sleeping parents would hear us lurch away into the dewy, predawn, humid Ozark mist.

Before we pulled away, I insisted that Summer and I bow our heads in prayer, the pounding of my heart drowning out my words as I choked out my prayer to God:

Dear Heavenly Father, I thank Thee for bringing me an escape. Father, I ask Thee, please, please protect Summer and me as we start this journey. I am very afraid right now because I'm leaving,

and I've never been alone and I do not want to reject Thy will.
Father, my dad says I will be raped and murdered if I leave, but
I do not believe this is true. Please guide me so that I stay virtu-
ous and remember Thee always. Please protect me from harm and
give me Thy Holy Ghost.

We drove to Summer's parents' house nearby, in the same city of Springfield, Missouri—the third largest city in the state. Her mom and stepdad had moved to the St. Louis area, nearly a four-hour drive away, so it was just us and another woman, a bit older, who was paying rent to Summer's mom. A nervous wreck, I felt racked with inner guilt and torment for running away from The Mission, and from God. I immediately fell asleep at Summer's place, grateful for my own room on the upstairs floor. The first place I went after waking up was the local LDS Institute building, the Mormon Church instruction building for young adults, to find out what time they met on Sundays (9:30 a.m.). I was planting my flag, and I wanted to remain spiritually grounded. From my journal on May 27, 2001:

I'll miss everybody, (including Maestro) and I love them all. I
hope & pray they don't hate me & forgive me & love me. I hope
they won't forget me but pray for me & think about me & that
I'll do likewise. My family is the only life I've ever known & I feel
scared and shaky about leaving for the unknown. I hope my faith
will keep me grounded and morally strong. I hope the spirit of the
Lord will strive in me & help me to grow into a more devoted and
stronger servant of the Lord. I want to keep my mind & heart pure
& undefiled & virtuous always. I hope to learn human relations

& how to speak well and communicate my thoughts. I hope I can
become socially mature in righteousness and learn to stand up
and speak out. I hope I will follow the Lord.

Summer's mom wanted us all to contribute to the housing costs, so I scrambled to find a job to pay my $175 monthly rent (that's $293 in 2023 dollars—thanks, inflation). After soliciting various shops within walking distance, on my first day of hitting up local businesses, I landed a part-time role as a hostess at Jun's Korean BBQ buffet, making $6.25 an hour with a promise of $6.50 with good performance. Jun was a kind Korean immigrant whose wife also worked as a hostess and cared for their adorable young son. It was just a three-block walk from the house, but it meant long hours on my feet, creating blisters from my one nice pair of shoes—strappy sparkly purple ones from Delia's, a '90s cheap fashion house phenom—and worrying about sweat stains through my DressBarn yellow short-sleeve suit top. I indulged far too often on the free soft serve ice cream with chocolate sauce allowed for staff. Jun's wife offered to give me a ride home during my night shifts. Jun kindly offered to front me cash if I ever needed it before my paycheck arrived. He said he treated his staff like family, and I felt it. They helped calm my nerves, with Jun telling me he thought my dad loved me since all fathers love their children.

While I was gone looking for work, Mom and Dad showed up and talked to our roommate Megan, handing over an envelope of $500 in cash, along with the nine handwritten goodbye letters I'd carefully crafted for my parents and seven siblings, one page for each person. They rejected this olive branch, the sin-stained ramblings of a satanic outcast. From my journal on May 27, 2001:

There was no note from them at all. I wonder if they read my notes. Maybe they thought I was just being a shallow suck-up. After I looked at my rejected letters, I started bawling. It's as though I were dead to them.

I filled my time working double shifts at Jun's, working twenty-five hours that week. I tried getting a second job as a server at a Carlos O'Kelly's Mexican restaurant, but they rejected me after I told them I couldn't work Sundays for religious reasons.

I tried calling and emailing my family multiple times but they didn't reply or pick up. The silent treatment killed me. I fretted they'd kicked me out of the family as a traitor, and I worried over whether I was sinning against God, since He placed me in this family.

May 30, 2001: I've been reading my journals that I brought that I've had since I was eight. I'm trying to kind of psychoanalyze, if you will, myself to see why I have left my family and at what point I lost my self-confidence, if I ever had any. I see my younger self saying so many things that my Dad always says. I never realized he was such a deep part of me. This is why withdrawal is so painful.

My panic and guilt overwhelmed me; I lasted only a week and quickly crawled back home after my parents staged an intervention and surprise ambush on my doorstep by Mom and two of my brothers. I left on a Sunday and returned the following Sunday. I felt embarrassed. But this wasn't surprising. Experts report that, on average, a woman returns to an abusive relationship seven times before she leaves permanently.[42]

June 14, 2001: I've been back with my family for about 2 weeks. On Sunday the 3rd, I went to the young adult [LDS Church] *branch. The people were really nice & I told them I was going to be going there for the whole summer. After church (I got a ride from a girl) I watched "Runaway Bride" again & "Braveheart". That night, Dad called and the whole family was there (but Mom, Peter and Benjamin) in Branson* [forty miles away] *while the other three were cleaning the house in Springfield. Dad said he had a revelation that my leaving was inspired by the devil & that if I were to stay there, something terrible would happen to me, like I would get pregnant or raped or something. He scared me. I was bawling & Mom came & Benjamin & Peter took all my stuff.* [My roommate] *Megan & Mike* [her boyfriend] *came while I was yelling & crying.*

We lived in the shed for about a week in the shed in Branson then left for Virginia in the Blazer with all 10 of us and Maestro. I was kind of rushed off w/o thinking, but I think I shouldn't have sneaked off early in the morning...

Ralph called Jun and left him a voice mail saying he could keep the $156.25 in wages I hadn't received yet because of the trouble I'd caused by starting and quitting so soon.

I felt ashamed, broken down without the harsh confines of a cult-like environment. It was Stockholm Syndrome, in some ways. Subconsciously, during my week of escape, I wonder if I missed being told that I was evil, unworthy, and that my dad's special spiritual powers meant his destiny must subsume any future plans or dreams.

May 29 2001: I've been thinking about Dad a lot today. He's such a complex man & I can't understand him. He says things which if I had heard them from anyone else, I'd think they had problems, but from him, they seem like they could be true. For example, he says our family has a mission to save our country, that the Lord considers him a prophet, that he follows the Spirit more closely than Gordon B Hinckley [the official Mormon prophet in Salt Lake City], *that the Lord told him to prepare to be president of the U.S., that I would become a traitor & try to delegitimize my family & lose my soul if I were to leave home, that President Clinton was personally trying to harm him, etc. But each of these and other like statements have stories behind them which I can honestly see happening. Except when he says I'm going to turn on my family.*

Isn't it strange to say a kid trying to go to college makes her a "traitor"? One who will sin irredeemably against the Holy Ghost and be damned for eternity because she simply sought the same path her parents trod?

One of the most touching scenes I've seen in film plays in *The Shawshank Redemption*, which I watched as a newly emancipated college freshman. During my rebellious phase, my first boyfriend (a non-Mormon) wanted us to watch *Shawshank*, a film that's rated R, a designation for films typically banned in Mormon homes (*Braveheart* won an exception in our family because of William Wallace's noble mission). The scene bringing me to tears came when the elderly inmate Brooks Hatlen, who served as the prison librarian, gets freed on parole and moves into a halfway house. After fifty years confined and suffering within a dysfunctional system, Hatlen cannot manage his freedom and hangs himself.

When his inmate friends discuss what happened, Red (played by Morgan Freeman), nails it: "These walls are funny. First you hate 'em, then you get used to 'em. Enough time passes, you get so you depend on them."[43]

Little did I know how close I would eventually teeter toward Hatlen's choice, multiple times over the years. With skyrocketing suicide rates in America, I know I'm not alone as our society struggles to cope with the breakdown of our bedrock institutions, which provide a healthy foundation for self-identity. That includes the family, organized religion, schools, and government institutions. We're floundering, turning to suicide, opioid addiction, violence, and crime because we are looking for meaning and purpose in the wrong places.

After whimpering back home, I told Ralph things needed to change if he wanted me to stay, including more stability for our family and no more yelling at us or getting into physical fights with my brothers. He rejected my demands, telling me that he led the family, and that I needed to repent and ask God for forgiveness.

"Carrie, you are not the priesthood holder in this home," he said, referring to the status of elder granted to all practicing LDS adult males. All lay male members are ordained in various offices, starting the year they turn twelve, not just a select few leaders as in Catholic, Orthodox, and Protestant traditions. "You have *no right* to force me under your authority. You are acting like a vixen filled with Satan's desires to destroy this Mission."

After a short shed sojourn (say that ten times fast), we drove back to the East Coast. I spent the summer locked in conflict, with Ralph cajoling me to permanently rejoin the musical group but then later, after other fights, banning me from playing with the family on street corners. Banished, I stayed at home alone while the Consort performed in the streets of Fredericksburg, Virginia, and elsewhere, as the family meandered in the motorhome from Boston to New York City and New Hampshire.

"Pack your bags," Ralph would threaten each time we had a flare-up, his way of threatening to kick me out and disown me.

Things eventually got so heated that I snapped and told him I wanted to leave for good and attend Truman State University.

July 2, 2001: I don't believe in what we are doing, and it would be fruitless & a fraud if I were to continue doing this indefinitely.

But I'm so shy & afraid & I don't want to hurt my family. A couple of weeks ago, I got a prompting [from God] not to quit. But maybe that meant just for the summer...

I do believe that Dad is being somewhat deceived in what he calls "the mission." Whenever he talks about how great he is or it is, I only feel revulsion, sadness and a wrong feeling. Would I be rebellious to tell people what Dad says about himself?

I'd waffled a bit in the immediate aftermath of my return, but by the end of July, it was settled: I'd move out for my freshman year of college.

While living at home previously during my junior year in the shed, I studied for the ACT test in the empty blue house on the Branson homestead and scored surprisingly high on practice tests. I knew I could attend a good school and get at least some financial help. I wanted to apply for Brigham Young University, but I didn't have money to pay the application fee, and it didn't occur to me they might waive the fee for financial hardship.

I'd applied and been accepted to Truman State, a small liberal arts state school billing itself as the "Harvard of the Midwest" or the "Princeton of the Prairie," ranked high by *U.S. News & World Report* because it's fairly competitive to enter, with students scoring well above national ACT averages. Truman was not my first pick; they simply didn't have that application fee. Looking back now, it seems absurd, but I'm definitely not alone. The *New York Times* and other venues reported that high college application fees deter poor applicants.

"In 2017, the median family income of a Georgetown student was $229,100, compared to the national median of $61,372 that same year," the Georgetown student newspaper *The Hoya* opined in 2020. "Georgetown's application fee is more than twice the $44 average college application fee in the United States, according to U.S. News & World Report. Georgetown should eliminate its application fee to increase the accessibility of applications and accommodate a more socioeconomically diverse applicant pool."

Also, because the BYU deadline landed months before graduating, part of me felt terrified they'd tell my parents, because the LDS Church is so centralized and a local bishop's approval is required for an ecclesiastic endorsement. Since I scored higher than the average Truman student, I landed a Bright Flight scholarship from the state of Missouri ($2,000), along with the Truman State University President's Honorary and Combined Ability scholarships. I still needed to work hard, but it looked like I could cobble together my future.

After I got my Truman State finances lined up and emailed with my soon-to-be dorm roommate, Mom gave a startling pronouncement.

"I prophesy to you, that if you go away, you're going to get pregnant," she said, also adding that I'd become an ex-Mormon heathen.

July 31, 2001: I'm scared, because although I would NEVER want or allow these things to occur, Mom is a very spiritual person & she's very close to the Lord. The only way I can prevent these tragedies is to pray, be humble, stay close to God and good people, so that I can keep my soul . . . God is so merciful & answers prayers. He's given me comfort & strength these past few days to get me through the loneliness.

My parents continued to ban me from playing with the family busking on street corners as punishment that summer leading up to my departure. It wasn't a punishment for me in terms of the actual street performances themselves. I found them embarrassing and ineffective at developing life-changing conversion relationships. I died inside when a former JV soccer teammate from Gaithersburg High School saw me playing music on the streets in Alexandria, Virginia. But I felt heartbroken to get cut off from my mom and siblings, sometimes for days at a time in their motorhome treks to New England and elsewhere.

As the summer waned, Ralph decided to escort me away himself, since it became clear I wanted out. He cited a concept of "shaking the dust off your feet" in Matthew 10:14 for missionaries, in which Jesus tells His disciples, "If anyone will not welcome you or listen to your words, shake off the dust from your feet as you leave that house or town."

Later, in 1830, Joseph Smith, founder of the LDS Church, revamped this in Doctrine and Covenants 24:15, in a revelation to LDS missionaries:

"And in whatsoever place ye shall enter, and they receive you not, in my name ye shall leave a cursing instead of a blessing, by casting off the dust of your feet against them as a testimony, and cleansing your feet by the wayside."

As a family called to a special Mission, Ralph said I was doubly cursed because, not only did I reject God like ignorant Gentiles in Scripture, but I proactively made this move as a former believer and someone fully warned by a prophet.

It was a risk I was willing to take.

Chapter 9

Liberated Life

You, my brothers and sisters, were called to be free. But do not use your freedom to indulge the flesh; rather, serve one another humbly in love.

—Galatians 5:13[44]

I felt petrified as my father drove away with Peter in the ancient white Plymouth Reliant sedan that muggy August afternoon in rural Missouri, leaving me to my own devices. We completed the roughly thousand-mile journey from Fredericksburg, Virginia, to Kirksville, Missouri, after experiencing car trouble.

Fearful that I would immediately have sex with the first male I encountered, I clung to my dime-store, purple spiral-bound notebook, which I had carefully inscribed with page after page of sober-minded quotations and scriptures from Mormon prophets and other inspiring leaders on virtue, humility, and diligence. Did

I follow these teachings perfectly? Absolutely not. But did I try? Yes, but with mixed results.

Friday, August 10, 2001: Monday night, Dad, Peter and I left F-burg in the Reliant. We had an argument, and I was feeling horrible. Sophie and Julie were so nice and helpful & Mom even said she would miss me, although she still says those bad things will happen to me. I pray they won't. On our way to Kirksville, the car broke down Tuesday night, so we got towed & spent the night at the garage. It got fixed & we proceeded north . . . I'm so grateful that Dad & I were able to leave on good terms. I emailed Sophie on Wednesday, but no word yet.

It was a surprisingly peaceful departure, but I eventually heard from my siblings that Ralph told the family later that I was a Daughter of Perdition and no longer part of the family. He wanted some dignity as he shook the dust off his feet at me. Perhaps he felt peace knowing he'd tried his best; plus, seven out of eight kids still under his control ain't bad.

The campus dorms weren't open yet, so I spent about a week for only $25 total in a two-story red-brick and cream-trimmed house owned by the Presbyterian Church, a women's group home of sorts catering to Truman students like me. Ralph miraculously found this place—I felt grateful to God. I wasn't Presbyterian, but the folks from the church next door at the First Presbyterian Church in Kirksville welcomed me with open arms. I hold special affinity for Presbyterians to this day. Ralph left me with a week's worth of groceries and $165, and I immediately spent about $90 on an iron, a hair dryer, a watch, socks, underwear, and clothes. I quickly landed a job at a Taco Bell off campus, though I got written up on my second day because I ended the day thirteen dollars above where my books showed.

"Don't worry, it's not a big deal this time, just a warning," my manager said. "But if this happens regularly, then this won't work out."

I was terrified. With a razor-thin margin for error, I desperately needed the money to survive and keep out of the motorhome. Over Labor Day weekend, I went to bed at 4:00 a.m. because I worked the Saturday night closing shift. Taco Bell closed at 2:00 a.m. but required heavy cleanup. I rode my bike home in the pitch-black night and caught a few hours of sleep before waking up at 8:00 a.m. to prepare for church.

During freshman orientation week, I donned a black tank top, the first time in my life I'd ever publicly exposed myself like that, except on a beach or pool. It was for some silly opening dance that each of the various dorm houses were performing in. I lived in the sole all-women's dorm on campus (dubbed "the Convent"), petrified of being physically close to so many males—and the songs we danced to included a medley of Madonna's "Like a Virgin" and the J. Geils Band "Centerfold." I had never heard these songs, and frankly, their sex-infused lyrics horrified me. But I felt determined to fit in, despite the jumbled mess of self-doubt and angst-ridden thoughts running through my mind.

Like many American college campuses, Greek life plays a big part for Truman State University, home of the Bulldogs. My dorm roommate had a boyfriend from one of the frat houses, some located in a strip on a street behind our dorm, so she dragged me to their parties. It was at a "foam party" in mid-September that I had my first kiss, in the basement of a fraternity house. A foam party is when a bubble-making machine fills the entire room, floor to ceiling, with foamy soap bubbles and everyone frolics and dances in the suds.

It was all fun and games until some fraternity guy who I'd briefly met with his friend a few weeks before pushed me back while we danced into the water stream feeding the bubble maker, dousing my hair, and then quickly pulled me forward before locking lips. He forced his tongue down my throat, his beard scruff scraping my chin and the smell of beer wafting into my nostrils.

It felt abrupt and startling, triggering a stab of guilt. It was not remotely as I'd dreamed my first kiss would be. I later wrote in my journal that it felt like a camel, with jumbo lips and a tongue forcing its way inside my mouth. Obviously, I'd never kissed a camel, but it felt animalistic to me—utterly unromantic and invasive. And yet, I knew I'd crossed the Rubicon; I'd never go back to VL status (virgin lips), as they say in Mormonism, and so I started to kiss him back. The cloistered motorhome maiden finally got some male attention, and even though it felt far from ideal, I was giving this a try. We kept making out and then he started groping me, an added shock, but I stayed. We walked back across the street and parking lot to my dorm room around 3:30 a.m. (my roommate stayed over at her frat boyfriend's place) and continued there, with him almost getting to third base before I kicked him out.

September 28, 2001: It was disgusting. He acted like he'd had a lot of experience with this sort of thing. Why did I let this happen? I haven't told anybody about that night . . . But still my ugly past is a scar which is hard for me to look at and think about. I know that I need to confess my sin to the bishop or somebody, but it's so much harder to put the scriptures into practice in real life situations. I know it'll make the Bishop uncomfortable & myself uneasy around him & I won't be worthy to go to the temple or to BYU. I know I must confess it, but I really don't want to. Will I ever be forgiven? Love, sex and marriage (maybe not the last one as much) were subjects which were not discussed at home. If my kids ever get ahold of this—please don't do what I did—you'll feel so ashamed and dirty inside. I wish Mom & Dad had been more open and allowing when it came to dating. I've still never gone to a formal dance w/a date, and my very first date ever is tomorrow...I wish they'd allowed me the experiences which would have given me social fulfillment, and maybe I wouldn't have plunged into the murky waters of immorality. But I'm not blaming them. The choices were mine, and I allowed myself to act like a beast, literally, w/o regard to the Lord's standards.

I pondered the five Rs of repentance in Mormonism: recognition, remorse, restitution, reformation, and resolution.[45]

How can I Repent from this sin? Well, the first R, I think is remorse. I feel horrible and I started crying a minute ago. Who can I give any restitution to? I can't restore my status, can I? The Lord says that He'll remember them [our sins] no more, but I can't forget & I don't think the bishop can either. Has he ever had to deal w/things like this? I grew up in the Church. I had all the teachings. So why did I rebel? I think maybe I'm depressed. Things appear so boring & lackluster, and I don't know what to do. I can't hold conversations very well, I'm socially inept, I have problems reaching out. People are just so annoying to me sometimes it seems. I mean I wish there were people who weren't the prissy, Molly-Mormon perfect, holier-than-thou type, and also

those who aren't the drunken, beastly, sex driven, loud, obnox-
ious maniacs. Who are the balance? Why can't I find people w/
whom I [sic] *comfortable with & with whom I can be myself?*
Except I don't even know who "myself" is, that's the problem.
And I don't know how to act & talk. Please, Father, give me guid-
ance! Help me know what to do. I need help really bad.

Now, I'm guessing some readers here are rolling their eyes at
my prudishness, but the truth is that sexually active teenagers are
more likely to be depressed and attempt suicide, and the confidence
of teenage girls especially plummets after sexual activity.[46]

Given my fragile state, I didn't want to mess around too
much, but full disclosure, even after that first camel-kiss, during
that freshman year I did my fair share of making out with other
men and toeing the line toward premarital sex. Yet I managed to
pull nearly straight A's and remain both a teetotaler and a virgin.
After so many awkward social encounters with men when I told
them I wouldn't have premarital sex and repeatedly realizing I'd
never truly belong as a Mormon, I decided to leave. Raised in such
a distinctly separate culture outside America's mainstream, I often
felt more comfortable with international students than my fellow
Americans. I passed the time with friends from Morocco, Bulgaria,
and Nepal.

Truman's campus, to me, felt like the dystopian fictional world
of Aldous Huxley's *Brave New World* that I'd read my junior year
of high school (on my own, outside my homeschool curriculum).
If you haven't read it, I highly recommend it—now, that author
was a prophet. Huxley published it in 1932, and it becomes more
prescient each year. It portrays a futuristic, materialistic, consum-
eristic, technocratic, soulless society in which youth is idealized,

there are no families, and children are created in embryo farms. Everyone feels happy endorphins because they're constantly drugging themselves with a narcotic called "soma" and engaging in orgies and random sex with strangers, because the concepts of love, God, and faith are totally irrelevant and society is completely secularized.

I felt like John the Savage, a man raised in the wilderness away from this technocracy, with a love for Shakespeare and a belief that loveless sex is meaningless. John stumbles into this "brave new world" (he's quoting Shakespeare there; an icon abandoned by society), feels horrified, and eventually dies, hanging himself in despair. "I don't want comfort," John the Savage says at one point before his death. "I want God, I want poetry, I want real danger, I want freedom, I want goodness. I want sin."[47]

I entered a mess my freshman year by stupidly trying to pet a dog in the back of a pickup truck parked at Walmart. In small-town America, Walmart is the central social scene, and Kirksville was no exception. I loved going there as often as my meager budget allowed. I dated a Walmart merchandise stock manager and fellow Truman student who shared scuttlebutt on how Walmart workers secretly gossiped about shoppers, including hotties.

Maybe that day I also felt at home, since our family often parked our motorhome overnight at Walmarts nationwide. There's no justifying what I did, but I felt so thrilled to see a dog since I desperately missed our family dog, Maestro. The truck was parked next to my car, and the dog seemed friendly. But as I reached in, he aggressively snarled and bit my right hand, ripping the flesh. It wasn't a huge gash, though shaken, I ran weeping into the store, where kind staffers got me bandaged up. Later, I was advised by medical experts that because this dog had been so aggressive unprovoked, it could be rabid. They said that typically, when a dog bites a human, it's held by authorities for a few days to check for rabies. But in this case, the truck vanished by the time I stumbled back into the parking lot with the Walmart employees. So the experts told me I could either chance it and assume the dog was not rabid, or get the expensive multi-shot rabies vaccine regimen. Unfortunately, I didn't have health insurance, and the cost approached $6,000 out of pocket. Panicking, I assumed I needed to drop out of college to pay this medical bill, because I didn't want to risk rabies. I felt deeply paranoid that God was punishing me for leaving my parents and there was a strong chance this dog was rabid. I frantically researched options and eventually found a resource from the state of Missouri, the Children's Health Insurance Program (CHIP). This CHIP program gave eligibility to children and young adults up until their nineteenth birthday. My birthday was approaching quickly— I believe only a few weeks away. CHIP saved my hide. Stupid and naive with the dog, my saving grace was my youth. I'm forever grateful to the taxpayers of Missouri for this CHIP program, which allowed me to remain in my studies. I got the vaccine with no side effects and continued on my way.

During Christmas break, Ralph enforced my quarantine away from my family, though he offered me one last escape hatch. As usual, it was an all-or-nothing, cult-like demand: to see my family, I must remain permanently. I turned him down.

11-26-01: Dad sent me a 7-page email saying the Lord would give me one last chance to come back & perform again. He said they were moving to Kansas City for the next semester & the boys &

*him are going to UMKC. He wanted to pick me up on the way
there. He said if I didn't come, the Lord said to give me $2700 of
my inheritance and that our relationship from then on would be
on a legalistic basis, and I'd be leaving the family.*

*I don't know why he's asking me to come back. A couple of
weeks ago he called. I wasn't here, [my roommate] answered &
got the message that they weren't going to let me stay w/them for
Christmas & that I needed to stay somewhere in Kirksville.*

Sick of Ralph's attempts to marginalize me, and feeling stronger from the independence offered by college and work, I decided he couldn't keep me suffering alone. I'd celebrate Christmas in Utah with my extended family, some of whom I'd reached out to immediately after leaving home. I felt mixed emotions about them, as I wish they'd done more to prevent Ralph from spiraling so far out of control and attempt to prevent his child abuse. Years after I'd left home, my cousin found a cassette inside her mother's (my aunt's) belongings, a decades-old phone call between my dad and his mother, Grandma Sheffield. Grandma recorded such calls at her family's urging, because Ralph made false claims about conversations. To save them drama, they began recording calls. In the recording, Grandma asked Ralph for a home address. He refused to give one. Ralph often kept his address hidden (this was pre-internet search engines), in part to keep us away from anyone who might give support. These are classic tactics of an abuser. I'd like to think if one of my siblings endangered his or her children, I'd be more proactive than my extended family was in attempting to rescue them. I can only speculate; perhaps they felt physically afraid for their own safety.

Now alone, I couldn't get preachy to my aunts and uncles. I bought myself a Greyhound bus ticket and hitched a ride with a kind Mormon classmate driving home to the St. Louis area, where the bus departed. Greyhound terminals are notorious for attracting shady characters, but I was willing to take the risk; the price was right, and this seemed far better than staying isolated in my dorm. One of my fellow passengers wore a long, dark, hooded cape cloak and claimed he was a warlock. Immediately suspicious but intrigued, I sussed out his divination skills. He tried to tell me facts about myself that, if I'd had a normal American teenage upbringing, might be plausible. But given my weirdo childhood, I immediately labeled this guy fraudulent, though I bit my tongue and remained pleasant (who knows what sort of chaos might ensue if I denied his "gifts"?) until we arrived. I felt enormously grateful when, after finding out I'd ridden in such company, my worried uncle used his airline points to get me a plane ticket home—the first plane ride of my life.

Aunt Charlotte, Dad's sister, encouraged me to come. She'd later endure years of harangues from my dad for hosting me during Christmas break at her home, accusing Charlotte of "stealing" his daughter. The truth is, Ralph rejected me and preferred I suffer in isolation rather than seek out support. He wanted to break me so I'd come crawling home.

Aunt Charlotte, a former Miss USA, was obviously gorgeous. As a young woman, she looked like Disney's Sleeping Beauty—statuesque, piercing blue eyes, and thick, wavy, golden locks. In her heyday, Charlotte's golden beauty rivaled Grace Kelly. And like Kelly, a Hollywood starlet during its Golden Age, Aunt Charlotte embodied elegance. Her powerful voice was velvet steel, alternatively soothing and commanding. Crowned Miss USA at the tender age of twenty, Charlotte burst into the spotlight, conquering the hearts of elite and everyday people around the globe.

She starred in various film, television, and radio productions, and traveled beyond the Iron Curtain to then-Czechoslovakia as the face of that country's Škoda Auto advertising campaign. She sang for nearly a decade in the famed Mormon Tabernacle Choir (now just called Tabernacle Choir), her coloratura soprano reverberating across the cultural fabric woven around our nation's milestones and world events.

She married early at age twenty-two, rebuffing the advances of wealthy and famous men in favor of a studious, homegrown man with a PhD in education who shared her Mormon background. They raised eight children together who, at her death, had produced fifty-four grandchildren and twenty great-grandchildren. Though they later divorced, and Charlotte remained single afterward, she never wavered in her passion for family, romance, and marriage. She refused to let heartache yield to bitterness.

During my Utah trip, I slept on Aunt Charlotte's couch at her downtown Salt Lake City home. I wasn't alone, as I shared the room with dozens of her fancy rental costumes and gowns. She'd launched a shop after her Miss USA and choral tours brought her around the world, and she picked up a local ethnic costume from each place. But what started out in joy became a source of stress. Charlotte constantly struggled under divorce and financial strain, including the demise of her beloved rental business, Charlotte's Attic. When she couldn't afford to keep the costumes in a separate facility, this gown and costume rental shop filled with bejeweled, mice-infested satin and lace dresses from bygone eras moved to her home. The sparkling tulle and whimsical costumes spilled into every corner of her home, crowding out the dining room, the basement, her bedroom—every spare inch, sometimes stacked floor to ceiling. The house belonged on a *Hoarders* episode.

Charlotte was endlessly compassionate and fabulous. The day after Christmas, Charlotte dressed me in one of her sparkly gowns, an ankle-length, long-sleeve forest-green number covered in forest-green sequins, with scattered crescent moons and magnolia-type flowers patterned in soft-white sequins. Of course, she had matching kitten heels (only slightly too big for my size six feet) in forest green—she had every shoe dye color imaginable. She rounded out my outfit with drop earrings with forest-green orbs atop golden dangling tassels. I felt like a princess. I'd never worn anything so fancy.

Charlotte wore a crimson-red pantsuit trimmed with black sparkles. She drove me in her ancient Cadillac—her Caddy—up the foothills above Salt Lake City toward Emigration Canyon, home to the area's most expensive houses, with stunning views of the valley glittering below, from Christmas lights and street lamps. We stopped at an enormous newer home, covered in glistening snow that sparkled under the driveway's foot lamps.

I drew in a sharp breath. *Breathe, Carrie.*

Aside from gawking at various tourist destinations like the White House, it was the most beautiful home I'd entered. It belonged to one of the singers in the Tabernacle Choir. During this jolly, festive mood, current and former Tab Choir singers jubilantly greeted each other while sipping eggnog and red punch. Most were quite elderly by that point; Charlotte was sixty-five. Bashful, I clung to Charlotte and simply flashed smiles and occasional hellos. It sounded heavenly to hear these veteran voices join together for a few Christmas carols. I don't remember which songs, but I felt on air as we floated in the car back home. It was pure Christmas magic.

Later that Christmas break, I trekked about forty-five miles south of Salt Lake down to Provo, where my cousin Becky showed me the snowy grounds of Brigham Young University. I fell in love, starstruck. It's a jewel of a campus, set against the majestic peaks of the Wasatch Mountains and home to tens of thousands of smiling, ambitious, normal young Mormons—a massive friend and dating pool. Plus, they incorporated their LDS faith into their studies— something my secular state school lacked. I felt hooked! Soon after, I chose to transfer there for sophomore year.

I would miss my Missouri journalism friends; Truman State University gave me my first paid journalism experiences, both as a writer for the university-owned yearbook, the *Echo*, and the student newspaper, the *Index*, covering the student senate. This filled me with a wave of confidence. I found a professional work home that wasn't Taco Bell or a buffet restaurant. In my paid role, my writing impacted dispatches of 4,500 weekly copies for circulation. I wielded my power over student government with a mix of pride and fear. I made the silly cub reporter mistake of asking the student senate leaders (mostly seniors) if they looked down on my status as a freshman. They're budding politicians; what do you think they said?

"Of course not," the senate president smoothly assured me, sending me off with a figurative pat on the head.

I also began interning for the local newspaper, the *Kirksville Daily Express*, which published six times a week and offered me more money (I believe $8 per hour). This was the newspaper by and for the local rural "townies"—or, the local community sometimes rightly annoyed by partying college students, many from bigger cities like St. Louis and Kansas City. But I was quiet, didn't party, and I felt grateful for their welcoming embrace. I burst with pride when the local police chief announced he was retiring and wanted to give *me* the exclusive exit interview.

By today's digital standards, the *Daily Express* was a dinosaur of an outlet in 2001—we hand-cut articles to lay them out on the page. But first we rolled them through a waxer that coated the paper with a thin layer of sticky wax on the back to assemble the pieces together neatly on the page.

My boss was the *Express* editor in chief, Judy Tritz, a middle-aged woman married to a professor at the Kirksville College of Osteopathic Medicine (now named A.T. Still University), birthplace of American osteopathic medicine. Judy was a lovely, dutiful, focused person and a committed journalist with short-cropped, gray-brown hair, who wore short-sleeve black work shirts and stuck a pencil behind her ear most days. When Judy was out of town for a week, she let nineteen-year-old Carrie fill her shoes and manage the front-page editorial process. Her trust in me built up my confidence. It was no coincidence that she shared the same first name as my mother and my aunt.

I sporadically corresponded over email with my sister Sophie during the fall semester. She'd wanted to leave home for years but hadn't carved out a pathway. I told her I could help. A generous family in my LDS congregation offered to give her a free bedroom to stay in.

Sophie came to stay in Kirksville that March, just before her eighteenth birthday. Dad brought her, accompanied by Peter and Thomas. They dropped her and her belongings at a local hotel. Dad said he didn't want to see me. I knew he hated me even more for "stealing away" a second child from The Mission. Though I invited her to various social events, Sophie, an introvert, wanted to take more time to decompress rather than rush into her sister's campus life. We didn't grow close, but I felt grateful I could assist her escape from the cult. A few months after arriving in Kirksville, she moved out to Utah ahead of me to live with our aunt and uncle. I left in August after my semester ended and a summer full time at the *Express*.

While my Truman journalism career flourished, I fled to BYU seeking personal cultural shelter and normalcy. At Truman, I grew tired of being the weird one, the girl who didn't drink or have sex despite the ambient fraternity beer parties and raging hormones. I felt alone in the world, since my parents wouldn't let me visit home for holidays or summer break. If I wanted to come home, it must be permanently, so I could help with The Mission, not corrupt my siblings during a free-spirited fling. So I moved to Utah, the living, breathing manifestation of Mormon ideology. I engaged in plenty of self-flagellation for making out with various men and my awkward social skills. I was ready to clean up my act:

> *July 29, 2002: I feel as though I have no personality, that I absorb in and blend into my environment without thought of what I claim as true. I am a two-faced, secretive bitch, who, if people truly knew who I was, would (and rightly so) flee at the sight of my crooked eyes and nose, my sensual, chubby face. I pretend to be interested in others, when all I want is something out of them in return. I am slow-witted, tongue-tied and unrestrained in my actions—unable to control my appetite, spending, emotions, facial expressions and thoughts. There are so many deep-rooted sins, tendencies and falacies [sic] in my character and life experiences that I feel unable to do anything about them. And they are not my parents fault, contrary to my pathetic justifications. They cannot be blamed for me going astray from God's path.*

Chapter 10

Mormon Exodus

If an idea is true, criticism will not destroy it, but strengthen it.

—James Clear

I drove the 1,100 miles from Kirksville, Missouri, to Provo, Utah, in my rickety 1994 cherry-red Mazda Protege sedan with black trim. I'd bought it off a guy in my Mormon congregation for a steal at $1,800 (around $3,054 in 2023 dollars), but it had many problems, including needing a new clutch, making it unable to move above maybe thirty miles per hour uphill in the mountains as I puttered along the I-80 freeway. It got so bad that my little Mazda gave out somewhere in rural Wyoming, not too far from Utah's northern border. I felt petrified, but glad it happened during daylight hours. However, it was Sunday, which meant most businesses were closed. I limped into a gas station area and pondered my fortunes.

Mercifully, there was a repairman at the gas station's garage.

He needed to pick up a tool and just happened to be there, even though the repair shop was technically closed. I felt immensely relieved when he offered to help me. I don't remember the problem, but he charged me just a fraction of the price after he quickly fixed it. That should have been a red flag right there, but I was ecstatic, so I didn't assume the worst.

He asked me if I had eaten lunch, and I said no. Still on cloud nine from the breezy repair, against my better judgment, I entered his truck's cab and we drove over to Wendy's. I ate a chicken salad, and it was quite delicious. We returned to my car, and I said I'd hit the road again, eternally grateful for his talent and generosity. He was a young guy, I'd guess early twenties, and I was nineteen. I thought he was decent looking, with brown hair and brown eyes, part of why I agreed to lunch. Then things got weird.

We exchanged email addresses—mind you, this was 2002, so emails were still a fairly new concept. His was something like xxxhotboyxxx@hotmail.com or an equivalent. That should have been another red flag! As I prepared to enter my car and pull away, he asked me to give him something to remember me by. I giggled and surveyed the cargo in my back seat, which, along with the trunk, contained all my earthly possessions. I had a navy blue-and-white Umbro gym bag in the front seat with a change of clothes for my hotel stop.

I racked my brain until I saw, dangling from the rearview mirror, my purple and green Mardi Gras beads that I picked up at some school event, perhaps handed out by student government. I asked him if that would do?

"I was thinking something a bit more personal," he replied, a sly grin on his lips.

"Oh, well what do you mean 'more personal'?" I replied with a nervous giggle.

"Well... I was thinking maybe a pair of your panties?" he said.

My inner alarm bells clanged loudly! Danger! This guy might hurt me. Must not provoke... must back away slowly and hightail it out of there!

"Aah I see..." I stammered. I had underwear in the gym bag, but there was no way this side of Hades that he'd get his paws on it.

"Well, I really don't know what you'd do with them, so I'd rather not," I practically whispered, afraid I'd choke on the words. I swiftly got into the car and backed out of the garage as rapidly as humanly possible. I failed my driver's license exam twice because of parallel parking—I was *terrible* at backing out in a straight line. I must've looked like a crazy woman, but I successfully escaped! Rattled, but with a working vehicle. The dude emailed me, and I replied, thanking him again profusely before blocking him and, hallelujah, never heard from him again.

My first night in my apartment (owned by my aunt and uncle— they generously gave me free rent; their daughter and two other girls were my roommates) near Brigham Young University, our downstairs neighbors hosted a birthday dance party, and I attended with my social-butterfly roommate Janelle. I felt excited; even though I was still socially awkward and tongue-tied, I finally would be surrounded by people who understood me. Unfortunately, my stomach didn't agree. Earlier that day at a family baby shower, I ate some leftover barbecue with South American spices that my cousin's husband learned to use during his mission abroad. The meat was rancid, even though I didn't remember it tasting strange. But I immediately felt sick the entire day, though by nighttime, I thought my stomach rumblings were manageable. Big mistake. I continued to feel queasy at the party but met some fun people from my church congregation, even feeling courageous enough to dance a bit in the darkened living room because I could hide in the shadows. Janelle's brother Ron was visiting, though he needed to leave to pick somebody up. Janelle and I offered to walk him to his car. My dancing must have accelerated the food poisoning like a blender. Outside on the sidewalk, I exploded a few seconds after I told them I needed to barf.

Vomit gushed up out of my mouth, all over the sidewalk and grass. I tried to stop the flow with my hands, but instead the orange and brown chunks just kept flowing. On my boots. All over my face. I felt disgusting and wretched. Ron continued onward, but Janelle escorted me back to the apartment, where I later threw up again in the toilet bowl.

There I lay, crumpled in a pathetic heap on the bathroom floor in my light purple satin pajama pants and white tank top. I quickly went to sleep but kept waking up for diarrhea runs to the bathroom. Magically, the next morning I felt much better and even made it to the 9:00 a.m. church service.

Despite these silly, inauspicious obstacles to the new school year, I thrived. At nineteen, I felt like a normal girl for the first time in my life, like I belonged. I was surrounded by my Mormon people, and I was away from my abusive father. Yes, I was painfully socially awkward and still suffered from depression, PTSD, and anxiety, layered over underlying feelings of self-doubt and self-marginalization. But I had an incredible Mormon leader, a kind British man named Bishop Lighten. The name fit him perfectly—he lightened my load. He was like a character from John Bunyan's *The Pilgrim's Progress* (Mom was rightly obsessed with the fabulous

1978 animated film adaptation of that late Renaissance book from 1678—the film's soundtrack is peak '70s music), no subtlety in their names! At my assigned congregation (a Singles Ward, married people banned), Bishop Lighten listened to my confessions and said he understood that abused women often let men take advantage of them because of low esteem.

"I know it's difficult to imagine this, but you have the capacity to break the cycle of abuse rather than passing it on to the next generation," he said.

Bishop Lighten encouraged me to get therapy; he said abused people who don't seek counseling are like cancer patients who refuse to get chemo or other medical treatment. He rejected any stigma in getting mental health services, and I completely agreed. The truth is, mental health is physical health. There's a biological feedback loop between your nervous system (physical) and your psyche (mental). *Anatomy of the Soul* by Curt Thompson, a neurobiologist and psychiatrist, explains this beautifully. Psychiatrists note that people suffering from PTSD are stuck in a permanent fight-or-flight state in their neurological wiring, their "limbic system." This inhibits their ability to handle normal stress and everyday life.

"One day, I hope to run into you at the airport with your beautiful babies in tow," Bishop Lighten told me. "And I'll smile and know that you were healed."

His words made me cry with joy and hope, sparking thoughts that breaking the cycle of abuse was possible. Sadly, he died before this could come to pass.

I found counseling on campus with a Mormon therapist, an empathetic woman who diagnosed me with PTSD and depression. We began to unpack my trauma, and she told me to invest in activities that brought me joy—roll down a hill singing, she said—to create a deep well of positive memories to draw from and create distance from the abuse. It would be well into my thirty-ninth year, a twenty-year journey, before I finally felt released from the trauma.

Around that time, I urged my dad to get counseling for the trauma of his childhood rape and feelings of depression and abandonment. We spoke sporadically on the phone and sometimes he'd snail-mail or email me pages-long annotated letters, complete with footnotes quoting Scripture.

"Dad, why don't you get therapy to help you heal from what Ada did to you?" I asked.

"God helped me. I don't need a busybody," he said, offended that his offspring was trying to tell him what to do. "And you are filled with Satan. You have no right to try to control me."

At BYU, I found new financial support from partial Pell Grants—direct government cash, rather than loans, for poor students. I received them after the federal government declared me legally estranged from my parents. After helping pay for some freshman-year schooling (only because he had to under Grandpa's will), after I transferred to BYU, my parents' support dried up, and they refused to provide the necessary financial documentation and their Social Security numbers that would allow me to obtain student loans.

That sophomore year before Christmas, Ralph briefly agreed to let me come home during the winter school break. Uncle Ivan booked a flight into BWI airport in Baltimore, near my family in Gaithersburg, Maryland (or was it Fredericksburg, Virginia? I don't remember. They were constantly moving). I called my dad to tell him when the flight arrived. He took the information like a normal parent. Then he called back half an hour later to recant.

"I'm prompted that you shouldn't come," he said.

Heavy silence.

"But why?" I stammered.

"When we first spoke, that was *Ralph* talking," he explained. "Now, it is *the Lord* speaking, and His will is that you keep away from The Mission because you have broken your covenants."

The rejection hit me hard, even though I'd grown somewhat accustomed to his ostracizing behavior. It felt extra painful in my new campus environment because of the heavy emphasis on family in LDS culture. Because Mormon doctrine teaches that your family unit transfers into the afterlife and your personal worthiness affects whether you're together, I heard infinitely more family talk on campus than at Truman. I felt constantly barraged with reminders of what I lacked.

Despite this rejection, I enjoyed a decent holiday with aunts, uncles, and cousins from both sides of the family. They showered me with Christmas gifts, which I didn't feel I deserved. They included a short-sleeve, floor-length, shimmering forest-green gown with a lustrous metallic floral brocade on the top half that Aunt Sue bought from the BYU Store (which sells a lot more than textbooks—they also specialize in stylish women's clothing that covers the shoulders and reaches at least the knee). By far the nicest thing I'd ever owned, this Jody California dress brought me to tears. It still fits me today (hope I can always fit into clothes from age nineteen!) and I wear it for special occasions and think of her.

December 31, 2002: I don't want to sit here & rag on Dad, and I hope & pray that he'll open his eyes. I asked him when we last spoke on the phone, that night of [Christmas break] rejection, if he had considered getting counseling to help him deal with his past issues, such as the sexual abuse, his controlling, harsh

father, his homosexual struggle, etc., but he told me that he
didn't need to, b/c the Lord was helping him through it. This is
just what Bishop Lighten said is not the way to do it. But if Dad
were to go see a counselor, to him it would be admitting that he
was wrong & be allowing someone else to have power over him.
He would feel like he's losing control. It's so sad. It seems unfair,
that my dad was afflicted with such torment and that he's react-
ing only in the best way he knows how. Why must he suffer so?
And why won't he let anyone help him? Why should he be allowed
to injure those he loves, to stunt their growth in countless ways?
Maybe God has given us these extra trials because they will help
us to understand and be empathetic to other people's struggles.
They have hindered me in my growth, but they've helped me grow
stronger in other areas. But for me now, the suffering outweighs
the benefits. Maybe someday it won't.

Dad never ceased sending nastygrams, hoping I would return
to The Mission. He'd send guilt-laden letters, including this one
where he accused me of aborting my unborn child, a grievous sin. I
was a virgin at the time, so this was scientifically impossible:

Nov 27, 2004
    ...To my great sadness, the Lord told me that you have
killed your baby, and that you travelled [sic] far away to do so,
because your pride was of more value to you than the precious
life of your child—and our grandchild. The seriousness of this
is beyond what your heart is capable of feeling at this time. But
know that we love you still and continue to pray for your welfare.
Joseph Smith once observed that there never was an adulterer
who wasn't a liar. Therefore, the temptation to prevaricate in

My Grandma Cora with her two oldest children, my father, Ralph, and his sister, Charlotte. The family lived in the heart of Salt Lake City, in a middle class, hilly neighborhood, reminiscent of the movie *A Christmas Story*—all the more fitting because the protagonist of that film was also a blond boy named Ralphie.

My Aunt Charlotte with her parents, my Grandpa Ralph and Grandma Cora. Crowned Miss USA 1957 at the tender age of 20, Charlotte was thrust into the spotlight, conquering the hearts of elite and everyday people around the globe.

Me as a toddler with my dad. Over the years, he gave me a deep love of our exceptional country, of intellectual inquiry, and of beautiful music. Though we've had many disagreements, I know his heart holds a deep desire to serve others through his work. I pray God's blessing on his life, especially during his struggles today with Alzheimer's.

Kindergarten school photo, East Sandy Elementary, Utah. Mom forced me to wear my dark auburn brown hair with bowl-cut bangs. I despised these bangs, not only for their uniform rigidity but because the girls at church had long, flowing hair and bangs they could sweep back in ponytails with enviable, frilly bows and curls pressed by their moms. Mom kept the back part of my hair slightly longer but cropped just above my shoulders. She wouldn't let me grow it too far because sometimes we didn't have running water to wash regularly, plus it'd get too tangled with rats' nests.

Dad holding me alongside my four big brothers. Nobody messed with me in elementary school—they knew I had backup.

With my brother, who shared a birthday month, and our cat Jumpy. Note my brother's Brigham Young University birthday cake. We were steeped at a young age in the culture of revering BYU, the crown jewel of the Mormon education system.

The Sheffield family's eight surviving children. I'm near the lower right side, brown skirt. I'm not sure where all we lived during our family's early years, but our birthplaces dot the map. Six out of ten were born in various Utah towns, the rest in Massachusetts, Maryland, and Virginia. In all, Mom gave birth to ten babies, delivered one stillbirth, and suffered two miscarriages. She followed the Mormon cultural standard of bearing as many children as possible to provide unborn "spirit bodies" with mortal bodies that would be raised LDS. (One LDS family I knew in Missouri had twenty-one children from the same mother!) Two of my nine live-birth siblings didn't make it past infancy, and some of us who did survive at times wished we hadn't. Those feelings came as we grew older.

Circa fourth grade, visiting family home in southern Utah. Mom's grandfather was a sheepherder in rural, south-central Utah, tending his flocks against a stunning backdrop of dramatic red-rock mountains.

Utah's legendary red-rock national parks draw millions of visitors from around the globe, including to Capitol Reef National Park—near Mom's family's small towns of Teasdale and Torrey.

With the family cat Buff, circa fifth grade in our Springville, Utah, mobile home park. From when I was about age 5 through age 11, our family lived mainly in Utah (except for a motorhome sojourn at a campground in 1990 in Missouri). These years were important in solidifying my identity as a Mormon. Despite our transient lifestyle, I loved Utah—its trailer parks, RV campgrounds, and houses. I loved being surrounded by people who thought like I did.

Seventh grade school photo, proudly wearing my LDS Young Women medallion around my neck. Dad regularly played orthodontist, using the broken stub of a Popsicle stick to move our teeth for better alignment. My left incisor tooth stood nearly at a 90° angle. My brothers mercilessly teased me over my "snaggle tooth." Dad's Popsicle stick pressure felt like torture, and it backfired. Today, the root of my top left incisor is completely dead, requiring a root canal, and the top of the tooth permanently discolored brown–despite attempted dentist whitenings–because of his botched ortho work.

Circa eighth grade, with a neighbor in Kansas City, Missouri. We uprooted from Utah and moved to KC when I was 11, when puberty was starting to hit, emotions were on overdrive, and math and science classes actually started to matter. It was pretty much the worst time to drop a shy white girl from the trailer parks of Utah into an urban, inner-city school that was around 90 percent black, where students threw chairs at each other, smoked pot (and God knows what else) on campus, and where sixth-grade homework was about at the level of first grade.

At that time, our family of ten lived in a modest, white, two-story house on Holmes Street, about equidistant between Troost Avenue (where things start to get sketchy/dangerous) and Oak Street (where houses start to get real nice). It was a fitting metaphor for how our family's life often careened from stability and calm into chaos and violence.

Summer after eighth grade visiting Plymouth Rock, Massachusetts. In eighth grade, I tried to fit in wit black classmates by dressing like what's known in the vernacular as a "wigger," a "white n*****," in the of rapper Eminem. This was Mormon-adapted wigger, which meant adjustments were made after arrivi school, away from prying parental eyes, dressing in baggy pants with tight shirts (tight from wash shrin not because of a sanctioned purchase) or overalls with my homemade boxer shorts peeking out o1 sides, pulling my hair in a skintight ponytail at a right angle on the very top of my head, and wearing c knockoff, Nike-looking black sneakers (we couldn't afford the real thing).

Suited up for JV soccer squad at Gaithersburg High School. After a blissful freshman year, Dad annou1 we'd be heading to the East Coast, where I'd start my fifteenth public school at GHS in suburban Maryl outside Washington, DC. This was a foreign environment: we'd leave Jackson County, home of Mormoni Garden of Eden and a much more religious state, to plunge head-on into secularism. It was a new mission for helping convert our peers to Mormonism.

During homeschool studies my sophomore high school year, standing outside our Fleetwood Jamboree RV. Life in a motorhome had its charms, but also its pitfalls. A big one: toilets. One small toilet for ten people, an inhospitable arrangement when the sewer hookups froze or the septic tank brimmed to capacity with urine and feces and needed an RV site dumping. It was also tough when my oldest schizophrenic brother locked himself inside the tiny, roughly two-by-four-foot bathroom for hours, meticulously wiping every body crevice and doing God knows what else. The stench of fresh sewage was commonplace enough that my nostrils would quickly grow accustomed. Ralph also tried to mitigate the putrid scent with the bright blue–colored chemical treatment, both liquid and powder—the kind you'd see in an outhouse. We basically lived adjacent to a permanent outhouse for untold gallons of ten people's waste.

My patriotic parents in front of the White House. Though I never thought it possible, seven years after I'd "disowned" him, I forgave my father for his abuse. I even visited his life celebration and sang "Happy Birthday," grateful for the gifts he imparted, and forgave the mental agony he helped create that made me want to kill myself. I'm grateful to Mom for her decades of selfless prayers for me, even when I didn't appreciate them. I know God was listening.

Credit: Screenshot of a video from the author's family collection

Playing violin during Young Women's group at my local LDS Church. I began to see our family mission as my outlet from the insanity at school and practiced my violin for hours to help save our country from utter depravity. By the time we finished our inner-city schooling our roving family orchestra played our musical ensemble on the streets of Kansas City in the downtown Plaza area during the school year, and during school breaks we rode in our 1991 Winnebago Warrior motorhome and played various street festivals, campgrounds, and LDS churches from Portsmouth, Ohio, to Stevensville, Maryland. Our repertoire included classical greats like selections from Bach's Brandenburg Concertos and Handel's *Messiah* and "Water Music," Mozart's Symphony no. 40 in G Minor, Edvard Grieg's "The Last Spring" along with "Somewhere" from the musical *West Side Story*, and even "The Pink Panther Theme" by Henry Mancini, just for fun. I didn't tell my classmates about my preaching musical escapades. I was mortified they'd think I was a religious nutjob and beat me up.

Parkview High School graduation day, May 2001, Springfield, Missouri. Songs, often at pivotal moments in my life, pop into my head—a soundtrack for my emotions. Perhaps it's a genetic feature as the daughter of a former music professor and a granddaughter of a music composer. That day of high school graduation, it was the Beatles' "Eleanor Rigby," a song about "all the lonely people" and how Eleanor Rigby wore a fake smile and "died in the church and was buried along with her name / Nobody came." That was my life, and where I'd end up at my current trajectory—scared, abused, and alone.

With Grandma Cora during my Utah trip during winter break freshman year of college I slept on Aunt Charlotte's red velvet couch at her downtown Salt Lake City home. I wasn't alone, as I shared the room wit dozens of her fancy costumes and gowns for rent.

Dad performs across the street from the White House in Lafayette Square. His beautiful classical guitar music attracted listeners, whom he would offer his free religious brochure bookmarks. Before he received much of his dad's inheritance money, Dad relied on the money people threw into his open guitar case. After staking out his street corner (which wasn't always easy—he got jailed for turf battles), he'd toss a few dollars inside the case to get the ball rolling. My father seemed to enjoy fighting in the streets, brawling with homeless people, panhandlers, and other musicians. *Credit: Courtesy of Grudnick on Flickr, 2008*

Our family musical ensemble, the official publicity photo used atop thousands of bookmarks. Our Dad called our chamber symphony group "The Sheffield Family Consort." Dad, naturally, was the conductor. Dad plotted this family orchestra years earlier through careful assignment of our instruments. We had no say in which instrument we'd play—Dad told us God carefully selected each one. He'd assigned me to play the violin when I was in fifth grade and oboe in eighth grade. One brother wanted to play saxophone, but Dad kiboshed that idea quickly. No respectable chamber symphony group had such a thing!

Evening gown competition during a 2006 beauty pageant. Encouraged by my Aunt Charlotte, former Miss USA, I competed as Miss Alexandria USA in Miss Virginia USA. This meant pressures of incessant tanning and skipping meals; I was 23 and felt old. It also meant pricey shopping: clothing, makeup, advice books, accessories, pageant fees, publicity shots, styling. All told, I spent around $5,000—added pressure to win. Perhaps I sought escape through pageantry, but ironically, it left me more insecure and deflated because I lacked self-confidence. During my pageant interview, I told unimpressed judges that the pageant world "was foreign to me" because it was. I was a novice against girls who'd competed for decades. I didn't advance beyond initial rounds.

With legendary newspaper journalist Robert Novak. Immediately after college graduation, I took a journalism internship with Robert but was quickly offered a full-time newspaper job in the cutthroat world of political journalism in Washington, DC. My internship supervisor encouraged me to snap up the full-time gig. "You moved here to get a job, not to stay an intern," she said.

Group photo after a guest appearance on HBO's *Real Time with Bill Maher*. I'd never heard of my co-panelist Nas, the world-famous, platinum-selling rapper. I told Nas I was from a family of musicians and asked if he knew the Mormon Tabernacle Choir, which several of my family members sang in. He said no. I got a chuckle, because the Tab Choir is similarly a global, platinum phenomenon—albeit in a totally different cultural context. *Credit: Publicity Photo by HBO/Warner Bros. Discover*

such matters must be quite stark. Please remember, however, that
devotion to truth (of which Christ is the embodiment) and taking
responsibility for what has happened, is the key to the door of
hope and building a future of blessing. We miss you.

Love as always,

Dad

Aside from Dad's emotional terrorism, those early days at BYU were the highlight of my life until then. Feminists will cringe to learn this, but I initially chose a print journalism major partially because I thought it nonthreatening to possible male suitors. Because I was really just there for my "Mrs." degree. An aggressive or threatening major meant something in the hard sciences, business, or accounting. A print journalism degree fell under the softer BYU Fine Arts school and meant I could perhaps run an amateur Mormon mommy blog while raising a brood of children as my husband brought home the bacon.

These days, college journalism programs are heavily multimedia; you study a combined curriculum of print, radio, video, blogging, and social media. But in my time, things were more bifurcated. You were either a print or a broadcast major. You could do both, but they were separate tracks. I had a strange inferiority/superiority complex toward my classmates studying broadcast TV journalism. I'd never say it openly, but I felt jealous and intimidated by their perfect, expensive hairstyles and wardrobes, their confidence, charm, and charisma. I had none of those things. My clothes were cheap (blue jeans, khakis, Forever 21 or Wet Seal tops), and I could barely muster a conversation without stuttering or turning down an awkward path. Yet, I fancied myself superior because I pronounced to myself that print majors were the smart ones; they did heavy investigations and wrote the substance behind the headlines those perfectly coiffed bimbos merely parroted off the teleprompter.

The print journalism program was short in terms of credit hours, and technically I could graduate in three years, but I didn't want to force myself quickly. I needed healing from trauma and wanted to stay in my cheerful cocoon. I chopped my course load to just one class when I took field journalism reporting so I could focus and minimize my stress. I thrived writing for BYU's student newspaper, the *Daily Universe*, where I eventually worked my way up to senior editor. It's a meaningful newspaper name, a nod to the metaphysical, extraterrestrial ponderings of Mormonism. I enjoyed bragging I was "senior editor of the universe"—ha! I also covered politics and crime for *Deseret News*'s Utah County bureau. I initially slept with the newspaper-issued police scanner in my room, but the noise grated too much, plus the crime rate in Utah County is remarkably low, so I eventually rarely listened. I also wrote for the local town newspaper, Provo's *Daily Herald*, covering the Utah legislature, where at age nineteen I asked then-Governor Mike Leavitt a question during a live press conference airing on statewide networks. I felt over the moon.

As I discovered in high school, journalism is a passion and calling. Independent journalism is a hallmark of a vibrant, beating democracy. Done properly, it serves as a check on power and a voice for the people (when abused, the press becomes a tool for partisan vendettas and egoism). Aside from the public policy aspects, journalism in some respects saved me personally. It helped lift me out of my destitute, abusive upbringing and gave me purpose during six journalism internships by age twenty-two—including at the major magazine *Newsweek* and for the venerable *Washington*

Post columnist Robert Novak. This field later allowed me to travel the world, study for free at Harvard through a journalism scholarship, and sit in the front row of history. I later became unhealthily obsessed with my media work, but during college, it was still a respite.

For my twenty-first birthday, friends and I took a road trip to Las Vegas, less than a six-hour drive from BYU. "Sin City" Las Vegas was founded by devout Mormon missionaries assigned there by Brigham Young,[48] and legend holds that some BYU students drive down there, get married, have sex, and get an annulment within the twenty-four-hour grace period, all so their copulation technically isn't premarital. Scandalous! And utterly disrespectful of marriage. That wasn't us.

My birthday fell on a Sunday, and our group attended the local LDS ward. Rather than desecrate the Sabbath and break God's Law, the day prior, on Saturday, I broke Man's Law and gambled (only a nickel) in a slot machine, technically at age twenty. I thought it a fairly harmless act worthy of a slap on the wrist (and ensured no casino employees loomed), but turns out, in Nevada, underage gambling carries a penalty of up to six months in county jail and/or a thousand-dollar fine. Serious stuff. Today, I'm way beyond the statute of limitations for prosecution, but if I'd been caught, there's no doubt Dad would get my crime inscribed on my tombstone.

Our group also accidently broke God's Law and imbibed a little rum. When the restaurant staff discovered it was my birthday, they rolled out a flaming dessert, a thrilling sight. We all dug in; there were maybe five or six of us scooping this large dessert. We thought it tasted a little funny but didn't think much of it and assumed the flames burned out all the alcohol—or so the boys in our group claimed. When we went to pay at the cash register, the server laughed and said, "Wow, that was enough alcohol to get an elephant drunk! I'm impressed at how quickly you got it all down!"

———

Perhaps this Vegas hooliganism foreshadowed my future apostasy from the LDS faith, though I didn't leave because I wanted a life of boozy, floozy benders and crime. My journey out of Mormonism began, ironically, at Brigham Young University—a Mormon college.

It started during a spring term class my junior year called Mass Media History and Philosophy. I thoroughly enjoyed our professor, who felt passionate about media and previously helped publish a magazine. As part of the course, we undertook what seemed like a harmless assignment. We descended into the bowels of BYU's Harold B. Lee Library (HBLL) and studied microfiche from the 1800s and early 1900s of the *Deseret News*. Founded in 1850 and owned by the LDS Church, it's the oldest continuously operating newspaper in America's West.

I'll never forget that shell-shocking moment in that beautiful building. The HBLL entry features a spacious, airy glass atrium evoking the French Louvre Museum on a smaller scale, with a square base supporting its pyramid-shaped roof. Downstairs in the archives section, I reviewed these old microfiche pages alone because this homework fell on our own time. As a political journalist, I took keen interest in the political coverage and other news events while I scrolled through the microfiche machine in the HBLL basement. The room was dark, so the microfiche is easier to view. It seemed a fitting allegory for the dark clouds I felt encircling me after my eye fell on something else.

They were advertisements from a department store called

ZCMI (full name Zion's Co-operative Mercantile Institution), owned by the LDS Church. It's now defunct, but ZCMI was the Mormon Macy's of its day, a general store selling everything from clothing to farming supplies.

I felt jolted that ZCMI was selling alcohol and tobacco. My jaw hit the floor. I knew LDS authorities didn't enforce the ban on smoking and drinking until well after the founder's death. And I knew that early Mormons enjoyed imbibing and some chewed loads of tobacco. It never occurred to me, however, that the Mormon Church proactively made money off the stuff, rather than quietly look the other way as secular vendors hawked their wares. The church I gave absolute allegiance enthusiastically commercialized vice!

I felt stunned. It became a seemingly minor rabbit hole that I fell down and never crawled out of. I voraciously started reading dozens of books and articles about LDS Church history. I felt saddened to learn repugnant things about the founder, Joseph Smith, who by many credible accounts, seemed a rather unsavory character. I knew there were multiple attacks against Smith's reputation, but I chalked it up to opposition from satanic forces.

But as a journalism student, I strove for objectivity while I studied this organization. I struggled after realizing just how much Mormonism's claims about anthropology, history, and other subjects contradict reason and science. While many faiths' irrational claims are obscured by centuries of myth and rubble, the LDS Church lacks the moderation and scholarship of its older peers. Thankfully, it's recently started to change this culture, but back in 2004, it stifled efforts to openly question church pronouncements, labeling such behavior as satanic.

Critics of Mormonism include geneticists, Egyptologists, and even the Smithsonian Institution, which stopped Mormon apologists from claiming that the institute viewed the Book of Mormon as a scientific document. I spiritually imploded after learning facts about Mormonism's origins—facts that fell outside the official church curriculum. Disturbed, I met with a high-ranking regional Mormon leader and BYU professor who told me to quit reading historical and scientific texts because they were "worse than pornography." Other leaders told me that questioning is acceptable, so long as it's done secretly.

I felt distressed and ashamed, suffering in silence, and fell into suicidal despair because my entire worldview and reason for living was crumbling before my eyes. Since Mormonism is highly centralized, without the local doctrinal flexibility that exists in Judaism and many Christian churches, I saw no place to live a moderated, reformed existence. It became time for me to take another leap of faith and leave virtually everything I knew behind.

I shared some of what I'd found with my sister Sophie but felt afraid to share everything because I didn't want to risk contaminating and damning her to hell if proved wrong. Sophie and I met with BYU's dean of religious education, who couldn't answer my growing list of about fifty serious questions that I left on his desk and requested responses to. The responses never came.

My faith was an unshakable part of my identity, and if I openly voiced my concerns, I risked rejection from the church I loved. After the microfiche moment, I desperately sought answers and community. As a BYU student, I feared expulsion for asking questions. Trembling, I logged on to the website ExMormon.org, terrified of what I might see. Little did I know, it held a portal to a new life. First founded in 1995, ExMormon.org is wildly popular, with more than two million posts in its main board and archives and more than 1,500 topics to read about—everything from discussions about life without the Mormon underwear to how to "come out" as ex-Mormon to your family. I left the LDS Church for historical and theological reasons, but the cultural freedom felt like icing on the cake. Clothes could fall above my knee. Tank tops were no longer banished; I could wear sleeveless sundresses during hot summers. I could drink alcohol. I wanted to try coffee and tea. Starbucks taunted me for years.

As a Christian now, I believe that message board is a mixed bag. It's where many understandably bitter and angry people hang out and anonymously commiserate about how to cope with leaving a deeply intense religious order. Many of them rejected God altogether, and I empathized. They're rightfully angry at the obfuscations fed to us about Mormonism's origins. And I kept leaning on these posts. I cared too much about what they were saying, desperate not to feel alone. I didn't have any ex-Mormon friends. I relied on these anonymous internet strangers to give me crucial life advice. But I wouldn't find salvation in an internet message board centered on bitterness. I'm grateful for ExMormon.org and the community it offered at a vulnerable time in my life, but I simultaneously should have turned more to God during this time. Because I didn't, I became more angry and bitter instead of more reliant on Him to guide me through this earthquake.

I will always be one of Mormonism's most ardent defenders and admirers, though also someone calling for transparency and critical thinking among its leaders and adherents. As a kid, I loved the lay-leadership structure of the LDS Church. I didn't realize until later that this volunteerism serves an important function: to reinforce the ideology of the volunteers. While I'm all for leadership development, most Mormons have no formal training in theology, genetics, history, or sociology. Thus, they unquestioningly repeat verbatim the whitewashed Sunday School manuals printed in Utah, where the unvarnished Church history is hidden from the average member. This perpetuates the cycle of opaqueness and creates stress and drama when a member seeks independent sources of information.

Most LDS sermons are preached by volunteers, with few exceptions from the top men running the nearly seventeen million–member church from headquarters in Salt Lake City. Unfortunately, we don't know their salaries or how they conduct Church finances because these figures aren't publicly released. As a journalist, this rankled me deeply, though a recent IRS whistleblower investigation filed by the twin brother of my friend shed some light.

A key factor in Martin Luther's Reformation movement was the excesses and financial abuses of the Catholic Church. While many of the men running the LDS Church no doubt have good intentions, they don't trust their members enough to let them see their good intentions on paper. This contrasts with many other religious groups, which voluntarily offer public accounts of how they spend their flock's money.

While I became disillusioned with Mormonism, I recognize that for every person like me, there are many others who feel the faith brings them hope, joy, and peace. I don't want to, nor can I, take that away from them; I respect their pursuits of happiness. But I'm articulating the feelings and experiences of many people alienated by Mormonism's rigidity who saw our pursuit of happiness at times frustrated by irrational and unflinching demands.

Today's LDS Church is reforming in many ways; for example,

the wonderful recent collaborations since 2020 by Deseret News (the LDS Church–owned media company) under the leadership of Sheri Dew and Robin Ritch, are exactly the respectful dialogues that heal divides. Yet for the first 190 years, the Church too often required dogmatic, controlling groupthink. And it damaged many people in the process.

I've lived in Catholic Boston, Jewish Israel, Anglican England, and America's Baptist Bible Belt. I've traveled all over the world—every continent, including Antarctica, by age thirty—visiting regions dominated by Buddhists, Hindus, and Muslims. But in all these places, I've never seen a billboard offering psychological support for people leaving these faiths (not surprising in the Muslim areas; such things could be a death sentence for the instigator).

But that's what we've seen in Mormon-dominated areas like Salt Lake City, Utah; Twin Falls, Idaho; or Mesa, Arizona. Some were sponsored by a group called Post-Mormons, and they featured photo collages of beaming people of all races and ages (disclaimer: I'm not sure if they're actually ex-Mormon or just purchased stock images) and bold letters cheering on the beleaguered dissidents. "You are not alone!" they shout. In 2020, similar billboards arose, sponsored by Mormon Stories, a group led by my friend John Dehlin, offering support through a Mormon faith crisis.

These ad campaigns caused some angst among Mormons, who believe they attack a traditional, harmless religion. Unfortunately, for some of us leaving Mormonism, the family-values facade carefully crafted through million-dollar Mormon PR campaigns rings hollow. Now, having made peace with Mormonism after time and distance, I don't expect perfection from that body—just like I don't expect perfection from any human-run organization.

My view is that the LDS Church has more than 62,000

full-time missionaries preaching around the world. They knock door-to-door and stop people on the street to share their message. I am one person typing on a MacBook alone, hoping to connect with like-minded souls. Surely, I should be allowed a voice as well. I love the quote attributed to Socrates, basically saying the only reason people think he's smart is because he realizes how ignorant he is. I know there are many faithful Mormons who are much smarter and more capable than I am, and they keep their faith.

There's much about Mormonism that I carry within me—the principles of self-discipline, introspection, and longing for a close-knit community. But I'm still discerning how to overcome the self-righteousness, the facade of perfection, and the isolationism ingrained in me during the years I devoted myself to an intensely demanding family and faith.

After mentally starting to question the LDS faith, I unleashed a war within myself. It became a war of hungering for the truth, but also a deadly fear of the unknown abyss.

"God, I just want to die because I want to know if the Church is true, and I'd rather be dead and be with You than to live without knowing if it's true."

I loved the LDS Church so much, and I wanted it to be true. I felt deep sorrow at the thought of leaving. The Church helped pull me out of my abusive family cult and begin the healing process. Looking back now, I know my feelings weren't from God. God wouldn't require that level of blind obedience and violence against myself. I wanted the breezy certainty that LDS Church members invoked during the monthly fast and testimony meetings on the first Sunday of each month. But it would never return. This was the standard Mormon litany of beliefs I'd hear during a testimony meeting:

"*I know the Church is true. I know Joseph Smith was a true prophet. I know the Book of Mormon is true and Gordon B. Hinckley is our prophet today. I know I will be with my family for eternity in heaven.*"

I used to rattle off this statement of beliefs easily. Never again.

A compounding difficulty of my inner war is that it raged in a foreign country. I finished spring term and flew to London for a summer study-abroad program at the BYU London Centre. Close to Notting Hill and Kensington Gardens, BYU's orange-brick row house is in a beautiful location, but the students are crammed like sardines in double bunk beds with maybe a dozen women to a room and a small locker-type closet for each to store clothes.

Not exactly a dream setting, but for how (comparatively) affordable it was and the modest scholarship I received to fund my studies, I'd paid for what I got. I felt ecstatic after getting accepted during winter term to this competitive program. Though still painfully shy and socially awkward, I couldn't wait to tramp through Piccadilly Circus, Abbey Road, and the streets of Edinburgh. But now, with this unexpected faith crisis, the jammed housing situation felt like pure agony. I wanted a quiet place to withdraw and wrestle with God. Depression set in, and I failed to attend some of the excursions, weary with brain fog and anxiety. I missed the official group photo because I couldn't stumble out of bed and told myself they wouldn't miss me anyway.

The days dragged on, punctured with moments of joy and sorrow. About a two-hour drive northwest of London, we spent a day in the medieval market town of Stratford-upon-Avon, the hometown of William Shakespeare. We saw the house where Shakespeare entered this world, his wife's childhood home, and the church where he and his family are buried. Finally, the weather wasn't drubbing rain, and I took a pleasant stroll under blue skies along the banks of the beautiful River Avon, filled with long wooden punt boats.

That night, we watched a theatrical production of *King Lear*, one of Shakespeare's epic tragedies. Deeply moving and intense for me, I wept in the dark, stifling my sobs near my classmates as we peered down from the nosebleed section.

I felt like King Lear's youngest daughter, Cordelia, the one who loved him most but, unlike her deceitful sisters, refused to falsely flatter him. Cordelia spoke plainly and truthfully, yet doing so triggered her father to disinherit her and cast her into exile. Lear's stupidity later costs him his sanity, Cordelia's life, and other bloody conflicts.

King Lear represented both my father and the LDS Church. I loved them both, but I couldn't say things I didn't believe. My emotions nosedived out of control.

I'd survived unstable poverty, sexual abuse from a schizophrenic brother, and my parents disowning me, thanks to my faith in the teachings and hope offered by the LDS Church. After I couldn't believe in the Church anymore, suicide ideation hit for the first time.

I fantasized about throwing myself in front of the London subway, "the Tube," as it's called. Realizing something extreme happened to my brain, I dragged myself on the Tube about half an hour away to Hammersmith Hospital, a major teaching hospital in White City in West London. I wasn't a citizen, but I appreciated their treatment in the British National Health Service. The dried blood smeared on the tiles in front of me didn't help my anxiety as I waited for maybe several hours. An empathetic doctor listened to my story, slightly puzzled by my religious devotion, and prescribed the antidepressant citalopram, also known as Celexa. I rode back to the bunkhouse with the medication, a sliver of relief, and an appointment for the following week.

I hated that I'd take a drug to alter my brain chemistry, but this situation became more than I could bear alone. I felt tortured because I didn't want to get expelled from BYU. If you're non-Mormon you can still attend, though non-Mormons are a mere 1 percent of the student population, or about three hundred students out of thirty thousand. You must go to some religious service every week and certify an ecclesiastical endorsement. I didn't even consider switching churches because I felt terrified of going public with my doubts. I was afraid of getting ejected from BYU and deathly afraid of talking to my bunkmates about the nuclear explosion in my life because I didn't want accusations of encouraging apostasy. God says, "I will never leave you nor forsake you," but that's not how I felt.

Ashamed and isolated, I felt like I was facing down the authoritarian Communist Party of China. I read George Orwell's book *1984* around then and completely identified with this dystopian science fiction novel, though that book is far more severe than my suffering. In hindsight, I let my anxieties snowball far beyond reality because I'd fought so hard to get to BYU and didn't want to give it up.

In the throes of my faith crisis, I could transfer out, just as I'd already done from Truman State, but that would be intensely disruptive, expensive, and I didn't know where to go. I now realize I should have leaned more on God, but instead I kept my focus on the human beings around me.

The BYU professors running the program offered mixed reactions. The leader seemed unempathetic and treated me like a drama queen. I remember him saying something like, "Oh, there's always one in every group. There's always one that has a meltdown."

He took minimal interest in understanding the roots of my debilitating state, which in fairness, I wasn't willing to completely divulge.

His colleague, however, proved supportive and willing to ask questions about my faith crisis, which I gingerly discussed around the edges but felt deathly afraid to fully reveal. I didn't want to get kicked out of BYU for apostasy, and I didn't want to lead anyone out of their eternal salvation if I was wrong about Mormonism. So I withered in near silence.

This kind, supportive professor, a brilliant MIT grad, told me it was OK to ask questions, that God was bigger than any doubts I had. He also gave me an extension on my lengthy research paper about the media giant BBC's Hutton Inquiry, which I didn't submit until I returned to the Provo campus.

The medication helped; I stabilized and began jogging to relieve my anxiety and get natural endorphins. I splurged on my most expensive haircut ever and chopped off my hair from below my shoulders to chin length, desperately wanting a jolt from my depressing routine.

Amid my isolation, I met a Catholic priest at Westminster Cathedral, the biggest Catholic church in London. I didn't care much for the architecture; I thought the dramatic external orange and white horizontal stripes from floor to ceiling were too busy and a little dizzying, like zebra stripes. The sprawling complex with multiple dome towers and a soaring 284-foot bell tower reminded me of Willy Wonka's chocolate factory.

But I wasn't there to critique building design that day, though I was taking a BYU architecture course at that time. I entered the confessional booth and told the priest I wasn't Catholic, but I desperately needed help. I got some dark comic relief when he said he'd never heard of Mormonism. He was the first clergy I'd met who didn't know about the LDS Church.

Wow. This guy's never even heard of this thing that I am willing to die for, I thought.

An Italian with a thick accent and visiting on assignment from Rome, he said he'd grown up in a Catholic enclave without exposure to my American quasi-Protestant sect. This was a thunderbolt moment for me because he was deeply spiritual, loved God, and was very compassionate. But he didn't know anything about Joseph Smith, the Book of Mormon, the Pearl of Great Price, or the Doctrine and Covenants.

His confessional hours were ending, though he showed no rush to hurry me away. We strolled around the cathedral grounds. He retrieved a small book he handed me, a pocket-size version of Australian meditation teacher Paul Wilson's *The Little Book Of Calm*, a collection of about 150 meditations and small anxiety-relieving suggestions like, "write down your worry," "breathe deeply," "avoid tense people," and "massage your forehead."

The Catholic priest and I email corresponded for a while after I got home. I tried emailing in 2020, but he didn't respond. I assume he's passed away, because this was 2004 and he was fairly elderly.

My time with him became a redeeming moment, though he

was only temporarily in London, and Utah beckoned. I returned home to BYU for my senior year and didn't want to jeopardize my degree. So I just kept my head down. I made an arrangement with God, telling Him, "I've got one more year here in the Mormon Church, and if you really want me to stay, I'm open. But I don't really believe it." That senior year, I coasted along, attending the LDS services and trying to see if I could stay Mormon.

———

In many respects, I give credit to my journalism professor for not hiding or censoring those microfiche pages. I don't think he realized the effect it had on me; I never discussed it with him. Enormous blessings happen in my life *because* of something but also *in spite of* something. I found the truth despite the Mormon system, but I also found it because of it. If I were more grateful for that, perhaps deep bitterness wouldn't have plagued me during my turbulent years after leaving the LDS Church. God is a reconciler, and He expressly tells us in Ephesians 4:31 to "get rid of all bitterness."[49]

I spent many years conditioned to give my authority to human beings. When I questioned God's structuring of this human religious institution, again I looked to human beings for answers. That was doomed to fail.

There are some profoundly spiritual Mormons in a deep relationship with God. I was more into religion as a ritual-based practice. And I wanted to be a good kid. I wanted to fit in with the Mormons. Part of my shame over leaving Mormonism came because I grew up in a cult on the fringe of Mormonism. As kids, we never fully belonged in Mormonism, because my dad—later excommunicated from the LDS Church—said they were terrible for elevating their prophet to their own version of an "infallible" pope.

When I transferred to the heart of Mormonism in Provo, I did pretty well for myself at BYU. I was still dealing with emotional upheaval, but overall, I adjusted well. However, this was essentially based on human beings—fitting into the social scene and feeling acceptance papered over my deep insecurities. Insecurity infected my whole upbringing, raised by a man who saw himself as better than the Mormon Church and everyone else. I felt that I was worse. I felt like a freak, like I didn't belong anywhere.

The true gospel tells us that it's a lie that we don't belong. Imposter syndrome is not from God; it's not what He's about.

Obviously, seventeen million people in the LDS Church don't get baptized without something special drawing them toward the H_2O. And while all those people aren't necessarily practicing Mormons, many are, and there's a lot that keeps them going back for church each Sunday, Family Home Evening on Monday nights, Scouts and Young Women activities on other weeknights, potlucks on Saturdays, stake conferences, general conferences, Relief Society, etc.

What do I miss about Mormonism? I loved being a Mormon kid. What kid wouldn't love to try a haunted house in the church gym on Halloween (lucky for us kids, Mormons don't get worked up about Halloween and Harry Potter the way some other denominations do) and touch fake brains made out of pasta?

I loved the teachings and core values that I learned in Sunday School, known as Primary for the kids. As a child, I didn't know about the Nicene Creed, the Trinity, or other theological disagreements between Mormonism and other sects.

All I knew, as my eight-year-old self wrote in my journal, was that I loved Jesus, and I hoped that I'd never forget how much I loved Jesus.

In Primary, we sang songs, colored pictures of Jesus, and got candy and baked treats from our teachers. We sang songs like this ditty, which nearly always made me choke up because of its sweet message. It's a song called "I'll Walk With You," in the LDS *Children's Songbook* by LDS artists Carol Lynn Pearson and Reid Nibley, about looking out for the little guy and being kind to people who are different:

If you don't walk as most people do,
Some people walk away from you,
But I won't! I won't!
If you don't talk as most people do,
Some people talk and laugh at you,
But I won't! I won't!
I'll walk with you. I'll talk with you.
That's how I'll show my love for you.
Jesus walked away from none.
He gave his love to ev'ryone.
So I will! I will!
Jesus blessed all he could see,
Then turned and said, "Come, follow me."
And I will! I will!

Chapter 11

Post-Mormon Pains

This is what the Sovereign LORD, *the Holy One of Israel,
says: "In repentance and rest is your salvation, in quiet-
ness and trust is your strength, but you would have none
of it."*

—Isaiah 30:15[50]

When I left home, and then Mormonism, I had no "normal" yardstick for measuring what constituted healthy or unhealthy behavior. My yuppie anxieties arose from dating debacles, workplace
bullying, a coworker's suicide, sibling conflict, a women's Bible
study group that turned shockingly dark, financial stress, body
insecurities, a minor car wreck, and an embarrassing layoff that
was publicly blared about in an industry blog. If these "normal"
issues had hit a girl with healthier self-esteem and family support, I
might have handled them in stride. Instead, desperate to run away
from the values I grew up with because I thought them antiquated

and irrational, I stumbled and struggled with isolation, self-hatred, and suicidal thoughts. It took many years for my stubborn heart to allow myself to dream, to flourish, to discover a deep, weighty anchor for my soul that could withstand and hold firm against the external turbulent ebbs and flows of emotional pressures.

When I graduated from BYU at age twenty-two, I wanted a complete reset away from Mormondom. As a girl, I never planned to work outside the home. I just wanted to be a mom, my only major goal in life besides getting married. With seven siblings, I adored the positive aspects of a big family (rare loneliness, instant playmates, etc.). Competitive by nature—call it passive-aggressive "Mormon nice"—I wanted eleven kids because the cousins I idolized had ten, and I aspired to beat them. After an itinerant childhood, I wanted to plant myself in a suburban Utah cul-de-sac and never leave, as my husband and I raised an army of children. But this dream evaporated when I realized I couldn't be LDS anymore.

After the Mormon pathway collapsed, I narrowed my life choices to three: teaching English in Ecuador, beach bumming in San Diego, or writing political journalism in Washington, DC. From South America, I wanted to see for myself the habitat that inspired Charles Darwin's groundbreaking book *On the Origin of Species* about the theory of evolution. I still considered myself a Christian, and I wanted to explore how faith and science are complementary, not antagonistic (something I still enjoy now as a recovered agnostic). I pondered San Diego simply for its paradisiacal beaches and weather, which I'd experienced multiple times with friends and family during BYU road trips after the five-hour drives past Las Vegas. But I knew the journalism market in that area was small, and I felt anxious to prove my father's prophecies of my destruction wrong (important life lesson: striving to prove someone wrong might get you short-term wins, but it's an unsustainable, destructive life philosophy). Lazing about the beach and working an easy job would give me space and time to heal from trauma. But it would entail endless guilt, navel gazing, and accusations that I was frittering away my life. Plus, I had Dad to thank for my deep interest in public service and civic life. He has a deep love of country that I respect. DC spoke and drew me in.

I moved cross-country that August. My immediate family, except Sophie, skipped my college graduation—it would validate my apostasy. Three aunts, my grandma, and an uncle attended the ceremony, and a few cousins showed up for a luncheon at a Brazilian steakhouse restaurant afterward to celebrate.

To Ralph's credit, and to my surprise, he offered to help me move. Refusing to see any of his own siblings, he rolled into town from Missouri with Peter and hauled all my stuff in their blue twelve-passenger Chevy Astro over the 2,100 miles from Utah to Arlington, Virginia, which lies right across the river from Washington, DC.

I took a journalism internship with the legendary newspaper journalist Robert Novak but quickly snagged a full-time newspaper job in the cutthroat world of political journalism. My internship supervisor encouraged me to snap up the full-time gig.

"You moved here to get a job, not to stay an intern," she said.

My sister Sophie said she wanted to leave Mormonism and move to DC also. We tried living together my junior year at BYU, but again, we didn't have great chemistry. We'd even tried going to group therapy at a battered women's shelter my sophomore year. It didn't seem to help.

"If you can't get along with your own sister, you can't get along with anyone," she'd tell me. That hurt, even if I didn't believe it. I wanted us to help each other heal.

Something about growing up in a cult-like environment kept us emotionally guarded and unable to bond. But I felt willing to try again.

Sophie and I lived in a one-bedroom, income-capped apartment, where the government forces landlords to accept poorer tenants like us. It was 2005, and I landed a 2002 forest-green Saturn SL1 car with tan interiors from two of my brothers, who gave me a sweet-heart deal—in part as penance for photoshopping me out of the family pictures. Things were looking up. I was making $30,000 a year and Sophie was in college full time at a Catholic university studying fashion design and selling luxury Tumi suitcases at the local mall. That was, until a creepy older coworker started hitting on her, driving her to quit. Using Craigslist, I helped her get a fashion design internship with a trendy, sequin-loving purse maker, but it was unpaid. Money was tight in one of the country's most expensive zip codes, but still, my salary—more than $45,000 in 2023 dollars—was an unthinkable fortune for a girl who barely scraped through college earning maybe six or seven thousand dollars in a good year. Since leaving home at eighteen, I'd always worked, including part-time student journalism and internships, janitorial work, and fast-food jobs. Surviving college was tough, but the real world proved far worse.

In DC and the cities that followed, I struggled to adjust to the "real world." From learning how to drink to dealing with office gossip and politics, I was a lamb before the slaughter. Like Cady Heron, the homeschooled protagonist in *Mean Girls*, I had limited reading of the social cues for survival. The newsroom held its own

Regina George–type bully, who viewed me as a rival and ridiculed my ideas openly in the newsroom. She spread slander behind my back, including mocking my family to a guy I was dating in hopes of turning him against me. Her confidant was a cynical, middle-aged divorcé who announced in front of the entire newsroom that he'd discussed me with his therapist, complaining that—despite nothing I'd done to him—I was a stuck-up bitch who "thought I was all that and a bag of chips."

I had a sexist, neurotic supervisor for a year who openly berated me and another young woman for minutiae, his edits returning to us in red ink as a savage, bloody mess on the page. Not only would he deliver the excessive handwritten blows, but they were offered up with condescending, cutting, snide remarks, sighs, and eye rolls. Meanwhile, if he was out, his boss—second-in-command of the entire ship—reviewed our work and offered a few tiny tweaks with a figurative pat on the head.

I almost snapped after the supervisor berated me for leaving work without his permission at 5:00 p.m. (i.e., not even early) the day we learned a coworker, whose desk stood maybe fifteen feet from mine, had committed suicide. The poor man killed himself at age thirty-six with carbon monoxide in his garage, weighed down under hidden sorrows likely exacerbated by the toxic work environment. Several years prior, another young man working at the same place, who I never met, hanged himself at home in Arlington at age twenty-eight. This was not a positive mental health environment. More than a decade later, I'm happy to say I've heard the culture seems greatly improved. But back then, it was a somber time.

My now-passed colleague had a quiet, cheerful spirit. Six months prior, he attended my twenty-third birthday party. I still have the cute, stylish birthday card he gave me, along with a gift card.

"It's a joy working with you," he wrote in the pink, blue, and cream-colored card with silvery, swirly "Happy Birthday" lettering. "Hope you get something enjoyable with this."

He was softhearted, volunteering to help edit *Streetsense*, the newspaper for and about homeless people, plus a newsletter published by housing charity Habitat for Humanity. He also worked at a summer camp for traumatized children. His death steamrolled me, contributing to the second time suicidal ideation struck me after it first appeared when I rejected the Mormon Church a couple years prior. After my colleague's suicide, I told a coworker I'd fantasized that it was me instead. This phenomenon of a "copycat suicide" or "the Werther effect" is where someone attempts or successfully emulates the suicide of someone they knew personally or heard about through the media or word of mouth.

I'd also been fighting with my sister Sophie; our personalities clashed, and our tiny apartment had no space to decompress. She struggled with her credit score, making her ineligible to join Blockbuster Video's rental membership (kids, google what Blockbuster is if you don't know), so I cosigned to allow her to use my credit. Without telling me, she failed to return several DVDs for an extended period, until one day I received a notice that a collection agency was coming after me. When I got upset, Sophie started yelling at me, even though it was entirely her error. She never apologized and began years of one-sided estrangement from her. I love her and pray for her often; I know all of us were deeply wounded by our upbringing.

Also painful was a women's Bible study group, affiliated with a large nondenominational Protestant church, that took a sinister turn. This close-knit group of women was highly supportive during my exodus from Mormonism and into a strange new city. We actually liked each other and socialized far beyond the weekly Bible lessons, including a very active daily Gmail group chat, coed happy hours, roller skating, and more. They didn't mind the old-school Elizabethan English in my prayers, where I said "thee" and "thou" when addressing God, the way a Quaker or a Mormon does. This Bible study group existed years before I showed up, and I felt blessed that a slot opened up for this popular group. But it all went wrong after one of my fellow members—who had shared with me privately, after I shared some about my family struggles, that she also battled depression—told us her mother was dying of cancer. She took family medical leave out of state to care for her ailing mother. She was living back home with her parents when the Bible study group leader flew to visit.

I don't know how it started or what exactly they said, but somehow the two women got into a vicious verbal fight. Vulgar profanity emanated from the caretaker directed toward the Bible study group leader, who returned and announced she felt like this group member had ruptured her trust. The leader said she felt a line had been crossed and that she would never feel comfortable if this woman remained in our Bible study. But as the group leader, she didn't want to act unilaterally, so she asked us to take a vote.

The TV show *Survivor* was new and highly popular, and I felt disgusted, like my Bible study had morphed into a cheap reality show. While this poor woman's mother approached death, she needed grace, mercy, and compassion. She needed the friends she'd relied on for years to get through this horrible family crucible. But instead, her

Bible study booted her out. I and a few others voted to keep her in, but we lost. Shortly after this poor girl got exiled, her mother died.

Now, I know that humanity and this world are inherently broken. That is a feature and not a bug of human existence. But the Christian church, at least so it claims and so Jesus commanded, should be a shelter and a respite from a broken world. Jesus says to His church in John 13:35: "By this everyone will know that you are my disciples, if you have love for one another."

This animosity was the exact opposite, and it was traumatizing—especially for my friend and also for me as an onlooker. I already felt skeptical of Protestant, Catholic, and Orthodox Christianity. Raised as a Mormon, I learned various talking points and doctrinal responses to the theological failings of any non-Mormon denomination. So after I saw this Bible study behavior, I declared my independence from organized religion. I thought that if my mother was dying of cancer, I would get better treatment from a yacht or polo club—pretty much any alliance except this nasty little book club. I washed my hands of these self-righteous zealots who claimed to be following God's will. For me, Christianity, and all religions, were sociological constructs, mumbo jumbo that made some people feel good and others behave like destructive cretins.

Around this time, another woman from that same church suffered a far worse brutalization. I didn't know her well, but I felt her sunny, kind, radiant warmth during a church friends' weekend trip to Duck Beach in the Outer Banks of North Carolina. She was the perfect all-American girl, with a captivating smile, golden tan skin, and waist-length, shimmering honey-colored blond hair. Her violent rape and murder by her apartment's leasing agent shook me and others from church, especially until the vile criminal was caught. This previously twice-convicted felon admitted to getting high on cocaine, using his building keys to enter her apartment, and bludgeoning her repeatedly with a hammer and a frying pan. He wasn't affiliated with the church, but during that period of investigation, we shuddered to think her killer might be lurking among our church pews. God didn't protect her from evil, even though she was highly involved in the church. Her death confirmed my desire to stay away from that traumatizing crowd.

I started to spiral downward. My loving extended Utah family two thousand miles away said the answer was to return to Mormonism, but that ship had sailed and things got awkward with their non-Mormon niece, financially speaking. They say sometimes poor lottery winners and professional athletes become bankrupt debtors, worse off than if they'd never hit the jackpot. It's because they have no idea how to manage their money, since they didn't earn it gradually. That was me, on a smaller scale.

My extended family sold the last big property in Grandpa Sheffield's real estate portfolio. It was the first direct inheritance I'd received, worth more than $307,000 (nearly $458,000 in 2023 dollars). It was an unfathomable amount. I felt simultaneously thrilled and terrified. With no idea how to protect this money, I felt gravely afraid I'd lose it.

Growing up like I did and then scraping by as a low-paid journalist, at age twenty-three, I ignorantly got roped into a shoddy tenancy-in-common investment in a multifamily rental apartment complex (known as a TIC, similar to a REIT, a real estate investment trust) by my uncle, through a member of his Mormon congregation. She seemed sloppy; she was ridiculously late to our breakfast meeting to discuss the investment, for starters, but I trusted my uncle since he invested, even though he had no formal training (and certainly didn't impart any to me) in portfolio management, asset class diversification, risks and illiquidity of private equity, etc. I learned later this can be considered "affinity fraud," exploiting your trusted social ties to a religious or other social group. I considered suing her but didn't have the time or money.

I ignorantly took this lady and my uncle's advice and invested $257,000 (that's more than $378,000 in 2022 dollars) in the TIC, an amount representing 84 percent of my inheritance from Grandpa. The other $50,000 I cashed out and used to pay for beauty pageant fees (more on that later) and living expenses for my master's degree program at Harvard. I'd studied hard for the GRE test and knew I could get into a strong school. The degree was a master's in public policy (MPP), a program common among DC policy wonks. Disillusioned and heartbroken by working in political media, I thought the degree would give me wiggle room if I wanted to change careers. After I received my full-tuition journalism scholarship to Harvard—the announcement landing in my email inbox like a lightning bolt—I knew my life's trajectory would majorly change. But I still needed housing, food, and transportation.

A few years after the initial TIC investment, the incompetent property managers demanded a sizable capital call—i.e., thousands more dollars squeezed from investors—after the stock market bubble crashed. They wanted almost $70,000 more from me, cash I didn't have. By that point, I struggled as a Harvard graduate student, working on campus to survive, and my anxiety accelerated. I thought I'd have to drop out to pay the capital call. It was never a serious inquiry, but I briefly considered stripping to make quick cash. My parents already thought that's what I did anyway after I left the cult. It seemed like an easy way to get a rapid cash infusion for the capital call, but I worried about the downward spiral that might ensue.

It took long hours of agonizing and studying up on the financial terms, but the aggressive capital call, which we believed was illegal, galvanized me to lead other investors to hire legal counsel to block it. I was proud to lead the charge even though I was less than half the age of many of the other investors, but it was a Pyrrhic victory—a big chunk of my investment evaporated. I felt deep shame and anger at myself for trusting my uncle, the one who helped shelter me after I fled the family cult.

Realizing how powerless and willfully ignorant I'd rendered myself, I changed my master's degree focus to business policy (I initially focused on foreign policy) and enrolled in a finance course in grad school to empower myself and later worked at finance giants Goldman Sachs and Moody's Investors Service on Wall Street. But the entire process left me financially traumatized on top of everything else and put a strain on my extended family relationships.

Back in DC, things got so bleak that Sophie finally called the police when I told her one night that I wanted to kill myself. Between a hostile work environment, failed dating relationships (I'd been dumped by multiple men, more on that soon), toxic church environments, and a conflict-ridden home, I felt like a cornered rat, filled with impotent rage and depression. Everything I'd tried to bring me stability and joy was traumatizing me. God didn't exist, or He seemed to hate me with a passion.

This time, I didn't have a specific suicide method in mind like the London subway, but that didn't stop me. I ran into my Saturn, but Sophie physically blocked me with her car, boxing my car between two other cars on either side, stopping me from leaving.

"Move your car!" I screamed. She refused to budge.

Thud! I backed up and left a small dent in her car, a black Nissan Altima, still stuck. Furious, I got out of the car and ran out on foot into the night.

She physically tackled me and we tousled around on the ground in front of a bus stop waiting area, screaming at each other as she pulled my hair and my red wool sweater half off, leaving my bra partially exposed.

"Let me go!" I yelled. "You don't even care about me. You say my writing isn't worth your time!"

"Carrie, you need help," she yelled back. "And you say my fashion designs are drab!"

Panting, heaving, adrenaline pumping. We stumbled back to the apartment.

The police arrived, and I flashed my Congressional press badge (a very stupid idea) to convince them I was not crazy, I was a productive citizen, but that I was severely depressed because I'd left Mormonism. It worked; the police bought it, and in fact, one of them asked if I knew some woman whose name I'd never heard but was also apparently Mormon. His question stunned me—it seemed like an icebreaker, parlor game–type question—but I played nonchalant and told him I wasn't familiar with her.

I calmed down and told the cops I wouldn't harm myself, that I just needed to cool off. Legally speaking, they couldn't take me in unless I verbally told them I planned to harm myself. I spent the night at a shady two-star hotel down the street. It was the worst night of my life (till then—it would spiral further later). I still have the Highlander Motor Inn receipt for $74.95. I didn't want to hide it in shame, and on the back of the receipt I took notes about how I'd gotten to this low point. I took the next day off work. Somehow, I'd injured my arm during our fight and showed up with my arm in a sling. My toxic supervisor didn't say a word about my absence or my obvious visible ailment, totally unempathetic and aloof.

———

I apologized to Sophie and told her our combustible relationship needed to change. I gave her money for her car repair and later fully paid off her nearly $7,000 in credit card debt as penance for dragging her through my trauma. I love Sophie, and I'm grateful she both stood up to me and for me while I was engulfed in a rage of self-hatred. She's one of my heroes.

I moved out to a much healthier living situation in nearby Alexandria with two other girls I'd met on a nondenominational Christian church housing website. We lived in a three-bedroom apartment on the third floor of a complex with a large swimming pool. These Christian girls were easygoing and clean, excellent housemates. Yes, I was annoyed with Christians, but right after graduating, I'd been denied housing by some secular women who asked for my résumé. When they saw I attended Brigham Young University, they assumed I was a Mormon prude and that I'd be hostile toward male overnight visitors. They had zero interest in learning the truth about my story, and that hurt. But I realized those sorts of uncurious, rigid bigots would make terrible housemates. I probably could have sued them for religious discrimination under the Fair Housing Act, but I felt too timid and exhausted.

The year after graduating college, seeking to escape my inner pain and satisfy narcissistic urges implanted by Ralph, I followed the footsteps of Aunt Charlotte, Miss Utah USA and Miss USA in 1957. In 2006, I competed in Virginia's statewide beauty pageant as Miss Alexandria. It became another embarrassing failure that I shared with almost nobody, including my parents. I finally went public in 2022 about what happened in an essay for the *New York Post*[51] after Cheslie Kryst, a former Miss USA, tragically committed suicide shortly after her reign ended. Before her death, Kryst wrote a piece in *Allure* magazine expressing fear of aging as she turned thirty in a society that worships youth. She also struggled with the pain from aggressive cyberbullies who attacked her looks and African American race. I shared my challenges with pageantry:

Encouraged by [former Miss USA] Aunt Charlotte, I competed as Miss Alexandria USA in Miss Virginia USA, and I've seen pageant-life pressures. The incessant tanning and skipping meals. I was 23 and felt old—no wonder Kryst said haters called her ancient at 28. And pricey shopping: clothing, makeup, advice books, accessories, pageant fees, publicity shots, styling. All told, I spent around $5,000—added pressure to win.

While we had signed away our lives under a mound of legal disclaimers, Miss USA didn't want to be accused of abetting eating disorders. They forced us to attend meals, but they couldn't force us to eat. From our box lunches, for example, most girls would take a couple bites of their sandwich and trash the rest, along with their cookie and chips.

Pageants help women grow confidence, but they also create insecurities without proper mental-health care. Catwalking in

front of thousands of people wearing four-inch heels and a bikini
does wonders for public-speaking fears!

    Perhaps I sought escape through pageantry, but ironically, it
left me more insecure and deflated. During my pageant interview,
I told unimpressed judges that the pageant world "was foreign to
me" because it was. I was a novice against girls who'd competed
for decades. I didn't advance beyond initial rounds.

After my workplace nightmare and failed pageant, I fled to a different company to escape the dysfunction, but it followed me. After a short period of respite, I eventually became one of maybe ten or fifteen people in a gradual wave of layoffs after new management came on board and cleaned house. It stung badly when an insecure middle-aged female manager asked me how old I was (illegal?) and told me I was too young to hold the job because when she was my age, she worked at a rural newsletter. She used brutal tactics with my other fellow twentysomethings and got them fired, then she herself landed on the chopping block. She tried to sue the company for wrongful termination or some other employment dispute, but I personally felt she deserved it, in part because she'd ruthlessly "edited" her way into oblivion by screwing us all over.

My name and several other twentysomethings' names were strategically leaked, publicly listed as newly laid off in a gossip blog widely read in the DC news media industry. This was a high-profile workplace, with management changes closely scrutinized. But I'd been laid off without any article retractions, and my pieces were featured by the *Wall Street Journal*'s "Best of the Web," and ABC News' prestigious morning newsletter, *The Note*. Meanwhile, a colleague hired by the new management kept his job, despite forcing the company to issue an embarrassing retraction covered by basically every major news outlet. It wasn't fair. I'd clearly failed to play politics correctly and maneuver the right patrons to protect me from the ax.

After work environments that felt brutally abusive, I developed a reactionary, antiauthority attitude and a chip on my shoulder. Totally emotionally decimated, I became suicidal a third time after this very public failure. Because everything else crumbled, I tied my self-identity to my career—my source of income and self-worth. My work in political media became my new religion.

Without properly putting God at the top of my life and knowing His view of me, instead of the world's, life wasn't worth living if I couldn't fulfill my highest purpose in life. I daydreamed about how I'd kill myself. I'd shoot myself with a handgun on the steps of the US Capitol with a suicide note naming the editors who ruined my life. Under the intense pressure of a competitive national newsroom environment, I constantly felt an unrelenting desire to drive newsreader traffic, especially by getting one of my articles linked to the Drudge Report. It's not as popular today, but back then, the Drudge Report meant peak reader traffic. You might get a quarter of a million page views or more if Drudge touched you with his golden Midas hand. I had not achieved that status, but I nihilistically thought Drudge would certainly feature me if I went out with this sort of bang.

Without fatherly or motherly guidance, I turned to pop culture and my peers for guidance. What a mistake. American mass media always says you're not having enough orgasms, not wearing the right clothes, not flirty enough. Women's magazines print reams of glossy pages filled with lies, deceiving young women and making them feel like they'll never be perfect enough. I was drowning in lies.

Around this time, Mom wrote me to say God told her I would get schizophrenia, a prophecy she seemed to relish. It reminded me of the schadenfreude Ralph displayed after Peter was struck with the debilitating disease.

July 27, 2008
Dear Carrie,

I am prompted to write to you. I've prayed so hard for you over the years. You are so special. It was difficult getting you here . . .

I have had many warnings about you. I have told you about them. You have disregarded God's counsel, becoming very prideful instead. You have made me very sad, though I try to help you. The devil tricks you to believe that you know more than your Creator, putting worldly ambitions, self-centered ideas, popularity, friends, and men, etc. before the Lord.

Now you have lost your testimony (the very seed of your eternal life), dressing immodestly, living a worldly, loose, and self-indulgent life style.

You always think you can "get by" by being tricky, like our cat "Houdini," who always sneaked off on escapades, until he was crushed to death on one of them. Now the Lord has told me he is going to come down on you. You will get schizophrenia if you don't repent. Ask Him if this is not true!

Pray always. You have been taught. You know too much. I don't want you to get schizophrenia, the dreaded disease Peter has. He was clearly warned by Dad, but did not hearken. PLEASE HEED THE WARNING OF GOD.

You've been blessed with many talents. Be humble, for with-out this, Christ warned, Satan "shall deceive the very elect."

Please be a better example, in righteousness, for your younger sisters. Do the Lord's will. Stop your wander-lust attitude. Repent. Remember Dad's quote in the Bookmark, "The wise learn by precept—fools by punishment, if at all."

We know we haven't been perfect parents, and hope you will forgive us. But we have tried hard, though. We hope the best for all our children, whom we have warned to leave the east coast. A disaster is coming.

Love, Mom & Dad

I plunged into the murky waters of anxiety because I was both negatively imagining my future without God and fantasizing about my own strengths and abilities without God. Author Amy Chua, who shot to fame for her bestselling 2011 memoir, *Battle Hymn of the Tiger Mother*, followed up with a 2014 book, *The Triple Package*, which explores her theories about why US Jews, Mormons, and Asians are disproportionately wealthy and successful compared to other Americans. She identifies what she describes as two powerful cultural traits: insecurity and superiority. There's the sense of, "I'm not part of the mainstream; therefore, I have an innate insecurity. But I also have an innate sense of superiority because of this tight-knit community."

This bedrock sense of identity formation in these communities allows members of the Triple Package to propel like rockets to new heights because of the intense mental fortitude forged by the double-edged forces of radical adversity and radical belonging.

When not tempered in a healthy way, those extremes become toxic. Yes, it's good to feel passionate and earn a good living for your family, but if you let these cultural attributes consume your psyche, it becomes unhealthy and destructive (like the movie *Black Swan*). After I ripped away my religious Mormon identity, I still kept this cultural trait of the superiority impulse:

"Oh, I'm hot stuff, and I'm smarter and better looking than almost everyone. I got a full-tuition scholarship to Harvard, and I regularly go on TV in front of millions of people to discuss war and politics because I'm brilliant. I worked at the most elite investment bank. I travel to exotic places and hang out with billionaires and famous people on their private jets because I'm both pretty and smart, unlike bimbo airheads or drab bookworms. People are jealous of me because they want to be me."

Followed by the subsequent inferiority crash and burn:

"I hate myself. I get dumped because I'm a clingy, shallow bitch. I'm a poor fraud. I brought shame on Grandpa's legacy by a failed investment. I weigh 112 pounds, and I need to lose five, I'm a fat disgusting slob. I'm not married, and I don't have kids; therefore, I'm worthless. I have disgusting blue veins popping out under my eyes—permanent bulging, periorbital bags. My family thinks I'm satanic and going insane. They're right. I should just kill myself."

This toxic stream of consciousness is polar opposite what the Bible tells us are the fruits of God's Spirit: love, joy, peace, patience, kindness, gentleness, faithfulness, and self-control. The Bible also teaches us the power of humility and a contrite spirit. Any achievement by mere mortals is tiny and fleeting compared to the scope of our universe and the expanse of eternity. Since we did not create ourselves, we can boast about nothing; we are wholly owned by our Creator. Everything in our lives, down to our body's subatomic particles and brain-wave impulses, belongs to God. We have no reason to beat our chests in vanity or to destroy and demean ourselves, because our loving Father in heaven cherishes us with a humble, secure bond.

Vacillating between hubris and self-hatred is not God's will. But it's where I lived for many years when I rejected God's grounding, healing, healthy love. Each of us will never fulfill our highest purpose and best serve God if we can't temper our human frailties by keeping our focus on Him.

Chapter 12

Queen of Lonely Hearts

Love is not a victory march, it's a cold and it's a broken hallelujah.

—Leonard Cohen[52]

Craigslist can be a lurking ground for serial killers,[53] human traffickers, and Ponzi schemers. So, of course, Craigslist was also the dating pool in which I immediately cast my net upon leaving Mormonism. In 2005, before this threat became clear, I was oblivious to these dangers.

At twenty-two, I didn't know how to socialize the "normal" (i.e., non-Mormon) way. Now that I'm older, I think the word "normal" is overrated and illusional, but back then, it was my North Star. The LDS Church provided everything—a ready-made group of friends, suitors, and service projects. Now, I was starting from scratch in a new city with a new job and a new worldview. After successfully vetting my prospects using call screening and an incognito email account, I went on a few Craigslist dates without any problems—just didn't feel any chemistry, though I did get a free dinner inside the restaurant at the infamous Watergate Hotel. I quickly ended my Craigslist romances, scaring the chaps off by telling them I wouldn't kiss a man (one went in for the kill on the first date, and I dodged his face) until I fell in love and that sex was completely off the table. You can take the girl out of Mormonism, but it ain't easy to take Mormonism out of the girl—and on some cultural matters, I think that's swell.

Singles Awareness Day, or SAD for short, falls every year on February 15, the day after Valentine's Day. It's a real national holiday, copyrighted and everything.[54] A group of high school kids developed the holiday in 2001 to celebrate being single and carried the tradition to college, where it grew like wildfire. It's a day to embrace half-off grocery store Valentine's Day chocolate and toast with other single friends.

Of course, it's no coincidence that SAD is also my birthday. I am the queen of miserable singlehood. For decades, I starred as the poster child for self-sabotage and rotten courtship. I'm pretty sure Lady Gaga wrote the song "Bad Romance" because she heard my pathetic tale. I should demand royalties one of these days.

I woke up at almost thirty-nine years old with a history of dating abusive, angry, manipulative, drug-using, controlling, callous, exploitative, narcissistic, dismissive men. How did this pattern start? I wasn't always this way. I struggled my freshman year of non-Mormon college and fled to BYU, where I dated healthy men. But when I realized I couldn't believe Mormon theology, I threw the baby out with the bathwater by rejecting men with good values, who loved God. Over time, I lapsed in my standards of who I let touch me, let into my life and heart.

At nineteen, my wonderful first boyfriend at Truman State cared about me deeply and found many ways to show his affection, from sending flowers and teddy bears often to fixing my car, and helping set up a dunk booth and walking overnight during a Relay For Life Cancer Walk fundraiser when I was captain. His fatal flaw: he was non-Mormon, so I dumped him.

6-30-02: He's an atheist, who compared Jesus Christ to [rapist death cult leader] *David Koresh & says that religion is the worst institution that humans have come up with b/c it makes people strap bombs to themselves like in the Middle East & kill & hurt & discriminate. He said that I discriminate against him, but last night he said he'd become a Mormon to make me happy & that he'd do anything to make me happy. This is so wrong, and yet sad, b/c it shows how much he loves me, that he's willing to make a life-altering change like that for me.*

During my years immediately after college, there were men who cared for my soul and treated me respectfully. But I shunned and dumped them, sometimes quite suddenly, without any warning— a trait of borderline personality disorder (more on that later). Instead, I went for the "bad boys." The ambitious, worldly ones. They used my body and lacked spiritual depth, with no intention of honoring me.

Working on Wall Street and in the TV industry, I spent years pretending, masking the dark abuse I suffered from my father and other family members. I didn't realize that by suppressing my past, I created a false perfectionism that neither I nor my romantic partners could ever measure up to. And while rejecting kind, stable, loving partners because of my false perfectionism, I accepted negative partners who told me I was not smart enough, not blonde enough, that I was damaged goods, that no other man would want me because of my "crazy" family. I stayed because abused women often marry abusers—we tell ourselves we don't deserve better.

My LDS boyfriend during my faith crisis at BYU was a kind, supportive, and positive influence. He was the first partner I'd seriously considered marrying. We lived next door to each other and took turns packing each other's lunches each week, swapping our navy blue-and-black insulated cooler and meeting on campus each workday for lunch together. This guy was a serious Romeo. He wrote me original poetry and songs about how much he loved me, which he'd sing while playing his guitar. He bought me a tiny diamond earring and necklace set to celebrate our one-year anniversary.

He fought for my mental health when the suicide demon first struck, sending me long, encouraging emails while I was in London and calling as often as possible amid the time-zone differences and limited phone booth availability in the cramped BYU student housing. But in the end, we couldn't reconcile that I was moving on from Mormonism, and he cut things off. A bishop from his hometown area jokingly tried to scare young Mormon men away from dating non-Mormon women, saying they were "wicked, evil, mean, and nasty." Sure it was tongue-in-cheek, but underlying the "joke" was a sentiment I shared when I was Mormon, too.

Early in my DC days, I also flirted with Catholicism, largely thanks to a brown-eyed Italian American boy who once belonged to the intensely secretive sect Opus Dei. This Catholic religious order is featured in the popular book and movie *The Da Vinci Code*, with the main Opus Dei character a freakish, red-eyed albino monk-turned–bloodthirsty assassin in God's name. It's a heavily dramatized and unrealistic portrayal of Opus Dei.

Before I'd met him, this short-term beau left full-time Opus Dei (I never learned if he was on the part-time track, which makes up about 70 percent of their crew and allows marriage and a secular day job) because of its strictness—for example, its permanent celibacy/marriage ban and that adherents lacerate themselves during prayer by strapping spikes to their thighs as punishment for sin. Drawn to this elite subsect while a college student, he felt miserable after becoming a full-fledged member living in New York City. Yet he was still a devout Catholic. I felt special kinship with this fellow intense sect survivor, and we bonded over learning to live in a secular environment.

I went to Catholic services with him, mesmerized by the Latin homily, elaborate gold statues and crucifixes, and colorful paintings adorning Old St. Mary's in downtown Washington, DC. It seemed exotic to a girl raised in LDS churches, which are typically bland and sensible, with neutral brown, tan, maroon, and creme colors (unless they were a hideous '70s orange), and crucifixes and crosses are banned. It felt like watching a National Geographic film, my jaw dropping inside at what I perceived to be pagan-influenced gold-plated iconography. After about a month of dating (though we'd been friends a few months prior), he left me to return to and marry his ex. I wasn't Catholic enough for him. It shattered me more than it should have, because I was fragile and brittle.

After I left Mormonism and abandoned dabbling in Catholic and Protestant Christianity that following year, I avoided dating religious men. At worst, they were dangerous or dopey sheep; at best, hopelessly misguided, naive, and sheltered. They lived lives of oblivious ease and shallowness that I wanted no part in. Some of them were phonies, claiming to be godly men but behaving otherwise. At the same church with the toxic women's Bible study, a young man in the same "Christian" friend group pressured me to have sex with him while I was tipsy from alcohol. Thankfully, I fended him off, but not without feeling demoralized and violated. He was another reason I left organized religion.

While a Mormon, I refused to seriously date anyone but devout members of the LDS Church. After departing, I thought that was narrow-minded. Sadly, I swung the dating door *way* too far open and made terrible choices.

In my early twenties, I got dumped by a two-timing guy who was hooking up with his ex behind my back, and later insisted we make out all night after my twenty-mile marathon prep run. I got sick from exhaustion and still ran the marathon—while on antibiotics. Instead of coming out and supporting me during the Marine Corps Marathon, the guy (who'd been one of my closest friends during the year before, or so I thought—he called me his "best friend") played Frisbee with his buddies on the Capitol Mall in the shadow of the Washington Monument.

The weather that late October day was perfect—crisp autumn air and radiant blue skies—as our running route weaved through the various DC monuments, ending in a slight hilly incline (killer for shins after running 26.2 miles) at Arlington National Cemetery at the United States Marine Corps War Memorial, commemorating the Battle of Iwo Jima in World War II. I wish I could have enjoyed it, but congested and clogged up on medicine, I hobbled across the finish line after taking walk breaks at every refreshment station, dragging my end time.

Shortly after, he announced he was getting back with his ex. The rigid perfectionist in me—who'd won or placed among top finishers in multiple 5K and cross-country races growing up and eventually thrice won the National Press Club 5K in the female members' category—beat myself up for my relatively slow finish time. It was a lackluster 4 hours 52 minutes, slightly below the approximately 4:44 average time among all of the nearly 21,000 finishers, and in the 50th percentile among women finishers.[55] I achieved something that less than 1 percent of Americans do in their lifetime—complete a marathon.[56] But it stung bitterly— I hated being "average," though I desperately wanted to be "normal." I felt so rotten about my completion time, combined with getting dumped, that I trashed my marathon completion medal. My heart and body ached mercilessly for days. The marathon took its toll—it made me skip my period and my knees permanently throb whenever I hit around forty-five minutes running. I resolved never to torture myself like that again.

A couple months before my twenty-fifth birthday, I lost my virginity during a trip to Miami with a drug addict who was slandering me behind my back to his ex-girlfriend and bragging to his best friend that I was naive and easily manipulated into buying him gifts and doing his will. I didn't believe I deserved better.

We'd been dating for around five months, and I'd started taking Yaz birth control pills in time to prepare, feeling proud and defiant—I was a modern, liberated woman. I ignored the red flags about his toxic behavior toward me, desperate to shed my sexually repressed religious nutjob identity. There probably was no God, and if there was, He sure didn't care about me, so the feeling was mutual. Why should I care what his abusive, brainwashed followers said about my premarital sex life?

We flew from DC that early December and stayed two nights in a bright white-and-gray three-star hotel, with a fusion of Deco and ultramodern ocean-colored decor in the center of the Art Deco Historic District. I'd bought some sex toys online for us, thinking that's what the women's magazine writers wanted me to do. Why do we women live by this chorus of strangers with no idea what's best for us?

When the big moment came, I felt crushed because he started yelling at me, telling me I wasn't performing right because I was tensing up.

I was a failure. I felt myself going limp and hollow as he finished the job. It felt a lot like my first kiss: far less romantic than I had dreamed of, dejected, and sad.

Funny how they don't talk about this hollowness in the same magazines shouting at you to have fifty orgasms a day as you casually float among sexual partners. The 1960s women's liberation movement achieved important and valuable ends, including opening for women the most basic pathways allowed to men, from getting a credit card or car loan without a man's approval to entering previously closed career fields. But in many ways, women threw the baby out with the bathwater. We accepted the male framework around human sexuality and deprioritized commitment. For thousands of years, humans embraced the order of love, marriage, and then sex. We switched the order to sex and possibly love or marriage later down the road. In that process, women lost out. Science tells us women are wired more deeply to be monogamous; "free love" popularized in the 1960s failed to bring women more satisfaction. As Louise Perry reported in the *Wall Street Journal*:

> The vast majority of women, if given the option, prefer a committed relationship to casual sex...In today's hookup culture the sexual playing field is not even, but it suits men's interests

to pretend that it is. Women are entitled to be angry... hookup culture demands that women suppress their natural instincts in order to match male sexuality and thus meet the male demand for no-strings sex... I've spoken to many women who participated in hookup culture when they were young and years later came to realize just how unhappy it made them. As one friend put it, "I told myself so many lies, so many lies." [57]

I was no saint in that relationship: immature, emotionally volatile, angry, and insecure. I learned some of his dirty laundry when I snooped in his email and GChats that he'd left logged in on my laptop—a total violation of privacy. I justified it to myself because we'd been fighting, and I was furious with him for continuing to meet up with his ex-girlfriend and bad-mouth me.

I found out this guy cheated on a work drug test by borrowing a friend's urine. He had an impressive résumé, though he lied to me about his ongoing drug use and eventually got fired because he spent all day playing video games while getting high instead of working.

Before I met him and without him even knowing me, he planted a hurtful article about me in a news gossip blog read by thousands of journalists in the DC area. I kept trying to leave him, but he was a bullying manipulator, and I felt insecure and terrified of being alone, so I stayed with him on and off for almost two years. I persuaded him to attend the twelve-step program for his drug addiction, though it didn't fully register until we permanently split. Years later, he asked to meet up to apologize. He'd typed out a long list of things he felt remorseful about and asked my forgiveness. It seemed that he'd become a totally reborn person, productive, healthy, and happy. The transformation was heartening. He'd been so successful with the twelve steps that he was helping others with their addiction recoveries, and that made me happy.

I told him I wholeheartedly forgave him, that we were both broken people when we met, so we both needed our own healing journeys. I carry no ill will toward him today, and I pray God's grace over his life. I now believe God's power healed him. The twelve-step program centers on a Higher Power helping break the chains of addiction. At the time, I thought that was simply a tool for weak people, but now I see it accesses the most powerful, vibrant, and everlasting source of permanent renewal. It made him wise, not weak. He found God years before I did, so in the end, he was far more mature.

My toxic dating patterns continued in graduate school at Harvard in my midtwenties, when I dated men who didn't care about me and used me for their pleasure flings. Meanwhile, I soundly rejected kind and stable men, thinking they were boring, weak, and unambitious. A supportive husband could have helped me resolve my inner demons and thrive, but subconsciously, part of me sought dysfunction because it's how I grew up. I don't know who said this, but it's infinitely true: "May you never become so familiar with pain that you reject anything good that tries to find you."

The movie *Redeeming Love*, based on a book that's sold more than three million copies, taps into this broken mindset. The modern story is inspired by the ancient biblical story of the prophet Hosea, who marries a prostitute named Gomer, instructed by God to love her unconditionally. It's a metaphor for God's relentless love for us, even in our wretchedness.

In the modern movie/book, the prostitute mother of a young girl named Angel dies when Angel is eight years old, leaving her to be raised by a pedophile who rapes her until she escapes at age eighteen. After Angel falls into prostitution, a loving, kind, and godly man rescues her and marries her, though she runs back repeatedly into prostitution because she doesn't believe a man could want her for anything but sex.

"Attachment theory" in the field of psychology, which scrutinizes childhood trauma from primary caregivers, explains part of what's happening here. Scholar and author Arthur Brooks also wrote an insightful essay for the *Atlantic* called "How to Stop Dating People Who Are Wrong for You," about how abuse negatively impacts dating.

Brooks explains the tendency of some people to choose partners who are substance abusers or have other destructive behaviors, particularly if they have been exposed to such behaviors in their parents. Even more telling for me, he outlines the perils of dating people with what's known in psychology as "dark triad" personality traits—narcissism, psychopathy, and Machiavellianism. Certainly my father embodied dark-triad traits throughout my childhood:

One of the best ways to snag mates with Dark Triad personalities is to date primarily based on surface-level characteristics, such as money, power, and physical attractiveness. If you find yourself with one narcissist after another, this may be why. Remember, bad people can be good at appearing attractive, charming, and persuasive. As researchers reported in the Proceedings of the National Academy of Sciences, choosing mates this way doesn't generally deliver the partner you really want. Good teeth and a high-paying job don't predict faithfulness and kindness. Seek out evidence of the latter.[58]

I fled to the arms of a man with dark-triad traits who later became my ex-fiancé. I thought he'd give me stability with his hedge fund job, sailboat, BMW, and two Ivy League degrees. I chose to move in with this guy—just one month after we met, under his heavy pressure and desperate for security—before establishing a solid, healthy friendship. Emotionally volatile and controlling, he screamed at me for small things like missing a subway train en route to a Yankees game. I'd never visited that train station before and needed time to read the signs, apparently an unforgivable sin.

He pressured me to move in together even though I wasn't fully comfortable cohabiting before marriage. He nitpicked small things, like that I blew my nose too loud and used too many squares of paper on the toilet. He called me a babbling airhead and stupid because I went to a second-tier, subpar undergraduate school. To prove his point, he printed out the *U.S. News & World Report* college rankings and highlighted how much lower my school fell than his. He was unmoved by the fact that I later went to Harvard, or that as a seventeen-year-old I was barely surviving, living in a shed without running water and avoiding getting raped by my schizophrenic brother, so applying to an expensive Ivy League school didn't cross my mind, even though my standardized test scores fit.

He also hated Mormons (called them the "American Taliban") and journalists, saying that I shouldn't bother trying to go back into the journalism field after my master's program ended because it was full of backstabbing snakes and paid peanuts. He helped me mentally leave Mormonism and endured much, but we lacked equality. He wanted me to be submissive, and I wanted an equal partnership.

He pressured me into the field of finance, where I worked for prestigious companies Goldman Sachs and Moody's Investors Service, which looked great on a résumé but stifled my joy. It felt like he wanted me to be a Stepford wife. He told me I wasn't blonde enough and needed to start highlighting my hair. He reflected the inner turmoil and self-loathing I felt over my tumultuous past. Depressed, I turned to my old coping mechanism of food and put on fifteen pounds of extra weight. After much protesting, I dragged him to couples counseling, where he clammed up and said as little as possible.

5/22/11: The counseling didn't produce the kind of insight and bonding I was hoping for. We weren't willing to act out how bad we really are in front of the counselor, we were so diplomatic that he thought our problems were minor. [Dark Triad] *thinks our problems are minor. I wish I could think that, it's just that I don't believe he respects me or treats me the way I wish to be treated. I don't feel like he values me or cherishes me, and I worry that he would berate and disrespect me in front of our kids and set a bad pattern for them. I'm sick of him making jokes about dating or sleeping with other women, I'm sick of how he continues to talk on a regular basis and meet up with his ex. I'm sick of him failing to listen to me and I feel sad when he cuts me off and tells me I am rambling and that I sound ignorant. We come from such fundamentally different backgrounds that we have very different norms and standards of acceptable treatment of a significant other. I don't feel like I'm significant to him.*

Finally, after two years of dragging myself through the relationship, I woke up and realized I was a depressed, overweight, blonde Wall Street financial analyst when my best self was a healthy, fit, brunette journalist. It was no wonder I felt so insecure. Thank God I broke that off before marrying him—a saving grace at age twenty-nine. My close girlfriends, former Harvard roommates, were thrilled when I ended things. They'd visited me when I was living with this guy and said I was a zombie, a shell version of myself.

Yes, I was free, but as age thirty approached and I was still unmarried, I felt a pervasive sense of failure and dread. I begged my sister Julie, five years younger, to live with me for emotional support through the relationship train wreck. I hadn't lived with family since my abject failure with Sophie seven years earlier. Julie was about to finish college and considering a move to Chicago for its legendary improv comedy scene, Second City. I rerouted her to pursue her comedy dreams in the Big Apple.

We shared a bed in a one-bedroom apartment on the twenty-seventh floor of a luxury, twenty-eight-story skyscraper built in 1958, called 45 Wall Street after its address—literally on Wall Street. It previously housed a bank and sits a block from the iconic Greek-pillared New York Stock Exchange, which is across the street from Federal Hall, the site where George Washington took the presidential oath of office in 1789. Megastar actor Charlie Chaplin emboldened a massive crowd at Federal Hall at the 1918 Liberty Bond Rally during World War I. Just steps from there stands the stunning Trinity Church, a Gothic Revival building with a 281-foot spire sheltering its sweetly melodic, pealing bells. Founding Father Alexander Hamilton, now of Broadway fame, rests peacefully in Trinity Church's cemetery.

My 45 Wall Street building's amenities made me feel sophisticated—a sunbathe-worthy wraparound roof terrace, a penthouse-level club with pool tables, plus a yoga room, basketball court, and gym. Each morning leaving the apartment, I'd step into the dark cobblestone streets, immersed in a bustling, thoroughly American scene that'd survived centuries. Because of its fascinating mix of Art Deco, neo-Greek, Art Nouveau, and Gotham City–style architecture, the financial district crawls with filmmakers—including the cast and crew of a live-action film version of *Teenage Mutant Ninja Turtles*. Eventually, I wouldn't bat an eye strolling past masked, black armor–clad ninjas toting costume swords and daggers.

Unfortunately, despite this inspiring setting, I was determined to be unhappy. That's what self-sabotage requires. Julie and I fought like cats and dogs over her late rent payments and clutter in common areas. I was rigid, rude, and bossy—I didn't realize it, but I was transferring my ex-fiancé's abuse onto Julie. Sure, I could blame him, but it was my behavior. I berated Julie, telling her she wouldn't survive in New York because she was lazy and hadn't accomplished anything notable in her career. I boasted that by her age I'd already earned a Fulbright fellowship in Berlin, an editorial board seat at a national newspaper, and I was about to land my full-tuition Harvard scholarship. She was a slob working menial jobs and loafing about in her signature baggy red sweatpants, freeloading off my sacrifices and unsympathetic to the trauma I suffered as a trailblazer—first to leave the cult. I felt ashamed of my family, wanting to leave those unstable losers in the dust. Of course, I was not stable, even if I had a shiny résumé. I wouldn't admit it, but my abusive mistreatment of Julie added to my feelings of depression.

In the aftermath of my failed engagement, and just after I turned thirty, for the fourth time in my life, I fell into the suicidal ideation pit. I felt miserable and dejected, aging without hitting the typical milestones of husband and kids.

The month after I turned thirty, I decided to "disown" my dad and started calling him by his first name, Ralph, instead of "Dad," after he sent me a letter calling me a seductress who tried to seduce my second schizophrenic brother Jonah for sex. Ralph wrote:

> *You immodestly exposed yourself in his presence (whether carelessly or provocatively, God will judge) but he didn't "take the bait," to his credit. A very insightful book to consider is Games People Play, by psychiatrist Eric Berne. One of the 'games' people sometimes encounter in human relations is called "Buzz-Off, Buster." It could be described something like this: An inordinately vain woman will flirt, boast, and even flaunt herself before certain men, seeking their notice, alluring their attention, until she feels she's finally gained her objective—a 'pride-thrill'—then she will suddenly brush them off with the announcement that she hasn't "any romantic inclinations" toward them. It's fine if one doesn't have these "inclinations," but one should not play 'bait-and-switch' games with the deep feelings of other people just to gain a sadistic 'ego-high' at their expense.*

This ranked high as the most disgusting, hurtful thing my father said to me. Not only was it completely false, but it was also profoundly disturbing that Ralph would even posit that his daughter's brain functioned this way. It disturbed me that my father created this narrative to support the diseased psychosis of Jonah, who first leveled the seduction accusation. Ralph's letter shouldn't have shocked me, given the horrific claims he made about his family of origin. But it still stung bitterly.

After Ralph took Jonah's side, a wave of shock and anger rushed over me. There was no arguing with an insane and highly medicated schizophrenia patient, nor his enablers.

In the same letter, Ralph also claimed ignorance of Peter's sexual assault on me back in 2000. Ralph thought I'd run away from home because I'd been beguiled by my friend Summer, the friend who'd tried to get Benjamin to lie about his age so he could attend homecoming with her. How's that for middle-child syndrome? Your oldest sibling, then a twenty-four-year-old man, gropes and tries to rape you, but as child number five and the first girl, your dad's too busy to hear about it. Ralph wrote:

> *Something else I need to apologize for is my unawareness of something you recently mentioned to mother—that one of your siblings had improperly touched you years ago, which may have thus been a factor (unknown to me) in your abandoning your family the way you did. I thought it was mostly a result of your having been manipulated by a devious friend who wanted Benjamin to be dishonest with her parents, and who, when he declined, sought vengeance upon us by beguiling you away from your family and our mission for God and Country. But now, upon learning of the incident only years later, I asked Mother, "Why didn't you tell me about it at the time?" She thought she did, but wasn't sure. To me, it would've been unforgettable. However, upon considering the matter, I now realize it may have been in the Lord's wisdom that I didn't hear about it at that time, for I might have over-reacted very harshly upon your brother, who, unknown to us, may have been already going through the incipient stages of schizophrenia.*

At least Ralph apologized, though at the time, it felt worthless. Plus, Ralph's timeline was also wrong—we all knew very well that Peter had schizophrenia for several years by that point. That's part of why I didn't blame Peter, though I knew I wasn't safe.

Now in 2013, I was tapping out. I decided either Ralph or I would die before I'd ever speak to my father again. The rare times I called Mom, Ralph hopped on the line, and I'd click the phone dead.

A few months later, Jonah got off his meds and booked a Manhattan flight. Clearly psychotic, authorities locked him in Bellevue psychiatric hospital. My parents drove to New York to rescue him and tried to see me, but I told the 45 Wall Street doormen not to let Ralph up. I would let Mom visit, but there was no way she'd come without Ralph.

This rage and unforgiveness against my father compounded my depression and anxiety over my failed engagement. I trudged to work each day, feeling trapped in a field that didn't bring purpose and excitement the way political journalism had, but it was stable and safe. I'd been bruised and abused in media, and working in credit risk management meant my job was stabilizing and risk averse. It gave me a steady paycheck—the biggest of my life—but weighed on my soul. I knew it wasn't my purpose, but I felt too paralyzed to leave.

Feeling like a failure on personal and professional fronts, I fell into depression, and one summer night, fantasized about dying. I didn't have a suicide plan, but I told Julie I'd leave and figure one out. I'm grateful Julie, who is much taller and stronger than me, blocked the door to leave the apartment that night I threatened self-harm.

She shoved a futon in front of the bedroom door and sat on it, staying with me until I fell asleep in a fit of rageful tears. Just as seven years earlier my sister Sophie blocked my car, it was another sister who saved me from myself. I still didn't believe in God, but He sent my angel sisters. In both cases, the suicidal ideation didn't progress beyond those dark nights.

I got myself into therapy and later found a life-changing book

about Stoicism that helped me gain at least partial emotional stability. This realization took many months to achieve and started
after I got dumped, shortly after dating a rebound guy following
my broken engagement. I wanted to seize control of my wildly
rampant emotions, so I started a one-year daily spreadsheet where
I kept track of one action for my mind, spirit/emotions, and body,
and at least one good deed for someone else. I called it my "master's
degree in happiness."

It was a great stabilizer because it brought routine to my chaotic world. I regained my lost physical discipline. I lost ten pounds
and had never felt more consistently healthy (when I ran my marathon I was very healthy, but afterward I lapsed). Performing an act
of service for someone else, even if small, got me out of my own
misery. Sometimes I felt horrible and unable to complete the tasks
well each day, but I wrote that down to own how I was feeling.
Sometimes it was just a couple words or half a sentence. But daily
tracking is powerful, a concept called the "quantified self."

Julie and I both agreed it was healthier if she moved out, and
she left for Brooklyn. I reflected heavily on the negativity I brought
to my failed engagement and wrote my ex-fiancé a lengthy apology
letter without any caveats or finger-pointing toward him.

Eventually, the clouds of depression lifted, crystallizing as I
calmly sat on a park bench overlooking the water between Manhattan and the Statue of Liberty. The park's called The Battery, after
the historic artillery fort used to defeat the British. There are heavy
winds in the park because it's at the very southern tip of Manhattan, receiving crosswinds from both the East River and the Hudson
River to the west. This breeze felt delightful that warm night as I
watched the golden sunset on the river. I felt released, at least temporarily, from my dating demons.

I took a break from dating and focused on my work. My career became my religion, my substitute for God. After several years working in finance, I transitioned back into my first love, media, but this time as an opinion writer and national television commentator instead of a neutral reporter. This switch allowed me to surround myself with more like-minded souls. I felt over-the-moon joy and purpose and was on track to become a spokeswoman for a presidential candidate or even the White House. These things helped stabilize me, but they didn't halt my bad dating choices.

I was single in Manhattan, caught up in the materialism and rat race for money and status. I was obsessed with finding a guy who graduated from Harvard Business School (HBS)—that would be the ultimate elite status symbol for me in my soulless grind. HBS men made good money. Yes, I wanted a man with a good heart who gave back, but after my impoverished childhood and affinity-fraud victimization, money mattered, too.

I felt wounded by the rejection of some HBS men my age who didn't love God (neither did I) and didn't love me. So rather than going for men my age, I opted for older. I compromised, figuring if they were more mature, I'd be willing to deprioritize physical chemistry, as that could grow with time. What a naive mistake. At age thirty-one, with a wealthy dark-triad man fifteen years older, I desecrated God's house as we fondled each other on a December night in the pews while listening to Handel's *Messiah* (at the very church of my baptism three years later) before our first time having sex. Eventually, it became clear this man had no intention of settling down and starting a family. And he'd been cheating on me the entire year we'd been dating.

I found out about his cheating from another one of his "girlfriends" who contacted me on Instagram to inform me that he was her boyfriend also, and she suspected we'd been played. She also suspected another "girlfriend," along with multiple random flings. Grateful for her warning (she even got his confession on video!), I told the creep to never contact me again or I'd call the police. Ironically, he is a successful entrepreneur who makes utterly hypocritical public pronouncements supporting "girl bosses" and badgering people for more investments in female-led companies. What a load of crock. He exploited women and viewed them as pleasure objects.

Through a girlfriend who connected us, I worked with a high-net-worth matchmaker who didn't charge women but set us up with wealthy older men. I turned down a marriage offer from a very wealthy entrepreneur with a private jet who was old enough to be my father. He wasn't a dark triad, but he believed Christianity is "primitive," and he had kids my age, so it just felt weird, plus he wasn't excited about having more kids. I kept entering failed relationships, going on dates with single, typically divorced, men with complicated setups that made compatibility tough. But I liked their prestige, their millions or billions of dollars. It made me feel elite and special that they sought my time. I shunned men my age who would have been a good husband and father. I thought they didn't deserve my time or they wouldn't understand me. I was narcissistic and materialistic. I was also terrified they would dump me, so I preemptively rejected age-appropriate men to avoid pain.

In this state of despair, a girlfriend recommended an insightful dating coach named Evan Marc Katz, who specializes in coaching high-achieving professional women. His writings focus on a powerful concept that seems commonsense but that millions of women like myself fail to grasp. We complain that we attract terrible and abusive men. But the truth is, we *accept* these men. We attract many different types of men, but we choose who we allow in our lives. To remain trapped in bad relationships is to undermine our own power and free will. Obviously, it's so much easier said than done, and so many abused women stay because they are physically afraid. Only one time in my life in a romantic relationship did I feel physically afraid, and yet I stayed with him for more than a year after that. Here's Katz:

> *Believe it or not, I'm not here to tell you that all alpha males are jerks and commitmentphobes. I WILL tell you, however, that the alpha qualities that attract you are the very things that create conflict in your life. Alpha males assert their wills, work hard, play hard, like to conquer, and have enough ego to fuel a rocket ship.*
>
> *Partnership is about finding someone who thinks YOU'RE worth sacrificing for. If you're the one making all the sacrifices because he's too stubborn or egomaniacal, you're just going to build up a lot of resentment. As you can already see. Attraction and chemistry are great relationship starters, but compatibility and compromise are the things that allow you to sustain it. So instead of going for the short-term sugar high that always results in the same exact crash, start thinking of what's healthiest for you in the long-run. Chances are it's not the guy you're most "attracted" to. It's probably the guy you're most compatible with.*[59]

Mother's Day became a difficult day for me, not only because of my strained relationship with my mom, but also because, as my trauma worsened with age, my dream of being a mom died. I didn't believe I could find a man who wouldn't abuse me like my dad.

I'm still learning to stop accepting men into my life who don't cherish me fully in mind, body, and soul. I pray other abused women and men learn the same lessons without accepting so many beatings, both emotional and physical. With time, lots of prayer coaching, and through God's love, I resurrected my dream of having kids. I'm learning to treat myself with compassion, trust a man, forgive my abusers, and know I could be a great mom someday. I'm breaking the cycle of abuse. I'm blessed now with some hot mommas in my friend circle, Wonder Women who balance career and motherhood beautifully.

A post, author unknown, went viral online that spoke to me on many levels:

> *A father said to his daughter "You have graduated with honors, here is a car I bought many years ago. It is pretty old now. But before I give it to you, take it to the used car lot downtown and tell them I want to sell it and see how much they offer you for it."*
>
> *The daughter went to the used car lot, returned to her father and said, "They offered me $1,000 because they said it looks pretty worn out."*
>
> *The father said, now "Take it to the pawn shop." The daughter went to the pawn shop, returned to her father and said, "The pawn shop offered only $100 because it is an old car."*

The father asked his daughter to go to a car club now and show them the car. The daughter then took the car to the club, returned and told her father, "Some people in the club offered $100,000 for it because it's a Nissan Skyline R34, it's an iconic car and sought by many collectors."

Now the father said this to his daughter, "The right place values you the right way." If you are not valued, do not be angry, it means you are in the wrong place. Those who know your value are those who appreciate you ... Never stay in a place where no one sees your value.

This story reminds me of my dad and Joshua Bell, the undervalued onetime street violinist. My dad owned the talent and skills to become a national treasure, both with his writing and his music, if only he'd stopped sabotaging himself and putting his ego ahead of his desire to love and serve others. I'm learning the hard way in my dating career to do the same.

Chapter 13

Faith Labyrinth

The truth is incontrovertible. Malice may attack it,
ignorance may deride it, but in the end, there it is.
—Winston Churchill[60]

Navigating the labyrinth of human faith and religion is complex. Before I joined Christianity in 2017, I spent many years exploring other faiths. Unfortunately, religious intolerance is one of the last acceptable injustices that is still commonplace in the US and abroad. A frenzy of anti-Jewish, anti-Christian, and anti-Muslim animosity has seized America. In Europe, leaders banned even moderate Muslims from wearing religious garb and building houses of worship. That said, pockets of intolerant Muslims preach with a fundamentalist zeal that inspires blind, violent faith, and Islam is riven by Shia versus Sunni conflict. Here in the US, secular people and other groups disqualify Mormon or Christian political candidates simply for their religious affiliation.[61] Utah Mormons themselves fail to elect to national office (and typically, state/local office) those who are non-Mormon or ex-Mormon. After centuries of persecution, Jews still suffer from anti-Semitism around the world, and Catholics and Protestants still clash in Ireland and elsewhere. Those who are nonreligious or choose to abstain from formal religious affiliation are often wrongly eschewed as amoral.

Data show that America and the rest of the world are secularizing, and religion is evolving to fit a postmodern worldview. Yet this great moderating influence has also triggered a fundamentalist backlash.

My hope is that, someday, the world feels the same aversion to religious bigotry as we feel toward racial bias or discrimination against the disabled. Unfortunately, that's not the case. The BBC reported in 2019 that global Christian persecution was at "near genocide levels."[62] The NGO Open Doors USA estimated that 360 million Christians in 2021 lived in countries where persecution was "significant." That year, an estimated 5,600 Christians were murdered, more than 6,000 detained or imprisoned, and another 4,000-plus were kidnapped. More than 5,000 churches and other religious facilities were destroyed.[63]

One big obstacle for me as I pondered leaving the LDS Church was the potential slap in the face this could mean to my ancestors, who sacrificed much for Mormonism. Mormon guilt about ancestors is pervasive, and while Mormonism is a much younger faith, it might rival Jewish family guilt.

But after traveling the world, my feelings changed as I took a more comprehensive view of my family history. I've got many British ancestors, and I'm a certified Anglophile. I share my last name, Sheffield, with a large English city, Winston Churchill is one of my greatest heroes, I adore tea and fascinator hats, the Beatles are

my jam, etc. During my study abroad through BYU's London program, we visited numerous chapels from the Church of England,
aka Anglicans, including entering the iconic Westminster Abbey
for British nobility. I saw the gravestone inside Westminster Abbey
of a man named Lord John Sheffield. My cousins who investigated
our genealogy said somewhere in the line we might be related to
him through his "bastard" line. Even if that's untrue, we absolutely
have many Anglican ancestors in my family tree. I began to ponder how those ancestors would feel knowing their subsequent offspring joined what they might perceive as a blasphemous, esoteric
sect called Mormonism.

Our BYU London group also took an excursion to Stonehenge,
that mysterious, ancient sculpture fashioned in a sundial, perfectly
aligned to the sunset of winter and summer solstices. It was slightly
deflating because widespread illusional photos make the thirteen-
foot stones look far more impressive than they are. Sure, at twenty-
five tons per block, moving those stones was miraculous for more
than five thousand years ago, but I expected something massive—
more along the lines of Rome's nearly 160-foot Colosseum or
London's 365-foot St. Paul's Cathedral.

We aren't entirely sure the purpose or meaning behind Stonehenge, but historians tell us it was likely mystically pagan, perhaps
a funerary monument or a ritual healing and burial ground. That
got the wheels in my head turning—perhaps my ancestors helped
build this pagan religious edifice! What would they say if they knew
I belonged to a mystical Christian sect born in America's frontier?
Oh, the shame.

Eventually, I realized I must stop living for my ancestors'
expectations. I was piling more guilt on top of the living parental
units, let alone centuries of previous ones. This I now know for

sure: God's love and grace don't require any human conduit. God is an everlasting and abundant source of love and mercy that no human can block or deny—even if they share your bloodline.

The relativism of religious morality hit me upside the head as an agnostic in 2009, while I stood on the porch of a Jerusalem home. I had ridden there that evening on the back seat of a moped, wind caressing my face at sunset as I drank in the rolling hilly vistas of the Holy Land's ancient stone walls, cypress trees, and the haunting, polished white tombstones of some 150,000 graves in a Jewish cemetery at the Mount of Olives. But as a stonehearted agnostic, I felt a tinge of anguish that so much blood was spilt over such a beautiful landscape, all over what I perceived to be the tribal fairy tales of organized religion justifying cultural conquest.

The moped driver—an acquaintance through my work as a summer correspondent for the *Jerusalem Post* during grad school, covering the Israeli parliament—had agreed to house-sit for a Jewish friend who kept kosher. Because my driver friend did not keep kosher and didn't live there, he needed to make sure he didn't contaminate certain pans and dishes. My friend brought a mechanical label maker to mark which pans were allowed meat, which allowed dairy. Ironically, as we stood on the porch waiting for his friend to open the door and receive the label maker, the kosher Jew's recycling bin on the porch overflowed with empty beer and wine bottles. You'd never see this sight at the home of a pork and cheeseburger–eating Mormon. It reaffirmed my agnostic, "registered independent" status on issues of faith.

Sometimes I'm asked what agnostic means. It's a fence-sitter—someone who is not willing to go full-blown atheist and deny God exists, but not someone who unequivocally believes in a Higher Power. You're basically in a permanent state of shoulder shrugging and saying, "I don't know." I thought it was the most humble and open-minded posture because it's not making audacious claims in either direction. Many faith traditions share universal views of God as an omnipotent life force and a loving Creator, who desires good for humans created in His own image. But because of the abuse I suffered at the hands of human beings allegedly in the name of God, I couldn't accept that premise. If there was a God, He seemed like an indifferent asshole, because He sure didn't seem to believe in me. I remained stuck in this painful agnostic limbo for nearly twelve years.

Later, during my summer in the Middle East, I visited the mysterious orange-rock temple building carved into the side of a sandstone mountain known as Al-Khazneh, or "The Treasury." It's one of the seven wonders of the world, created by the ancient Nabataean people at Petra in the modern-day country of Jordan. The Treasury building, featured as the exterior of the Temple of the Sun in *Indiana Jones and the Last Crusade* with Harrison Ford and Sean Connery, was likely the mausoleum of a Nabatean king in the first century AD. Initially, the Nabataeans, a nomadic Bedouin tribe, followed a pagan religion that required human and animal sacrifice. Nabataeans later converted to Christianity under the Roman Empire and their distinct culture eventually disappeared, their lands divided among various Muslim Arab tribes. It seemed to me that religion entailed pure sociological constructs and political power, that whoever owned the guns and the gold dictated God. The Nabataeans were simply another group of monkey-evolved Homo sapiens who saw their sacred rituals trumped by their more powerful Roman rulers. It all seemed so man-made, fleeting, and contrived. This reaffirmed my interpretation of religion: it could be a good thing to help people feel nice when done right, but ultimately was just another tool for mind control.

I agreed with atheist Karl Marx when he called religion the "opiate of the masses." Marx, who didn't believe in God, claimed religion was constructed by humans to calm uncertainty over their role in the universe and society. Though I wasn't atheist and disagree strongly with his political philosophy, I shared his views on religion. Boy, was I ignorant. The cavernous difference between God and religion is the difference between heaven and hell. God is love, truth, and light. Religion is corrupt, fallible, and human run. Marx rejected religion because he didn't understand that religion isn't God. Marx didn't understand that you cannot erase God, and that religious people doing evil in God's name is not God's will.

As a reporter in China covering the Beijing Olympics in 2008, I visited numerous Buddhist temples, many officially run by the atheist Chinese government. The beautiful coloring, towering pagodas, incense smells, and elaborate gold lettering enchanted me. During graduate school, I stayed overnight in a Buddhist monastery at the Golgulsa Temple, high in the mountains of South Korea, about a three-hour drive southeast of Seoul. We followed a strict regimen, sleeping on yoga mats on the floor and rising before a chilly dawn for a silent, single-file meditation. We weren't allowed to speak, but our breathing made puffs of frosty, misty clouds in the darkness. We hiked about the rocky terrain of the monastery, which featured a large Amida Buddha carved into the side of the mountain. It's a designated national treasure, an image of a peaceful seated figure with eyes closed, hands folded in front, and a circular hole in the figure's forehead symbolizing the third eye. We drank hot tea with a Zen master. After a rigorous course of martial arts, we ate a sparse diet of kimchi, soup, rice, and vegetables.

Before and during eating, we followed a strict protocol, sitting cross-legged on the floor, speaking not allowed except for the pre-meal group chant. Marx might say this chant is evidence of religion being used for self-flagellating mind control to accept meager provisions:

Where has this food come from?
My virtues are so little that I am hardly worthy to receive it.
I will take it as medicine to get rid of greed in my mind
　　and to maintain my physical being in order to achieve
　　enlightenment.

Other instructions, in English:

Be careful not to make noise while eating or using your spoon, chop-
　　sticks, and bowl.
Always hold your bowl while eating.
Do not put food other than rice in the Buddha bowl (the big bowl) or
　　mix rice with the side dishes in the Buddha bowl.
Do not let your eyes wander while eating.
Be mindful of equality, purity, and tranquility.

I felt enthralled by the ritual, the simplicity, and the exotic setting. When I got back home and moved to Manhattan, I started attending a Buddhist temple near my house on the Upper East Side. Initially, it went well because the monk was a woman about my age, originally from Michigan, and we had some peaceful and enjoyable conversations before and after the meditations. But that was while the founder was away on sabbatical, and when he returned, things went south. He didn't speak much English, and he nitpicked the way I sat on the meditation cushion. My knee was injured while rollerblading—scabbed over from a bloody fall on the pavement— so I couldn't cross my legs properly. That bothered him in a decidedly non-Zen fashion, and he tried to physically force me to cross my legs according to his desires. When I tried to explain what happened with my injury, he banished me to sit in a normal chair with my back against the wall, away from the meditation group.

I felt sad to get expelled, because even though I didn't believe in God, I wanted to learn more about this tradition and had heard business leaders and other high-performing people, not to mention scientific evidence, rave about the physiological and psychological benefits of meditation. But that monk left a bad taste in my mouth, so I stopped attending.

Searching, seeking, I still felt depressed and angry at my circumstances: my birth, my abusive, impoverished, and transient upbringing, at my choices made early in my career and in relationships. But I finally reached an epiphany, a moment of realization and brutal self-honesty that gave me what I thought was a replacement for religion: Stoic philosophy.

During my reflections after my failed engagement, I began reading many helpful and enlightening books; I wished I had done so earlier. The book that brought me a moment of lightning is called *The Philosophy of Cognitive Behavioural Therapy: Stoic Philosophy as Rational and Cognitive Psychotherapy*. Yes, a title as bone-dry as the Grand Canyon.

The author, Donald Robertson, is a professional therapist who writes on the similarities between Stoic philosophy and modern-day cognitive behavioral therapy. I was already a fan of Marcus

Aurelius's Stoic *Meditations*, so I found it particularly compelling. The way this author explains the similarities finally spelled out explicitly how I could control my mind and emotions. The development of this self-control is something that occurs each day and can be practiced in the same way that a gymnast practices to strengthen muscle. Stoicism, in a nutshell, is the "serenity prayer" (except I wasn't praying to God): *God, grant me the serenity to accept the things I cannot change, the courage to change the things I can, and the wisdom to know the difference.* Stoicism was founded in ancient Greece around 300 BC. (I prided myself on it preceding Christianity) to train emperors and other elite rulers to govern virtuously. Stoicism is not a religion; it's a philosophy and way of teaching detachment from pleasure or pain. Stoicism also entails radical honesty with yourself. Roberts's best excerpt from Aurelius: "Ambition means tying your well-being to what other people say or do. Self-indulgence means tying it to the things that happen to you. Sanity means tying it to your own actions."[64]

I realized I'd been dishonest with myself when I would have emotional eruptions. I would continually compare myself with others, and I refused to acknowledge my mortality and character flaws. I behaved self-righteously and didn't admit that, many times, I behaved egotistically and self-indulgently. I constantly blamed my father, Mormonism, coworkers, ex-boyfriends, etc., for my failures when, as Aurelius says, I needed to tie them to my own choices. For months, I would wake up and go to Wall Street and hate my job, hate my family, hate the world for the toxic and unstable circumstances I grew up in. The Stoics would say this type of hate toward my upbringing is totally irrational and self-indulgent. It was as fruitless and illogical for me to hate myself and hate the world because I was not born with wings, with five eyeballs, or the ability to leap through walls. It was a waste of energy and harmful for me to spend another precious moment hating the universe because I was not given a loving and kind home. That's just the reality, and I needed to accept it.

Through Stoic readings, I understood I made my own choices that brought me to my place of depression and despair. I chose to date men with dark-triad traits. I chose to leave journalism and work in finance, which left me miserable. I chose to date a drug addict who slandered me and manipulated me. And each day, I chose to self-indulgently let my passions control me by feeling jealous of other people, their accomplishments, and their loving families. I chose to let my powerful emotions cripple me.

Though I later ended up careening away from those principles, this book, for a time, taught me to capture the upside and minimize the downside of my strong, passionate emotions. As the daughter of a world-class musician, hypersensitivity is in my DNA. I never achieved Dad's heights in music, but I received respectable music awards and first chair violin placements in various schools growing up. We musicians are highly passionate and sensitive (often overly so). Artists are often "histrionic," another word for dramatic. There are healthy histrionic traits and there are dysfunctional ones, and the toxic ones manifest themselves as histrionic personality disorder (HPD), a psychiatric condition within Cluster B personality disorders that Mayo Clinic states "are characterized by dramatic, overly emotional or unpredictable thinking or behavior."[65] Cluster B also includes antisocial personality disorder (aka sociopathy), borderline personality disorder, and narcissistic personality disorder—all mental illnesses in my family.

After reading Robertson's book, I started training myself and stopping myself each time my thoughts began to run like an untended train. I trained my mental reflexes in the same way I trained my body to crave healthy food and exercise. I made huge strides in my career and started landing spots in front of millions of people on marquee television programs. But I didn't let it get to my head (not yet). I kept my Stoic grounding. That grounding wouldn't last, but it gave me some temporary stability.

There's a wonderful book that explains what happened to me during this period. It's called *Counterfeit Gods: The Empty Promises of Money, Sex, and Power, and the Only Hope That Matters* by a brilliant pastor, the late Tim Keller, a well-known author who many people described as a modern-day C. S. Lewis. His book came out in 2011, but sadly, I didn't get my hands on it until 2021, well after my December 3, 2017, Christian baptism (influenced by Keller's other works and his Manhattan church). But it's a useful retrospective that crystalizes how my life careened out of control each time I tried to build on a sandy foundation rather than the eternal Rock. Each chapter in Keller's book describes a false idol that humans pursue as false gods: love and sex, career, power, money, etc. I tried nearly all of those, and they kept failing.

After leaving Mormonism, I tried putting my career as my idol, but then I got laid off. I tried dating relationships and kept meeting heartbreak. Finally, I settled on a god that I thought wouldn't fail me: the god of politics and public service.

I graduated with a master's degree in public policy, paid for with a full-tuition journalism scholarship from the Harvard Kennedy School, named after former President John F. Kennedy. In some ways, I subconsciously put JFK as a messiah figure for me, same with Abraham Lincoln and Martin Luther King Jr.—all men who sacrificed their lives in the bloody battle for justice.

It was a meaningful religion for me; my calling, my higher

purpose in life. Many people, especially secular liberal young people, worship the same thing. It's less frequent among conservatives,
but I shared this commonality with my secular progressive friends.
I called myself a secular conservative in national newspaper essays
in the *New York Times* and *USA Today* and cheered the rising secular-
ization of America.

By the time I'd navigated the labyrinth of the major world
religions, I convinced myself I needn't rely on some fairy-dusting
eternal being. But I was only fooling myself. Contrary to God's
will, I still hadn't forgiven my father. I was suppressing my anger
toward him while building up a massive ego because I was thriving in my professional life in ways that he could never imagine.
While he made his family suffer in destitution, he'd paid hundreds
of thousands of dollars over the years to publish his writings and
political messages in paid advertisements and billboards nationwide. Meanwhile, I got paid for my journalism, to write for national
newspapers and speak to millions of people on these same political
and economic matters.

Early each morning, I'd rise and meditate on Stoic principles,
how to incorporate the core Stoic principles of courage, temper-
ance, justice, and wisdom. I'd do a little yoga. Even though I didn't
believe in God, I prayed to Nature, to the Universe. It brought me
peace. My mom said it was "disgusting" that I prayed to the Universe. Pagan.

Even though she disagreed with my spiritual choices, she never
stopped praying for me, and for that I'm eternally grateful, because
I know it eventually helped lead me back to God.

Our human species is permanently seeking to fill a "God-
shaped hole" in our hearts, and I finally thought I'd filled it with
Stoicism. In technology, software updates get stronger with each

version, from 1.0 to 2.0 and beyond. I thought that yearning for a god was a bug in our human system that we'd eventually work out with enough man-made economic, technological, and educational progress. The truth is that on this broken earth, we human beings are the bug, and God is the only pathway we reach peace. Religion is a tool, and any tool can be used for good or evil—like the internet, or any other human-run institution. God gave us the gift of the Church, but people abuse the Church, just like they abuse their children or their spouse.

In my quest for purpose, I'd traveled the world—every continent, including Antarctica, by age thirty—but it still didn't bring me lasting inner peace. Peace comes from within, through connecting with the Divine. It was a brutally hard lesson I still needed to learn, and it would take supernova forces to humble me enough to receive it.

Chapter 14

The Peace of Christ

" 'A new heart I will give you, and a new spirit I will put
within you, and I will remove from your body the heart
of stone and give you a heart of flesh.' "

—Ezekiel 36:26

My conversion to Christianity happened because of two powerful forces: Donald Trump and science. People laugh when I say this, but it is God's honest truth. I'll explain how it happened, but first must disclose I never thought I'd return to belief in God or to organized religion. My flinty heart remained closed for nearly twelve years because I felt angry at evil things I'd seen done in God's name. The God of Judeo-Christianity seemed a vengeful, angry being, not one of love. The Bible lied to me in 1 John 4:8 when it claimed that "God is Love."

When I decided to leave Mormonism, my entire purpose in life after a traumatic childhood imploded, and I fell into suicidal depression. I hadn't developed a healthy faith in God and instead put faith in man-made religion. When that religion failed me, I threw myself into my job, schooling, dating, friends, and travel as ultimate sources of meaning. I earned a master's at Harvard with a full merit scholarship and worked on Wall Street, earning unthinkable sums for the girl from a motorhome. Yet, I had never felt so poor because of the disease of comparison. These earthly gifts and accomplishments aren't wrong, but they didn't offer me the deep spiritual fulfillment I found through prayer, meditation, and fellowship with others who centered their lives on something eternal rather than temporal.

I turned to Stoic philosophy, the ancient rationality method for analyzing life, to bring me peace and stability, and in many respects, it did. But it wasn't enough during the 2016 election, when I felt an existential crisis. I realized that because I lost my faith in God, I allowed politics to become a substitute "religion." I worshipped at the altar of nasty, brutish, man-made politics.

And then something revolutionary and disruptive happened. Donald Trump happened.

I won't delve into any partisan analysis of what happened in both the 2016 primary and general elections. I only mention it here because it was a potent force in my faith journey, and I see similar patterns in the lives of many others. I pray every person can know that God, the eternal source of purpose and meaning, fills a deep void that mucky, grimy politics never can.

When Trump came down that golden escalator in the atrium of Trump Tower in June 2015, I'd built much of my career (my substitute religion) toward working on a campaign or working in the

White House. It would be the pinnacle and a crowning success. I was ready. I knew the economy inside and out after managing billions of dollars in credit risk exposure for major Wall Street firms. I'd appeared in front of millions of people on CNN, MSNBC, Fox News, Fox Business, and other networks and sparred on HBO's *Real Time with Bill Maher.*

Behind the scenes, a campaign brand strategist and later a lead Trump campaign surrogate both became impressed by my TV debating skills and asked me if I was interested in a role with their team during the primary, but I politely declined. I couldn't endorse what this guy said about women or that he had no policy track record. To me, there wasn't any daylight between Trump and Democrat Hillary Clinton, to whom he'd previously donated. I had no faith that he would achieve the policies he promised. I was a "Never Trumper" through the end of the 2016 race; as a New York voter, I wrote in then-Senator Ben Sasse, a Republican from Nebraska, as my protest candidate.

During this crisis of meaning, I didn't become suicidal, but I felt distraught. Leaving Wall Street and returning to political media in 2013 as a conservative commentator fighting for the GOP helped stabilize me after my failed engagement. My career brought me the meaning and purpose my love life couldn't—or so I thought. With the tectonic turbulence of a 2016 candidate I couldn't endorse, I needed something else to fill this existential void of purpose and meaning, since Republicans couldn't do it for me.

That's when I started to go to church, first to Redeemer Presbyterian Church, founded by Pastor Tim Keller, at various campuses in New York City, and later to Saint Thomas Episcopal Church on Fifth Avenue, where I eventually got baptized on December 3, 2017. I kept showing up for God, and God kept showing up for me. Each week, I generally either attended church or a Bible study, known as a "small group." In surrendering my prestigious political perch, I thought of Mark 8:36–37, which asks, "For what will it profit a man if he gains the whole world, and loses his own soul? Or what will a man give in exchange for his soul?"[66]

I gradually discovered why Christianity supplanted Stoicism (and other Greco/Roman schools of thought like Epicureanism). Stoicism, which contains elements similar to Buddhism, teaches detachment as a means of relieving human suffering. We are in pain because we irrationally attach ourselves to things, and true liberation comes from detachment. There is much truth to those sentiments, but I found as I left Wall Street and returned to politics, Stoicism didn't offer me sustaining community or comprehension of the depravity of the human condition and its possibility for redemption.

I liked Pastor Tim Keller's intellectual approach in his many books and sermons. He said his church welcomed skeptics, atheists, and agnostics like me. He had a great answer to the anger I shared with Karl Marx toward organized religions like Christianity.

"Karl Marx and others have charged that religion is 'the opiate of the masses,'" Keller writes in his book *The Prodigal God*. "That is, it is a sedative that makes people passive toward injustice, because there will be 'pie in the sky bye and bye.' That may be true of some religions that teach people that this material world is unimportant or illusory. Christianity, however, teaches that God hates the suffering and oppression of this material world so much, he was willing to get involved in it and to fight against it. Properly understood, Christianity is by no means the opiate of the people. It's more like the smelling salts."

In Christianity, Jesus took on a physical body, performed

physical healings, and promised a physical New Jerusalem. It's no accident that the most wealthy, healthy, and stable societies in history have been rooted in Judeo-Christian values. Christians are the tip of the spear in the fights against natural disaster, disease, orphanhood, hunger, and lack of education. Our Western education system—the best in the world—was founded by Christian leaders in both Protestant and Catholic traditions. The motto of Harvard University is "veritas Christo et ecclesiae," which means, "truth for Christ and the church." Harvard is America's oldest college, founded in 1636 as the first university in the American colonies. It was created to train Christian clergy in the pursuit of knowledge and truth.

On the science front, in parallel to my theological studies, I began studying metaphysics. It happened after a publicist for Deepak Chopra approached me to interview him on my digital television show about his 2017 book, *You Are the Universe: Discovering Your Cosmic Self and Why It Matters*. Deepak is an MD, and his coauthor was Menas C. Kafatos, a brilliant scientist with a PhD in physics from MIT, America's most prestigious science university. Like a glorious hurricane or Moses' burning bush, this book blew away any last vestiges of agnosticism and gave me a good overview of the science supporting the existence of a Divine Creator.

Their book laid out the insanely small probabilities of our universe and planet earth behaving as they do, 13.7 billion years after the big bang. Statistically speaking, there is essentially zero chance that earth exists this way merely by chance. It's like the probability of a tornado ripping through a junkyard and accidentally creating a perfectly formulated, complex nuclear weapons system. It would never happen randomly. Some atheists claim there could be multiverses with enough simulations to create our universe, but there's no evidence for multiverses, and the idea breaks the principles of Occam's razor: simpler explanations of observations are preferred to more complex ones. To quote the 2004 book title by Christian leaders Frank Turek and the late Norman L. Geisler: "I don't have enough faith to be an atheist."

As Deepak and Kafatos lay out, myopic human understanding of physics is completely unable to answer questions about the "observer effect," or the unknowable subatomic events laid out in the Schrödinger's cat principle, for example.

I am not a metaphysician, and I won't delve more deeply into this science here, but I highly recommend a ministry called Science + God created by former Harvard physics professor Michael Guillen and his wife, Laurel. Michael is a dear friend with a brilliant mind. An atheist when he entered Cornell University, he left as a Christian, graduating with PhDs in math, astronomy, and physics before teaching at Harvard and joining ABC News as their chief science correspondent. He's written many books, but a good one to start with is *Amazing Truths: How Science and the Bible Agree.*

The more I studied science, history, anthropology, and other disciplines, the more my faith in God and Christianity grew. It became exactly opposite of my experience with Mormonism, where the more I studied, the more distraught I felt. It felt like uncovering buried treasure discarded by intellectuals and Ivy League types who had not fully grappled with the intellectual heft of Christianity. A couple good books to start delving into the solid logic and evidence for the life of Jesus Christ are the books *More than a Carpenter* by Josh McDowell and *The Case for Christ* by Lee Strobel. *How We Got The Bible* by Greg Lanier, a professor with a Cambridge University PhD, is a short but powerful guide to understanding the Bible's history.

I examined my deep doctrinal concerns—the Mormon Church teaches numerous doctrines that fall far outside the Bible, which the LDS Church teaches is correct only "as far as it is translated correctly." My take on Mormonism now is that it's theologically wrong, but culturally strong. In 2010, I completed a formal renunciation process of Mormonism, and I doctrinally believe it contains man-made theology about who Jesus is: Mormons believe He's just our biological "elder brother,"[67] not divinity incarnate in a trinitarian God. They also believe in many other things like polygamy in the afterlife, baptisms for the dead, etc., that I don't agree with. But now, instead of wrath toward the LDS Church, I'm happy to calmly discuss these disagreements. There's much we Protestant Christians can theologically dialogue about with Mormon brothers and sisters, building redemptive bridges of mutual understanding and compassion.

I also see Mormonism as culturally strong. Utah, for example, is top ranked for income mobility and low income inequality,[68] driven by strong social capital.

Unlike the LDS Church, which proactively helps with matchmaking and preengagement support, the Protestant Christian Church overall does a terrible job taking care of its single adults and connecting them with each other. I think that's part of why Pew Research Center shows the LDS Church keeping a steady market share in America while Protestant demographics are falling off a cliff and Catholics are dipping slightly.[69]

When I looked at historical figures like Abraham Lincoln, MLK, Gandhi, and Mother Teresa, who ushered in exceptional moral victories, they came from faith traditions and used messages of universal truth to achieve these victories. I believe many universal truths can be expressed through many different religions and denominations, though Jesus is the fulfillment of all truth. Through Christianity, I chose to follow Jesus, who I believe is the way, truth, and life. Jesus put self-sacrifice ahead of self-aggrandizement, humility ahead of pride, compassion ahead of judgment.

I was baptized into the Episcopalian Church under the spiritual guidance of Presiding Bishop Michael Curry, the preacher from the Royal Wedding of Meghan Markle and Prince Harry. More than two billion people watched his electric sermon on the power of love in spring 2018. But I already knew the power of this small, bespectacled, energetic man. I was taken by Bishop Curry in summer 2017, when one of his chief advisers, Reverend Canon Chuck Robertson, became a spiritual mentor after we met in Manhattan at St. Bartholomew's Church on Park Avenue. Reverend Chuck gave me a copy of the bishop's book called *Crazy Christians*. It's an inspiring narrative about the power of love—a power to heal all racial, socioeconomic, gender, generational, or any other divide. Bishop Curry is black and partially grew up before passage of the Civil Rights Act. Though he'd seen segregation, his father brought his family to the Episcopal Church because it served communion from the same cup for both black and white parishioners—revolutionary for that time. He saw that, per Galatians 3:28, "all of you are one in Christ Jesus." His words touched my heart and set me on this new faith journey.

My baptism day, December 3, 2017, was the happiest day of my life. Held at Saint Thomas Episcopal Church in the heart of Manhattan, this enormous church boasts deep-blue stained-glass windows adorning the ornately carved front altar and a flamboyant limestone rose window designed in the French High Gothic

Revival style. The Anglophile in me enjoyed learning the church hosted the marriage of a Vanderbilt woman to the first cousin of Winston Churchill. Poetically, the original 1957 Norman Rockwell painting of Saint Thomas is housed at the Museum of Art at my alma mater, BYU:

> Rockwell depicts New Yorkers with hunched shoulders and downcast eyes passing St. Thomas Church on Fifth Avenue and 53rd Street. A male figure posts the message "Lift up thine eyes" by the portal doors—a wry comment on the loss of religious faith in America. The Gothic portals, tympanum arches, and statuary of the church are inspired by European cathedrals. Rockwell studied Monet's renderings of Rouen Cathedral before painting this work.[70]

Leading up to my baptism, each Sunday felt like visiting Carnegie Hall, as my ears bathed in angelic choruses from the Saint Thomas Choir of Men and Boys. This choir of professional adult singers and boys is the only church choir boarding school in America.

The priest, a cerebral, contemplative man with a PhD from Columbia University, baptized me in a side "chantry" chapel after the morning service. I wore a navy-blue Fuzzi midi tulle dress with a boat neckline that I borrowed from Rent the Runway (for my fifth anniversary after my baptism, when I could afford it, I treated myself to purchasing the exact style dress). I loved the dress's elegant sash and sheer long sleeves. I paired it with my silvery gold, sparkly Jimmy Choo kitten heels that I'd bought at T.J. Maxx for a fraction of their original retail price. My brother and his family drove up from

DC for the baptism, and two LDS cousins (and my cousin's young daughter) attended, plus a friend and her daughter flew in from Utah. All told, about thirty people came to support me as I vowed to "serve Christ in all persons, loving my neighbor as myself" and "strive for justice and peace among all people, and respect the dignity of every human being."

I love my brother, and I'm grateful he brought his family to the ceremony. Though I felt devastated when he pulled me aside just after the baptismal service.

"Carrie, I want you to know that if you ever try to push your religion on my kids, I'll cut you out of their life," he said softly.

This was the same brother who'd photoshopped me out of the family pictures at my dad's command. However, I understood his hurt that day; he was confusing my delicate, revived faith in a loving God with toxic, egomaniacal interpretations of religion. I've done my share of inadvertently hurting him, so there's no point in escalating. It hurt, but I bit my tongue. The day was too special to let it devolve. He was abused, too, and God loves him just as much as me and everyone else.

My mom didn't come, but she was happy to hear I believed in God again and was attending a Christian denomination, though it saddened her that I wasn't LDS and didn't believe in the Book of Mormon like she did. I thanked her for praying for me all those years I walked away from God.

My devout LDS cousins were supportive and glad I returned to faith. They wished I was still in the Mormon Church, but they felt empathy for my abusive childhood and were not judgmental of my choices. A few years earlier, they even made the trek to Manhattan to celebrate my thirtieth birthday with me, joining my friends for a fancy prix fixe group dinner and a viewing of *The Book of Mormon* musical on Broadway. The show is vulgar and crass (and has Mormon cultural inaccuracies), but they laughed at the savage wit in other areas. They took the whole evening in stride.

In my Christian walk, I've been mentored by an incredible pastor, A. R. Bernard, who leads the Christian Cultural Center megachurch in Brooklyn and spiritually counsels celebrities like Oprah Winfrey and Denzel Washington. Disowned by his white father and raised by his single black mother and the streets of Brooklyn, A.R. immersed himself in Harlem's 1960s Black Power community. He joined the Nation of Islam, which did not take kindly to him parting ways upon his departure for Christianity. Early on, A.R. spent time wrapped in anger toward white racists and felt heavily influenced by Malcolm X, Louis Farrakhan, and the Black Panther movement. Besides paternal disownment, we shared another similar experience: he allowed politics to become his religion.

"It was difficult to practice it as a religion, because what I discovered is the Nation of Islam really is a social protest movement that took hold of Christianity, Islam, a little bit of the Jehovah's Witness doctrine," A.R. told me over brunch one morning. "I didn't buy into the apartheid thinking that was present in the Nation at that time because they wanted a separate nation within the United States. But the discipline, the order, the strength, all of those things that I needed as a young man, those things appealed to me."

I asked A.R. to help me understand the difference between God and religion.

"We're religious because we're spiritual by nature. We have a sense of the transcendent," he said, pointing to man's moral compass, the ability to reason, and things that cannot be measured by science: love, anger, and other feelings. "What religion attempts to do is codify that spirituality into ritual practice, and through observation and recording, pass it on from one generation to another. I understand the function and the place of the institution, but the most important thing is a relationship that the institution should foster with God and with people living out the big questions that God answers. What does it mean to be human? What does it mean to live in this world? Who or what is God? Is there life after death? Does life have meaning and purpose? All of those questions, Christianity answered for me more than any other religion."

For A.R., that relationship is specifically with the person of Jesus, citing Matthew 11:29, where Jesus says, "Learn of me."[71]

"Come and learn of me, not the institution, but learn of me," A.R. continued. "And I understood that it was about an invitation to a relationship to a very specific person," he told me. "And the relationship with the person is what has fed me and sustained me all of these years. I function within the institution, I understand its role, its purpose. But the institution is secondary to the person of Christ."

More than six years since my baptism, my faith foundation is distinct from my politics. In my Saint Thomas Episcopal confirmation class in Manhattan, we learned the divine order of things:

God
Man
Things

In putting politics first, i.e., man-made society, I was living a messed-up order:

Man

Things

Indifferent to God

The truth is, any politician or party or policy process is a false idol. False idols like politics can never fulfill the human pull in our soul toward the Divine. Politics is a shoddy substitute, just like abusive, man-made religion is a shoddy substitute for divine Relationship. This distinction between loving relationship versus human religion, sadly, wasn't clearly delineated for me growing up. I was looking for God in all the wrong places. But after years of mistakes, I'm learning to stop looking for God among human jars of clay.

My faith is deeply rooted in my experience with seeking God and is separate from my politics (and all other man-made constructs). Dr. Alveda King, niece of civil rights hero Martin Luther King Jr., had the right order of things in a news statement about the 2016 election: "While I voted for Mr. Trump, my confidence remains in God, for life, liberty and the pursuit of happiness."

I also know many faithful, devoted Christians who are politically liberal, including one of my baptismal sponsors, Michael Wear, who was President Barack Obama's faith director, and Bishop Curry, who is a vocal Trump critic but welcomed me after my baptism into the Episcopal Church. I have a healthier separation from my politics than I did as an agnostic because it is not my highest purpose. God is much bigger than puny, man-made politics, and we are all brothers and sisters.

I newly appreciate Thomas Aquinas's words: "To one who has

faith, no explanation is necessary. To one without faith, no explanation is possible."[72]

As I returned to a walk with God, I feel enveloped with a sense of peace that surpasses all understanding. My renewed admiration for the mission of Christ to unify and heal breathed new life and joy into my heart. I recovered a sense of confidence, not in myself but in my purpose and identity as a child of God.

Chapter 15

Shattered Glass

Do not conform to the pattern of this world, but be trans-formed by the renewing of your mind.

—*Romans 12:2*[73]

Usually, parents want a better life for their kids than their own upbringing. Though he'd deny it, Ralph made me feel like he wanted his kids to have things worse, and in most respects we did. Ralph's toxic behavior appeared to be classic "destructive entitle-ment," a pattern identified by Ivan Boszormenyi-Nagy, a psychia-trist and pioneer in family therapy. An example of destructive entitlement is a child with cancer suffering an unjust, seemingly random, horrific fate with his disease. Because of this affliction, the child acts out at school, bullying and punching others, hitting or verbally lacerating his parents and siblings far more explosively than a typical child without cancer would.

Boszormenyi-Nagy calls destructive entitlement "a huge problem in child care. It has a long history in warfare between nations and ethnic populations within nations. And it plays a major role in destroying marriages…Entitlement resembles a right, something earned either through contributions that benefit another or through suffering. It is an ethical accumulation or surplus."[74]

In the middle of me disowning Ralph, he sent me a note, dated October 19, 2018:

> *Dear Carrie, we love you and pray for your welfare. Let us both ask God to help me see if I have severely wronged you in any way—and for you to see if satan is beguiling you to misjudge me for his evil purposes. Let us both heed God's warning (Haggai 1:7) before it's too late: "Thus saith the Lord of hosts: consider your ways."*
>
> Love, Dad (Oops, Ralph)

He thought I was still full of Satan and he was the victim. As a child, he turned to God and self-reflection to recover from childhood sexual assault, the death of a close friend, would-be abduction, and a basement dungeon. He did this because the adults around him failed to protect and heal him.

It seems to me that Ralph felt destructive entitlement because his parents didn't take him more seriously when he cried out for justice over his traumatizing child sexual abuse. Because they made him live in an isolated cellar while the rest of the family lived upstairs. Because they weren't devout enough in their Mormonism for his liking.

Ralph's parents papered over his childhood assault; thus, he diminished my sexual trauma, telling me I provoked my brother's sexual assault and another's sexual fantasies about me. His parents made him live in a cellar; thus, he made his wife and offspring live in a shed, tents, and motorhomes. It all had perfect symmetry. Abuse begets abuse. And it won't stop from generation to generation without proactive, assertive healing.

Boszormenyi-Nagy said, "If you were exploited, abused as a child, you feel angry, suspicious, psychologically entitled to revenge. You also have a right to be revengeful, ethically."[75]

This is what Ralph did to us, using religious language—his "ethical" cloak for his destructive abuse. Because he suffered, we must suffer, too. He said God assigned him to perform music on the streets, in harm's way. Therefore, we must put ourselves in danger too—in dangerous schools and living situations. Ralph as a boy ate steady meals and grew up in stable housing, while we lived in constant motorhome chaos, eating grass from the town square and weevil-infested oats. He received millions of dollars in inheritance to spend on promoting his political essays and itinerant lifestyle while his children lived in squalor.

Ralph said suffering brought us closer to God. Yes, it's true that anguish and misfortune can lead us closer to God's presence. But the Bible tells us God will never give us more than we can handle. Unfortunately, humanity piles on far more suffering than God ever designed. God says His yoke is easy, and His burden is light. God does not endorse self-sabotage. Ralph's burdens on himself and those he placed on his kids were suffocating, heavy, and dark. Ultimately, I believe they helped push two of my brothers over the cliff into insanity—definitely not God's will.

What's worse is that Ralph told my brothers they essentially *deserved* their schizophrenia for being sinful and rebellious against The Mission, against Ralph's prophetic call. What utter garbage. Ralph's lies about this filled me with rage.

For most of my adult life, I used Ralph's dark prophecies of my demise to fuel my ambition. *He thinks I'll crawl back home? I'll prove I don't need him. Then I'll surpass him in achievements.*

Sure, I'd never win a scholarship master class with phenomenal classical guitarist Andrés Segovia, and I couldn't win a national young composers competition, but I'd find a way to outshine him. Even as he meticulously assigned us various musical instruments and taught us each piano, he refused to teach any of us guitar. I think he secretly didn't want us to eclipse him on guitar, though statistically it would have been unlikely.

Growing up, he'd claim credit for our achievements rather than lift us up and congratulate us.

"You're my *daughter, so it's my prize,"* he'd say, whether it was a cross-country running trophy or a violin medal. After he disowned me when I left home, I told myself he didn't deserve to revel in my successes (though I did note that after I landed my full scholarship to Harvard, I magically reappeared in the family photos atop his bookmarks).

I thought I'd surpassed this man in sophistication and worldliness when at twenty-six, through my Harvard connections, I won entrance into Middle East journalism programs that took me to Jerusalem in Israel, Cairo in Egypt, and Doha in Qatar.

Around that time, I spoke occasionally by phone with my parents, though I didn't dare tell Mom before my travels—she'd likely say God told her I'd get my throat slit in the sandy desert of a faraway Muslim country.

"What's Doha?" Ralph asked on the phone as I sat on the steps of my blue-gray off-campus house that warm, humid August night when I told him where I'd been.

"What a loser," I thought. *"He doesn't even know what Doha is."*

Not only did I get a full scholarship to a higher-ranked graduate school than my dad (though these days, Harvard is, sadly, largely void of wisdom and basic common sense), *it was taking me places this religious zealot couldn't even fathom.*

Was this a healthy train of thought against my dad? Absolutely not. Swinging from one ditch of cowering fear into another ditch of superiority and arrogance is doomed to fail. Competition and rage against your father are not sustainable motivations. I set myself up for a spectacular fall, one that I was genetically predisposed to make.

My dad's side of the family struggles with mental illness.

These genetic predispositions, combined with a traumatizing childhood, brought me diagnoses of PTSD, depression, and generalized anxiety disorder. I nearly died from hyponatremia—severe sodium loss—after botched drug treatments for fibromyalgia, a nerve pain disorder with patients that are ten times more likely to die by suicide than the general population and about three times more likely than other chronic pain patients, according to a Copenhagen University study.[76]

A helpful parable explains why abused kids who don't fully heal from trauma embrace self-sabotaging behavior that amplifies their abuse. The parable illustrates how holding your burdens only makes them worse, like compounded interest grows money with time in your bank account. The same holds for unresolved trauma: it compounds and crushes like snowballing credit card interest.

Here's the parable: If you hold a glass of water for just a minute or two, it's light and easy, the way Jesus tells us His burden is light. But if you hold a glass of water for an hour straight, the weight makes your arm ache. If you hold it for an entire day without stopping, your arm will likely feel completely numb and paralyzed, forcing you to drop the glass, which will crash and shatter on the floor.

The weight of the glass doesn't change, but the longer you hold it, the heavier it feels. Our personal anxieties are like this; the longer we hold them, the more negatively they affect us until we feel completely numb and paralyzed—incapable of doing anything else until we drop them.

Don't hold the glass too long—it makes it feel heavier than it is, makes you feel more alone than you are. God is with you always. Maintaining control and perpetual shame is denying God's sovereignty. Nobody's mess is too big for God.

Holocaust survivor Corrie ten Boom said it well: "Worry does not empty tomorrow of its sorrow. It empties today of its strength."[77]

Bold TV was my shattered glass. It's a digital television network I started on November 30, 2015 (Winston Churchill's birthday— remember I'm an Anglophile?). We lined up a national cable deal before launch; however, it suddenly got canceled after that network suffered severe financial hardship. Thus began four years of tumultuous and traumatizing attempts to keep Bold TV afloat. I started Bold TV because I wanted to reach a younger audience with fresh, new ways to talk about politics. As the country grew deeply polarized in 2016, we viewed our mission to help heal the country through bipartisan dialogue. As a conservative Republican, I cohosted our bipartisan show with my dear friend, singer Clay Aiken, a progressive Democrat (also born on November 30!). We tried to model for the country how to disagree but still love each other. We enjoyed editorial success, with millions of social media viewers and our videos shared across numerous networks, from Fox News prime time to *Good Morning America*, CNN, and MSNBC, and cited in many national newspapers. A profile of my work with Bold TV appeared on the *Wall Street Journal* homepage and in a feature podcast with *Entrepreneur* magazine. Ultimately, there wasn't enough financial support for our media company with this mission. It saddens me how divided the country is, and I pray we can choose a better path.

Unfortunately, I took on my father's messiah complex. Bold TV became my new cult, my drug. It became my version of Ralph's Mission. Just as he obsessed over converting people to Mormonism, I obsessed over forcing bipartisanship and converting people to my political view. There was always just "one more meeting," one more quick hit to keep Bold TV going, even as I sacrificed my health to pursue my false idol, my startup. Fibromyalgia is called a "central pain amplification disorder,"[78] meaning the volume of pain sensation in the brain turns up too high. Years of heightened panic led my body to pull an intervention on my brain.

I started Bold TV as an agnostic and became a Christian during the process, but I sadly got intoxicated with what's known as "prosperity gospel." This dangerous ideology within the Christian faith basically claims prayer can make you rich—that if you surrender your money to God, He will bless you with more money. It's trying to use God as your personal vending machine. In practice, that meant waking up each morning and ordering God what to do, because I felt so stressed about the startup's finances, rather than quietly sitting in His presence and asking Him for guidance.

I kept holding that glass because I felt too ashamed to set it down softly. So, instead, it completely fractured when the pain grew too great. I felt ashamed to shut down Bold TV because I didn't want to admit I'd failed. I felt afraid of what people would think.

I also displayed textbook traits for borderline personality disorder. I showed every single BPD trait outlined in the Diagnostic and Statistical Manual of Mental Disorders (DSM-5), something I was in denial about. My father exhibits most, if not all, BPD traits but is in complete denial. Generational curses repeat unless we proactively reject them.

As with many startups, it was a deeply unstable work environment due to the uncertainties of funding, personnel, and building entirely new processes from scratch. I kept meeting with executives from large technology, media, and investment companies but could never get a major deal over the finish line. I existed in a constant state of fight or flight, which eventually overloaded my limbic nervous system. I kept holding that glass cup for nearly four years, in denial about how long I could continue to hold it. It shattered on May 24, 2019. In the process, we poured around a million dollars into Bold TV—all of my savings, plus years of personal cash and sponsor revenue. My credit score fell into the toilet. I felt deep shame, regret, and pain.

After my dangerous emergency Cesarean birth that almost killed Mom and me, I spent the next thirty-six years in generally good physical health, never staying overnight in a hospital since. Yes, I had binge eating episodes and dark mental health times, including visiting a London emergency room for suicidal ideation, but I walked out with my antidepressants later that day and wasn't admitted. I generally took care of myself with yoga, rollerblading, and other workouts, albeit inconsistently. I'd run a marathon and various 5Ks, 10Ks, and a 15K race over the years. Running gave a natural source of endorphins, i.e., natural antidepressants.

This general good physical health collapsed in 2019, when I was hospitalized seven times, including multiple overnight stays. I woke up that May 24 morning with a searing, pulsating nerve pain in the back of my neck, at the base of my skull. It felt like an implanted Taser gun permanently emitting constant shock waves throughout my body. I felt terrified. I first thought I suffered terrible dehydration and kept downing water and Gatorade, hoping sodium, electrolytes, and liquid would get me hydrated. My vision appeared blurry because of the shock waves, making reading or writing difficult. I was scheduled to cohost a bipartisan talk show that morning with the president of the National Urban League, a powerful civil rights organization. I'd angled for months to get that conversation. But I couldn't go, too paralyzed and fearful that I might collapse live on the air. So I canceled and tried to determine what the heck was going on.

This feeling of pulsation lasted nearly four months, causing severe insomnia, migraines, and chronic lower-back pain. Initially, a chiropractor diagnosed a disc herniation in my vertebrae near my brain that caused the nerve pulsation. But an orthopedic surgeon examined me later and said I had no herniation, only minor spinal wear and tear, normal for my age. He said it shouldn't cause me this excruciating level of pain.

My seven hospital visits over that summer included two from allergic reactions to drugs pumped into me by hospital doctors during prior hospital stays. The first reaction is called akathisia, which I got responding to a common ER drug called Compazine. Akathisia felt like napalm pulsating in my bloodstream, with severe pain shooting through my veins making me unable to sit still or lie down. I kept pacing the floor, riddled with fidgeting, restlessness, chills. While pacing, my anxieties shot up, and I had my first panic attack. I lived on the tenth floor and fantasized about jumping out of the window to stop the pain. My sister Julie visited me that night, and she rode with me in a cab back to the same hospital that injected the Compazine. The nurse hooked me up with an IV Benadryl drip, which quickly lowered my panic levels and dissipated the akathisia.

By mid-August, I thought I'd stabilized enough to visit my former Harvard roommate, Natalie, in Boston, who needed help with a family crisis. Big mistake; no good deed goes unpunished, as they say. The pain came roaring back, and I fantasized about hanging myself on Natalie's dangling white attic rope to stop the Taser-level pain throbbing at the base of my skull. Natalie called us an Uber to the ER, and I transferred to a psych hospital, spending three days alongside drug addicts and alcoholics, all of us clawing our way back to life and mental stability. Of course, God was with us on this journey. As Psalm 40:2 says: "He lifted me out of the slimy pit, out of the mud and mire; he set my feet on a rock and gave me a firm place to stand."[79]

After I entered the psych unit, a female guard strip searched me and attendants confiscated and stored away my possessions, except for a few clothes and a Bible devotional book. We slept two to a room; funny enough, my roommate was a married Mormon woman whose adorable kids showed up with her husband a couple of days later. We couldn't sleep with the door closed, which made me nervous because of male patients shuffling around. Thank God we didn't encounter any problems.

The health care providers aren't even sure which one or ones of their drugs caused my second hospitalizing allergic reaction, as the psychiatric hospital pumped me with a cornucopia of pharmaceuticals. This nearly killed me by triggering severe hyponatremia, a condition generating a sharp drop in sodium levels, causing the brain to swell and leading to death.

After I'd just been released from the psychiatric unit, hyponatremia hit and my sodium levels severely dropped, triggering another panic attack and an ambulance showing up after Natalie called 911. This time, a different IV drip administered saline to bring my sodium up to safe levels. Today, I have two small, round, white scars, one inside the joint of each elbow, from the IV needles poking inside me for days at a time. The scabs made me cry when I got home. The scars will be there until I die. But I know they won't be there forever, and the beautiful Christian song "Scars in Heaven," by Casting Crowns tells us who will bear the only scars—our Savior:

> And the thought that makes me smile now, even as the tears fall
> down
> Is that the only scars in Heaven are on the hands that hold you
> now

I got caught up in MRIs, CAT scans, physical therapy, specialist appointments, X-rays, ambulance trips, insurance battles, etc., all while dealing with intense pain and exhaustion. Besides this epic career failure, my personal life was in shambles. Although I was baptized as a Christian a couple of months before my thirty-fifth birthday, I felt angry with God because I couldn't find a Christian man my age who attracted me spiritually, emotionally, physically, and intellectually. I felt angry at God for my abusive family and the terrible Christians who drove me away from Him years ago. But I deceived myself. I had not repented, forgiven my family and myself.

I was demanding, snippy, and closed off. No wonder I didn't attract the man I was looking for; I hadn't become the woman he'd want.

Each week, the congregation at church in New York summoned kids up for a pastoral blessing before dismissing them to Sunday School, and I felt horrible inside. It reminded me how I was unmarried without kids, like they were flaunting them in front of me. I knew that "suffer the little children" in the Bible meant something completely different, but I felt so heartbroken that I wasn't a mom it took on an entirely different meaning.

After everything collapsed in Manhattan, I fled NYC on January 26, 2020—less than two months before COVID hit—finally, some good timing.

Unfortunately, shortly after arriving in DC, I started dating someone I consider a hardcore dark triad. For nearly a year, a "religious but not spiritual" man emotionally and spiritually abused me. I did not listen to my heart, which warned me months before things ended—but I felt too petrified to leave. Headstrong because I felt sick of running from committed relationships, I felt afraid to leave a book-smart guy my age with an impressive résumé who called himself "Christian." And I thought he'd be a good father. But after nine months together, he dumped me, justifying himself with a doctrinally perverse script. A hypocritical, religious zealot, he fetishized virgins and dismissed me because I wasn't one. Raised in a stable, loving home, he was unsympathetic to my childhood trauma and viewed me as damaged rather than resilient and worthy of compassion.

He mocked me for wanting kids, calling me a desperate old maid. Just like the NXIVM cult leader Keith Raniere who fantasized about virgins, this guy obsessed over dating younger virginal women. For these men, it's about power, status, and control. They're always prowling for another notch in their belt. This guy labeled me tainted because of my past, calling me unreliable, untrustworthy, and undeserving of him. Yet, he carried his own baggage—premarital sex with more women than I'd had with men, even proudly taking the virginity of the girl just before me. I made wrong choices when I wasn't a Christian, but he supposedly was his entire life. The sexist double standard was maddening and irrational.

A few months into the relationship, he refused to help when I bled profusely after a terrible rollerblading fall, the worst of my life. Blood gushed from my knee and a deep gash on my elbow, which today has a permanent three-inch scar. The guy shrugged his shoulders and went back to drinking beer at a bonfire with his friends.

Ironically, after I dumped this guy but took him back the next day, his best friend jokingly said, "Well, it's not like she sent you a photo of her bleeding." Yes, I had, and yes, he ignored it, pure dark-triad style. But I returned to him because that's what abused women do. We don't believe we deserve better.

I liked that he was traditionally masculine. He opened my car door like a gentleman—refusing to let me do it myself. But on the other hand, he emotionally abused me. He was like the mafia mobsters of The Godfather series: upstanding, devout religious men on Sundays who mowed down legions in Tommy gun bloodbaths during the week.

One day, almost nine months into the relationship mess, he had another meltdown during a bout of road rage. While I still mucked in indecision and disrespect for my past, he yelled, "I hate my life. I hate my job. I don't know what to do about us."

I wanted to break things off for my own happiness and peace, but I lacked strength. He repeated those meltdowns fairly regularly without any provocation—it was internal. He was unwilling to trust and love beyond his fear and judgment. Sadly, as I spent more time with abusive men, I struggled with my own dark-triad battles. Like attracts like.

In our free country, we're blessed to enter relationships under free will, but he told me my nonvirgin status was the *only* thing holding him back. To me, it made zero sense, because he claimed to be a Christian, and since I had premarital sex before my baptism, my past was forgiven. Even after my baptism, through repentance, Hebrews 8:12 tells us God will remember our sins no more, and Romans 8:1 tells us, "Therefore there is now no condemnation for those who are in Christ Jesus."

His spiritual director priest, the Catholic version of a life coach, told him to get over it, but he refused.

"It's not a *spiritual* thing, it's a *guy* thing," he'd repeatedly tell me.

We tried couples counseling, and he flamed out, refusing to finish our booked number of sessions. He tried a Catholic therapist, who enabled his misogyny. He dumped me unceremoniously three days after Christmas. He even quoted the Bible, saying he didn't want trouble, citing Matthew 1:19 involving Joseph, the fiancé of Mary, the mother of Jesus: "Her husband Joseph, being a righteous man and unwilling to expose her to public disgrace, planned to divorce her quietly."

Every Catholic woman (and every other woman, period) I've described this guy to agrees he's emotionally abusive, and I dodged a bullet. I agree. "Man's rejection is God's protection," the adage goes. So true. I stubbornly refused to quietly listen to the depths of my heart, my body, my soul. They warned me each time I dated one of these dark-triad boys. I ignored them—making my self-deceptions louder than the truth. After that failure, I prayed to God:

> *Please give me the courage to continue and not be bitter and jaded. Give me faith, hope, and a future with a husband and father of my kids—if that's what you want for me. Nevertheless, not my will, but Thine be done.*

From the cross, Jesus' last words were "it is finished." In the Gospel of John, the original Greek word is "tetelestai." It's an accounting term meaning "paid in full." As Jesus uttered those words, He decreed any debts owed to God were fulfilled.

Sometimes, we need to say, "it is finished," and humbly exit, whether it's a damaging relationship, startup, or job. God provides us soft landings and off-ramps to prevent tragedy. Too often, we blow past these ramps, blow past red flags warning us of danger ahead.

If my father set aside his grandiose ego about The Mission and gave his family less abuse and more stability, I believe his sons would not have developed schizophrenia. He could have been a blessing to me instead of significantly contributing to my suicidal ideations.

If I'd escaped these dark-triad men immediately after sensing their nature, I could have saved years of heartache and loneliness. If I released Bold TV before the glass grew too heavy, I would have prevented financial loss combined with intense, searing pain, scars, and permanent ringing in my ears, known as tinnitus. I wouldn't have wasted years without a husband or children because Bold TV took over my life and consumed every waking thought.

After my hospitalizations, I gradually emerged with my health intact. Though some acquaintances tried to mock me, I felt no shame or stigma for needing mental health care, because the searing, Taser-like pain also caused depression as months of pain with no relief dragged on.

But after many years of self-sabotage and spiraling, I finally reached a place of joy and peace. I learned the difference between needing professional help and pathologizing yourself—magnifying and compounding your problems through self-sabotage.

Of course, this wasn't easy. It was a deadly battle.

Since these losses, multiple friends separately shared this passage from the Old Testament, and its promises penetrate my heart deeply:

"So I will restore to you the years that the swarming locust has
  eaten,
The crawling locust,
The consuming locust,
And the chewing locust,
My great army which I sent among you.
You shall eat in plenty and be satisfied,
And praise the name of the LORD *your God,*
Who has dealt wondrously with you;
And My people shall never be put to shame.
Then you shall know that I am in the midst of Israel:
I am the LORD *your God*
And there is no other.
My people shall never be put to shame."

—Joel 2:25–27[80]

The locusts devoured my physical, mental, and financial health, but with amazing healing partners, family, and friends, God is restoring what I've lost. There are millions of Americans right now experiencing joblessness and health complications due to the locusts of COVID, and mental health care needs are skyrocketing. I will never stigmatize or shame anyone who takes the important step of seeking mental health care. I pray our society is more compassionate for those needing restorative mental health care and assists them on the path to healing.

Chapter 16

⟶

Forgiving Dad

"He will turn the hearts of parents to their children and
the hearts of children to their parents."

—Malachi 4:6

Standing near my grandparents' graves, I wondered if I'd just desecrated their final resting place. If the dead could move, would this saintly couple who devoted their final years as mission presidents for the LDS Church be rolling below this funeral plot soil in disgust at their heathen, agnostic granddaughter? Above ground, on a breezy and overcast April day, generations of Sheffield offspring weaved carefully around manicured gravestones that include Martin Lafayette, my older brother who died at only ten months from sudden infant death syndrome.

We were there to bury Aunt Charlotte, at Wasatch Lawn Memorial Park, filled with soft grass, whispering oaks, stalwart pines, and soothing fountains. The Wasatch mountains tower in the distance of this Salt Lake City suburb, silent guardians for our beautiful queen about to enter her last repose.

At the local Mormon chapel, just before we visited the gravesite, her eight children, their spouses, and their children, sang a weepy yet touching version of her favorite song, "Somewhere Over the Rainbow." They stood in front of her coffin, draped in flowers and her sparkling Miss USA sash.

Legionnaires' disease is no obscure illness; this strain of pneumonia hospitalizes thousands and kills hundreds of people each year, victims contaminated by air conditioners, hot tubs, and other seemingly benign appliances. The Legionella bacteria spreads through mist, including through air-conditioning units for large buildings like the one Charlotte lived in. I had no idea this lethal sickness would strike our family matriarch.

I think about Charlotte often; she let me sleep on her couch during Christmas break in Utah my freshman year of college and encouraged me to continue forging my own path away from Dad's abusive control. Charlotte served as a sage counselor for many younger women, including me. She intervened on my behalf at a vulnerable time in my life while I was a teenager suffering estrangement from my immediate family. Her gentle guidance, love, and savvy gave me courage to recover and thrive. I was but one of thousands enriched by this bold woman.

Now, here at her final resting place that beautiful spring day, I furiously tried to avoid an encounter with Aunt Charlotte's ex-husband, Richard (or "Dick," as I called him). I worried I'd verbally lacerate the man who divorced Charlotte after she became overweight and their eight kids grew up. Dick then married a younger, slimmer woman. I wasn't intimidated by him like when I was younger. Now, I was a grown woman who'd spent years going toe to toe with formidable figures on national television in front of audiences of millions. Also, as an agnostic, I wasn't fazed by his religious claims of priesthood authority.

Some fourteen years earlier, when I was nineteen, I ran into him as a correspondent covering the Utah legislature. He was attending the same education committee I was writing about for the Provo *Daily Herald* newspaper. Proud of the media credentials around my neck, I looked official with my photo badge and media outlet listed. Dick condescendingly told me he felt shocked I turned out to be a success, given how mentally disturbed my father is.

"I really think you should find a kind, caring mentor to help guide you through your father's damage," Dick said. "It can't be me, but I hope you can find that person."

What an uncaring schmuck, I thought.

After finishing my Harvard master's program, I was in town in 2011, and Dick's granddaughter considered buying my car, so she asked him to check the engine and kick the tires. He asked me what I'd been up to and sneeringly inquired how much my Harvard master's cost me. He was flat-footed when I told him I'd won a full-tuition scholarship. I later heard he'd tried to push his grandkids to try for Harvard scholarships, though nobody yet followed in my footsteps.

At Charlotte's funeral in 2016, I saw Dick across the way. I didn't want to cause drama, but, boy, inside I wanted to scream at this guy. I despised him with the passion of a thousand burning suns.

Yes, every divorce has two sides, and I've never heard his side. But according to LDS theology, in the afterlife, Dick receives both his younger, slimmer wife and my aunt, since Charlotte never remarried (to her endless heartbreak) and is technically still "sealed" to him. Mormons believe you can't enter heaven's highest level unless you're sealed in the LDS temple to a fellow worthy Mormon. So, I thought, *allegedly Slick Dick got his second ticket to the next world while Aunt Charlotte is stuck with this creep.* I wasn't Mormon anymore, but it saddened me that my aunt died believing this was her future.

I also fastidiously avoided Ralph. I hadn't spoken to him in three years, since he took Jonah's side and falsely claimed I tried to seduce my own brother.

But in 2016, Ralph tried to pretend this didn't matter—he never apologized for his lie—and approached me as I stood speaking to my uncle near Grandpa and Grandma's graves. I felt torn because Ralph and Charlotte had been close, even though he'd been angry at her for taking me in for Christmas some fifteen years earlier. Charlotte was the eldest of five children, with Ralph just a year and a half younger. As children, the criminal babysitter Ada locked Charlotte in a closet while she assaulted toddler Ralph. Charlotte hoped Ralph and I would reconcile someday, though I blamed Ralph for driving my two brothers over the brink of insanity and inflicting deep wounds on the rest of us.

That day at the funeral, I wore a slimming, elbow-length, dark forest-green Diane von Furstenberg dress and bejeweled Ted Baker black satin pumps with gold soles. Ted Baker is a subtle British designer, so the jewel brooch, a black flower the width of the toes, is tasteful, not too flashy. I felt proud when I bought them at Bloomingdale's in Manhattan with my own money. I knew I'd made it. I wore them in Aunt Charlotte's honor, as she adored dressing up and getting others gussied up at her costume and gown shop, Charlotte's Attic.

Ralph would never let me own those shoes under his roof—too slutty. He thought his sister shallow with her pageantry. It recently rained, and I feared the pumps would sink into the muddy gravesite dirt and get stuck. I felt mortified when Ralph walked over and grabbed my arm at the elbow. I yanked it away, rebuffing him completely, refusing to speak, turned my back, and walked back to the car.

Am I wrong for doing this, rejecting my grandparents' son literally at their grave?

Ralph traumatized and abused me for decades. I could not merrily prattle away about small things, like my flight over, as he wished to discuss. I could not phonily pretend that all was well, or that I enjoyed his presence in the least.

Yet, I felt no emotion, neither sadness nor pleasure at the entire encounter. It felt as though Ralph no longer existed in my heart and psyche.

It'd been the cleanest and sanest period of my life, at least professionally, no doubt in part because he was quarantined away. Pulling away at the gravesite was self-preservation. Perhaps someday I would be strong enough to protect myself from his presence, to embolden my mother and remove her and my schizophrenic brothers from him.

Should I hold him to the same standards I hold a normal human being?

Ralph was emotionally unwell, but he was not mentally disabled like my brothers Peter and Jonah. Ralph was plagued by narcissistic personality disorder, but I didn't believe he was completely insane. Like his siblings and Aunt Charlotte's children, who refused to give him the microphone at the funeral (allowing him only to play the guitar the day prior at her wake), I felt uncertain where he would take the conversation at the gravesite.

Will he create a commotion, begin raising his voice, become agitated?

The potential downside of speaking to him near the grave seemed infinitely greater than the potential upside. I couldn't bear the thought of shattering the tranquility of the moment for others.

During a visit to New York City shortly after, my uncle assuaged my fear of desecrating my grandparents' grave.

"If Grandpa were alive, he'd be ashamed and sad about how his son treated you," my uncle said. "He'd be proud of you."

I was thirty-three. It was my "Jesus Year." A time of crucible. I believed my grandparents would understand why I refused to speak with Ralph. Even if they didn't, I'd lived more than three decades of disappointing my own parents. The bitter nihilist in me thought, *Just one more episode of disappointing my family members can't hurt.*

Though I never thought it possible, seven years after I "disowned" him, I forgave my father for his actions against me, my mother, and my seven siblings. An unlikely series of events allowed me to visit this man and sing him "Happy Birthday," grateful for the gifts he imparted and able to forgive the mental agony he helped create that made me suicidal.

My forgiveness journey started with my Christian conversion, a decision that began the process of opening my heart to God's healing balm of forgiveness. Shortly after my baptism, Reverend Anthony B. Thompson became a spiritual mentor in my forgiveness journey. Anthony pastors Holy Trinity Reformed Episcopal Church in Charleston, South Carolina, and authored *Called to Forgive: The Charleston Church Shooting, a Victim's Husband, and the Path to Healing and Peace.* Anthony's wife, Myra, was murdered by a white supremacist in the shooting of nine parishioners at the pre-dominantly black Emanuel African Methodist Episcopal Church in Charleston in 2015. Mother Emanuel Church, as it's called, is a his-toric church with a venerable history in the struggle for civil rights. Anthony and other family members of the Charleston Nine who suffered their loved ones' murders shocked the world with their miraculous story of forgiveness for this evil white supremacist who committed such a heinous act.

It's rare, but in the bond hearing, the judge allowed loved ones to speak directly to the accused. Dylann Roof was a scrawny twenty-one-year-old neo-Nazi, druggie kid with an allegedly vio-lent father, and he'd driven more than one hundred miles across the state from Columbia, South Carolina, in hopes of sparking a race war through his vile deed.

The messages of forgiveness from the victims' families to this murderer stunned the world.

During the bond hearing, Anthony was second to speak to Roof, after Nadine Collier, daughter of victim Ethel Lance, who told Roof, "You took something very precious away from me. I will never talk to her ever again. I will never hold her again. But I for-give you, and have mercy on your soul."

Then it was Anthony's turn.

"I forgive you, and my family forgive you," he said. "But we would like you to take this opportunity to repent. Repent. Confess. Give your life to the one who matters the most: Christ. So that He can change you and change your ways, no matter what happens to you. And you'll be okay." Wanda Simmons, granddaughter of vic-tim Daniel Simmons, told Roof: "Although my grandfather and the other victims died at the hands of hate, this is proof, everyone's plea for your soul, is proof that they lived in love and their legacies will live in love. So hate won't win. And I just want to thank the court for making sure that hate doesn't win."[81]

Other cities like Baltimore, Ferguson, and Minneapolis burned (destroying predominantly black neighborhoods and black-owned businesses) in the aftermath of shootings, but not Charleston. Instead of sparking a race war as this shooter desired, through the transformative power of forgiveness, Charleston grew more united than ever—love and unity reigned. These victims' words carried enormous weight, and even with deep anguish in their voices, their message came loud and clear: hate and vengeance had no place in their hearts.

Then-President Barack Obama traveled from Washington, DC, for the funeral of one of the Charleston Nine victims, a state senator named Clementa Pinckney. Obama's heart felt so touched by this wondrous act of forgiveness that he started singing that immortal song, "Amazing Grace."

As a pastor, Anthony followed up with the murderer and visited him in prison to reiterate his message of forgiveness and urge this intransigent monster to pray, ask for God's mercy and submit his life to Jesus.

Not long after my baptism, a Bronx pastor friend named Dimas Salaberrios invited me to a Manhattan screening of a documentary movie called *Emanuel*, coproduced by Viola Davis and Steph Curry, which told the story of this phenomenal forgiveness. At the screening, I met Anthony, and we immediately connected over our shared passion for discerning God's call on our lives. I devoured his book about forgiveness, and I felt convicted.

Anthony's book is gold, a guide to forgive. It knocks down all the myths around forgiveness, including that by forgiving you downplay or excuse sin and harm. Or that forgiving makes you weak and passive. Or that forgiving means you must let them hurt you again. None of these are true. First and foremost, forgiveness is an act of obedience to God. And even if you don't believe in God, science proves forgiveness is a powerful, healing antibiotic for victims. It releases us from the cancerous emotional and mental diseases of vengeance, insecurity, rage, and fear. It obliterates the power your abuser maintains over you by releasing the abuser's control over your mind and heart. Though you still might suffer bodily, financial, or other harm, you resist the dangerous self-sabotage of unforgiveness.

The Emanuel shooting was far from Anthony's first experience with remarkable forgiveness. He grew up in the Jim Crow South, encountering nasty racism on a regular basis. He said he spent much of his youth angry, bitter, and filled with rage at the racists around him. But he gradually realized this was not sustainable. He immersed himself in the Bible, his guide to freedom and forgiveness. Jesus suffered betrayal and a brutal crucifixion, but He prayed: "Father, forgive them; for they know not what they do."

Anthony built an exemplary life as a pastor and is a symbol of God's redemptive power for millions of people. I knew that if he could forgive, then I could, also.

In 2020, seven years after I stopped speaking with my eighty-one-year-old father, I decided to forgive him. I was about to enter my dad's house and have dinner with him.

I made sure I wasn't alone, in part for my own physical safety. My youngest brother, John, now a strapping, muscular US Army captain, joined me, along with my nephew, still in elementary school and dressed in an adorable bright yellow-and-red Pikachu hoodie.

My parents lived in Jackson County, Missouri, in a small apartment in a white-siding triplex bought with Grandpa Sheffield's inheritance. They mainly lived off Social Security and government disability payments for my brothers, who cannot work. I feel no shame or judgment for their modest circumstances. People from impoverished areas, including Third World countries, are often the happiest because they experience joyful, unconditional love. In our home, we were both poor and without healthy, unconditional, life-sustaining love.

John knocked and my parents answered the door. Mom and Dad both looked older and frail, starting to hunch over; I hadn't seen them in four years, since Charlotte's funeral. At seventy-one, Mom dressed in one of her practical, sturdy outfits, usually black sweatpants, black hoodie, and black or red turtleneck. Long ago, her hair turned gray, but she kept it near her natural auburn as possible using drugstore DIY hair dye.

Dad, his thinning hair and mustache practically snow white now, favored collared shirts and denim cargo pants—he loved the multiple pockets to stash his handheld Book of Mormon, day planner, and Swiss Army Knife.

We sat down in the tiny kitchen, crowded around the table with Mom, Dad, and my two schizophrenic brothers, Peter and Jonah. We sat at the small, rectangular, cream-colored tile table and ate defrosted frozen Mexican food and iceberg lettuce salad, while two cute little dogs and a cat scampered underfoot.

By this time, my parents felt proud I was appearing on national television. Peter and Jonah, who years ago demonstrated bizarre sexual inclinations toward me, stayed calm and nonconfrontational. Their medication regimes stabilized them, and I didn't feel physically unsafe, though I'm sure it helped that John was there.

Dad kept on his best behavior, but Mom told me he'd also developed Alzheimer's, and he seemed much more relaxed and placid than I'd ever seen him. Previously, my sister—a former stand-up comedian in Manhattan, so she's well-equipped with a zinger—joked that "he forgot how to be an asshole." Most of my siblings shifted in various stages of estrangement with Dad, though one "golden boy" brother remained the "Nephi" of the family. Nephi is a Book of Mormon prophet, the most righteous of six brothers who stood in stark contrast with their rebellious first-born brothers, Laman and Lemuel. For years, dad called my sister Sophie and me "Laman and Lemuel," since we first escaped The Mission.

Aside from our Nephi, who lived near my parents, none of the other siblings living away were on good terms with Dad. We all had mutual understanding about why. Only Mom consistently pleaded for me to forgive Dad for what she called "rough edges." To me, they were sins far more grievous than ill manners to be softened through etiquette training at finishing school. Mom, who believed wholeheartedly in her husband's prophetic calling, prayed for nearly twenty years for this day to arrive—when both parties would reconcile.

Until then, Mom's pleas fell on my figuratively deaf ears, and now Dad faced near physical deafness. Despite his hearing aids, Dad pulled his signature move of cupping his hand around his ear as an impromptu gramophone to help him hear.

Still coherent and able to hold a conversation, there were

moments when he drifted off and his sky-blue eyes glazed over. There were no recriminations, fire and brimstone accusations, no hateful sermons.

"Carrie, I was sitting in the living room, and I had a prompting from the Holy Ghost," he began.

I started to tense up, bracing for his latest diatribe but unafraid of combat—or to bolt.

"The Spirit told me to quickly turn on the television. So I quickly obeyed, and you were on the air!" His eyes gleamed with pride. "The Lord *knew* you'd be there."

Who was this man? I felt a wave of calm flood through my body. It was the first time since my childhood baptism that Dad's divine revelations about me didn't involve some religion-laced condemnation. God is the master of the universe. He manages colossally more important matters than transmitting the cable news schedule of the seventh-born child of a homespun Midwestern prophet. Yet, He also notes when the tiniest sparrow falls from his nest. Perhaps He wanted to give Dad that tiny spark of joy and us this brief moment of connection.

The whole thing felt surprisingly, blissfully anticlimactic. In some respects, these family members felt like strangers, yet there was a feeling of peace.

I released my visceral hatred of the man who brought me endless shame and regret. The man who spoke curses over me, abandoned me, and likely drove my two sweet brothers to insanity, stealing any possibility of a normal life. God will hold Dad accountable for his sins, just as He will hold me accountable for mine.

We often get our view of God from our fathers. That's why our crisis of fatherlessness hits society so hard. Numerous studies show fatherlessness and paternal child abuse is a crucial factor in whether a child drops out of high school, falls into drugs and gangs, commits crimes, or becomes a single teenage mother. Whether we suffer the trauma of abuse or abandonment, this often makes us forget who our real father is—God, our infinite source of love, joy, and purpose.

Reverend Billy Graham said, "A child who is allowed to be disrespectful to his parents will not have true respect for anyone."[82] He's right. My rage against my father manifested itself in how I disrespected myself, my romantic partners, and others in my life. I needed to forgive everyone in my life (including toxic coworkers, various LDS and other church leaders, cheating exes, and even Aunt Charlotte's ex-husband) and ask God to forgive me. There were LDS Church leaders who hurt me, but many others who helped me. I needed to forgive all the hurt and release my anger.

Graham also wrote: "The Bible clearly says, 'Honor thy father and thy mother' (Exodus 20:12[83]). This passage sets no age limit on such honor. It does not say parents must be honorable to be honored. This does not necessarily mean that we must 'obey' parents who may be dishonorable. We must honor them. Honor has many shapes and affections."[84]

In many ways, my father lived a dishonorable life, but that doesn't allow me to retaliate and dishonor him by mailing a package of sperm or yelling at him on my grandparents' grave. It means I live a life that brings honor, both to him and my family. The more I study the effects of childhood sexual and emotional abuse, the more my heart grieves for his pain.

I also see how we both became "Worksaholics"—workaholics who believe they must work to receive God's love and prove to the world that we are valid and "special." But while God is no respecter of persons—e.g., He tells us not to live in boastful pride—he also gives us unconditional love. We are always worthy to Him. The Jewish, Asian, and Mormon cultural practice identified by Amy Chua of vacillating between inferiority and superiority is not sustainable when taken to extremes.

The song "Jireh" by Elevation Worship explains how we should view God:

I'll never be more loved than I am right now
Wasn't holding You up
So, there's nothing I can do to let You down[85]

We have no need for insecurity. God is not insecure and doesn't need us to "hold Him up." Our parents should not be insecure and should instill confidence in their children. Instead, my father was deeply insecure. I "let him down" by running away from The Mission. I was "holding him up" when I lied to the social workers about our abuse, when I shielded him from his stalker. I was "holding him up" during the years I played music on street corners to fulfill his false motorhome prophecies.

Jesus says in Matthew 7:9–11, "Is there anyone among you who, if your child asked for bread, would give a stone? Or if the child asked for a fish, would give a snake? If you, then, who are evil, know how to give good gifts to your children, how much more will your Father in heaven give good things to those who ask him!"

My father gave me stones and serpents. I went out and bought myself baskets of my own rocks and snakes, too. If you've been hurt by someone you love or trust, the worst thing you can do is hurt yourself more through self-destructive behavior. It only gives your abuser more power over your life.

Many know Jesus' parable of the prodigal son. The story of

Joseph in the Bible is rich with plotlines, including one of a prodigal father and prodigal brothers. Joseph's dad attacks his spiritual abilities, and his brothers kidnap him, consider murdering him, and sell him into slavery.

My dad was like Joseph's family members, and while I'm not an adviser to Pharaoh, I praise God I could forgive and embrace Dad, just as Joseph forgave his family. Joseph's own weeping during his family reunion in Pharaoh's palace reverberated so loudly that it bounced across the palace, and Joseph's attempts at secrecy failed. I wonder if God's reunion in heaven when a prodigal child returns sounds similar. We know Jesus weeps.

Enormous blessings happened *because* of Joseph's family but also *in spite of* his family. "Even though you intended to do harm to me, God intended it for good, in order to preserve a numerous people, as he is doing today," Joseph tells his brothers in Genesis 50:20, when they unknowingly come to beg for food during a famine that he masterfully defeats, saving untold thousands or millions of lives.

I'll spend the rest of my life discerning how God will transform my abuse for His service. And I'll be praying for all others facing a similar journey.

Chapter 17

Wrestling with God

Commit your way to the Lord; trust in him, and he will act. He will make your vindication shine like the light and the justice of your cause like the noonday.

—*Psalm 37:5–6*

In October 2021, I moderated a lively debate on the campus of the University of Texas at Austin. While I waited to return home at the Austin airport departure gate, a passenger on our flight swaggered up wearing a shocking T-shirt that read: "Jesus is a cunt." Wow. The profane message sparked an audible, hushed buzzing among my fellow passengers. Eventually, a flight attendant called the man up and convinced him to turn the shirt inside out before letting him board the plane. I felt grateful the guy didn't erupt into launching fists, because he was clearly a troubled soul.

I strongly reject the message of that guy's shirt, and felt glad I wasn't seated next to him. Jesus is the Way, the Truth, and the

Life. But some Christians do behave in the most wretched fashion, and I wondered who, while invoking Christ's name, might have hurt this man? After all, the most religious people used political pressure to get Jesus killed, and the apostle Judas, one of the first Christians, lethally betrayed the son of God. Human nature doesn't change. Why should we expect better from Christians today? As former-slave-turned-abolitionist Frederick Douglass put it: "Between the Christianity of this land, and the Christianity of Christ, I recognize the widest possible difference."[86] I myself often fail to acknowledge my own flawed nature; my sharp tongue and temper sometimes make me a terrible ambassador for Christ.

Indeed, there is a cavernous difference between human-run religion and Divine relationship. Divine relationship with God is not religion. Mathematically expressed: lowercase **religion** ≠ uppercase **Relationship**. Our society today—young people especially—is turning away from institutions. Trust across the board is crumbling, whether it's in government, schools, medicine, or religion. As someone deeply abused by very religious people and agnostic for almost twelve years, I thought if God exists, He's probably an asshole because He allowed this to happen to me. Or He's indifferent, or He's proactively hurting people, since humans use His name for horrific deeds. But evil deeds done in God's name are like a knockoff Gucci purse with a big fake G. Clearly a false, flimsy imitation.

Pew Research Center found that far more Americans (55 percent) think religion is a force for good rather than bad (20 percent), while 24 percent said it lacks much impact.[87] Following the COVID-19 scourge that killed millions of people and devastated global economies, Pew also found in November 2021 that this didn't shake Americans' faith in God.[88] Pew reported 80 percent of Americans say most of the suffering in the world comes from people—not God. Just 14 percent of US adults said, "Sometimes I think the suffering in the world is an indication that there is no God." In my dark walk as a bitter agnostic, I fell out of sync with most Americans. My suffering came mostly from human beings: my father and other family members, myself, indifferent and sometimes harmful church leaders, toxic coworkers, and toxic dating partners. Rather than leaning into God for help, I rejected the very source that would help me heal.

Unfortunately, I'm far from alone. Young people in record numbers are turning away from God, the life force that brings lasting hope. And it's killing us. Women who attend religious services at least once a week are 68 percent less likely to die "deaths of despair," including suicide, drug overdose, and alcohol poisoning. Men are 33 percent less likely, according to 2020 research led by Harvard University's School of Public Health.[89] A January 2023 National Bureau of Economic Research (NBER) working paper found that states with pronounced drops in religious attendance correlated with sharper upticks in deaths of despair, and vice versa.[90] NBER is one of the most prominent economic research bodies in America, serving as a talent pool for many chairs of the White House Council of Economic Advisers.

I learned through my conversion that God can handle all our anger, rage, sorrow, and fear. He is bigger than any questions we have about evil deeds done in His name. So it's good to ask questions, it's good to scrutinize the behavior of Christians and people of all religions. As Ronald Reagan said, "We must be cautious in claiming God is on our side. I think the real question we must answer is, are we on His side?" That's a question I'll be asking my entire life.

I understand the need to shine a bright searchlight on America's sins and not ignore or hide them and their generational effects. But sin is not the end of the story—redemption and the pursuit of "A More Perfect Union" gives me hope for the future. We are a country that has broken generational curses, and while we can't change human nature, we can, as Dr. Martin Luther King Jr. said, bend the arc of the universe toward justice.

God is not about controlling us; He gave us free will. In Matthew 23:37, Jesus says "O Jerusalem, Jerusalem, thou that killest the prophets, and stonest them which are sent unto thee, how often would I have gathered thy children together, even as a hen gathereth her chickens under her wings, and ye would not!"[91] God desires our inner peace and wants us under His protection, but He will not force us. That's a process we must willingly start on our own, though He will help us each day as we humbly ask for help.

Of course, there are rules to life, and sometimes parents go way too loose toward the other end of the spectrum. As *The Ten Commandments* filmmaker Cecil B. DeMille said, "We cannot break the Ten Commandments. We can only break ourselves against them."[92] Or as John 10:35 says, "Scripture cannot be broken."[93] Good parenting is teaching your kids the right principles and rules, but letting them make mistakes. That's partially why I made so many adult mistakes—I couldn't make them as a kid. I was a feral cat after leaving home. Stuck in a shed and motorhome, I didn't have normal high school experiences. I struggled not to freeze in the winter and to avoid getting raped by my schizophrenic brother.

My prayer in writing my story is to help stop passing trauma to future generations. I moved from a place of despair, poverty, and illness into a place of stability, peace, and joy. This painful process always got worse when I focused on ways I felt like a victim, when I compared my situation to others and burned with jealousy at their loving families.

The *Wall Street Journal* in January 2023 ran an essay from the directors of the Harvard Study of Adult Development, which for eighty-five years "has tracked an original group of 724 men and more than 1,300 of their male and female descendants over three generations, asking thousands of questions and taking hundreds of measurements to find out what really keeps people healthy and happy." They reported:

> *Through all the years of studying these lives, one crucial factor stands out for the consistency and power of its ties to physical health, mental health and longevity. Contrary to what many people might think, it's not career achievement, or exercise, or a healthy diet. Don't get us wrong; these things matter. But one thing continuously demonstrates its broad and enduring importance: good relationships.*
>
> *In fact, close personal connections are significant enough that if we had to take all 85 years of the Harvard Study and boil it down to a single principle for living, one life investment that is supported by similar findings across a variety of other studies, it would be this: Good relationships keep us healthier and happier. Period. If you want to make one decision to ensure your own health and happiness, it should be to cultivate warm relationships of all kinds.*[94]

If strong, positive relationships are the lifeblood of longevity, the reverse logically must be true: lack of positive relationships—or ongoing toxic relationships—are severely crippling and damaging to physical health, mental health, and longevity. Early in my young adulthood, I knew this was true, yet I sacrificed deep, positive personal relationships for my career.

For years, I'd constantly compare myself to who I might be if I hadn't made terrible choices. I'd compare myself with people in my cohort before I launched my startup, and measure their lives against mine. They're getting married, snagging TV contracts, having children, landing a White House job. Meanwhile, I visited the hospital nine times as a troubled adult, my business failed, I lost a million dollars, I remained unmarried and without kids. It made me hate myself. I believed if I hadn't started the business, I could be where they are. I didn't want to feel jealous of them, but in doing so, I turned the hate on myself.

God helped me release the envy. There's a constant daily barrage of seeing friends' success pop up on social media. That sparks normal insecurity, but for me it's amplified because of the insane things baked into the cake of my childhood. Later, my own terrible choices, not my childhood, held me back. I remained mired in a web of self-victimization and self-sabotage. This web ensured I relinquished my own power to change. Once I took ownership of my mess, things turned upward.

In my public policy and media work, I constantly pushed for the social changes I thought the world needed, even while I rotted away inside. My family relationships remained strained, and my anger toward Dad ate at me like cancer. Persian poet Rumi had it right: "Yesterday I was clever, so I wanted to change the world. Today I am wise, so I am changing myself."

Colossians 3:23 tells us, "And whatever you do, do it heartily, as for the Lord and not for men."[95] If you're in deep emotional pain and suffering under a permanent burden, chances are you're living life for men. God tells us His burden is light. We inflict suffering on ourselves because we put human approval, money, career, relationships, or any other man-made priority ahead of God. This emotional suffering can lead to deep physical pain, including fibromyalgia.

If we reorient our lives toward God, our pain goes down because we're centered on the right motivation. We won't get crushed by failure because there's less at stake without our egos involved. This doesn't mean we should shy away from attempting difficult, even seemingly intractable challenges. It means that the journey will be far less harrowing because we aren't weighed down by excess man-made baggage.

I'm still sifting through the rubble of my 2019 collapse, and I'm still uncertain how God will fulfill His promise that nothing will be wasted. In John 6:12, Jesus told the disciples, "Gather the pieces that are left over. Let nothing be wasted."[96] Jesus fed thousands of people until the entire crowd was full. He was generous, but he was also resourceful and a prudent steward. I've struggled my whole life feeling like an outsider, careening out of control from my foiled schemes. Reaching my late thirties unmarried, with my fertility window shrinking, my entire life savings evaporated, many professional ties incinerated, and my health deteriorated, I would lie and agonize for hours, wallowing in insecurity, lack, and doubt. I knew God forgave me, but I couldn't forgive myself. I failed to honor myself as a daughter of God and forgive myself. Instead, I condemned myself. I was obsessed with my failing startup, that I squandered all these gifts God gave me, and I had nothing to show for it.

Time dragged on, and after my borderline personality disorder–induced sudden dumping of a loving and supportive boyfriend, I fantasized about falling under the wheels of a moving car. It jolted me. I felt sick of my dark fantasies. I was playing the victim and needed to stop or I'd die alone. At age thirty-nine, I *finally* resolved to see myself as a blessed person and shut out the noise. For several weeks, I didn't ask God for anything. All my prayers were prayers of gratitude. Until then, my posture of pleading for what I wanted from God simply compounded my feelings of lack and insecurity. The more I spoke about what I was missing in my life, the more I felt bitter, aggrieved, and jealous.

This taught me how, like Job in the Bible, we must praise God in the middle of chaos and misery. President Abraham Lincoln realized this in 1863. For the first time in seventy-four years and amid the tumultuous and bloody Civil War, he called for a day of Thanksgiving and gratitude, even when all seemed broken and hellish. Gratitude is central to our civic fabric. The National Park Service tells the tale:

> *In July 1863, the Battle of Gettysburg resulted in more than 50,000 American casualties. Despite these losses, the United States gained a great victory during these three days. On October 3, 1863, with this victory in mind, as well as its cost, President Lincoln issued a proclamation:*
>
> *"I do therefore invite my fellow citizens in every part of the United States, . . . to set apart and observe the last Thursday of November next, as a day of Thanksgiving . . . And I recommend to them that while offering up the ascriptions justly due to Him . . . , they do also, with humble penitence for our national perverseness and disobedience, commend to his tender care all those who have become widows, orphans, mourners or sufferers in the lamentable civil strife in which we are unavoidably engaged, and fervently implore the interposition of the Almighty Hand to heal the wounds of the nation and to restore it as soon as may be*

consistent with Divine purposes to the full enjoyment of peace,
harmony, tranquility and Union."
  This proclamation is viewed as the beginning of the national
holiday of Thanksgiving Day.[97]

I imagine some people during Lincoln's day took severe
umbrage and offense at this notion of giving thanks during this
catastrophic American Armageddon. For many years, that would
have been me. I likely would resent Honest Abe.

But now I embrace the power of gratitude—it is a potent
weapon against depression, doubt, and fear. I thanked God for my
physical and mental recovery, for my citizenship in such a wealthy,
blessed country, and for those who paid the ultimate sacrifice for
me in this land. I delighted in the seemingly smallest things (but
that are really huge): clean, running, fresh water. My dishwasher
to alleviate my First-World sanitation issues. That I can stroll just
a few steps down the hall and dump my trash down a chute rather
than burn my garbage on our farmland as we did in Branson, Missouri. I am safe, protected from the outside elements, and living in
a comfortable apartment in a thriving neighborhood.

I work in a field meaningful to me that allowed me to rebuild
my credit score and financial safety net. I bought my first home—
no more rent!—thanks to my hard work and supportive clients. I
found quality friends in a strong church and community. The more
I thanked God for my blessings, the more blessings I received.

———

Beautiful Aunt Charlotte, Miss USA 1957, came of age before today's
social media onslaught, our often crass and materialistic digital
Wild West that decimates public figures and belittles idealistic

dreamers. That includes the 2019 Miss USA Cheslie Kryst, who committed suicide by jumping from her Manhattan skyscraper apartment after enduring severe online bullying. It's heartbreaking to know that Cheslie collapsed under this burden, though my faith tells me that now, she's in a better place, free from pain.

Yet, even if the tools around beauty pageantry have modernized, there's "nothing new under the sun." Charlotte withstood those same negative forces and superficiality of her era. Her grace, family values, and belief in mankind's innate goodness drove this woman of faith in an era of doubt.

Charlotte endured health problems like leukemia, candida, and trauma as a pedestrian victim of an auto hit-and-run, among other sorrows. The years furrowed her brow and weathered her face as she struggled after a painful divorce. Yet Charlotte remained a fount of cheerfulness, positivity, and light. Even as she limped by financially, she always gave more than she received: to the homeless, the outsider, the lonely straggler. She lived by the mantra of Sydney Smith: "It is the greatest of all mistakes, to do nothing because you can only do little."[98] She saw treasure and gold in those society tossed aside, giving them jobs at her costume shop, Charlotte's Attic.

My aunt passed away in 2016 at age seventy-nine, surrounded by her loved ones after a brief battle with Legionnaires' disease. During her memorial service, one of her daughters read a poem Charlotte previously wrote to her grandchildren. Called "Your Choices," it was borne out of concern for a troubled teenage grandson who has since healed. It's a call to ponder the ripple effects we have on others—an excerpt:

Remember my loved one—the choices you make
Will affect generations to come

And all your decisions whether foolish or wise
Will show all where you have come from

Charlotte's a shining example of a faithful life well lived and a model example of following the command in Ephesians 4:31 to "get rid of all bitterness."[99] When we rid ourselves of bitterness, our souls are cleansed and light. When we rid our families of bitterness, we break cycles of abuse from older generations. When we rid our society of bitterness, we heal nationwide trauma.

Charlotte could have been bitter about many things, but she knew that our lives are not our own. We are made by a Creator, who gave us stewardship of our thoughts, bodies, and souls. But a steward is not an owner. It's someone entrusted with managing someone else's property.

Parents are stewards of their children. My parents pronounced destructive prophesies over my life. I internalized them and compounded them, creating my own venomous prophecies about how I'd self-immolate. Proverbs 18:21 tells us: "Death and life are in the power of the tongue," and I'd add the power of thought. Helping abused people learn to healthily steward their thoughts and words is a near-Sisyphean task. But with God, all things are possible.

In the Book of Genesis, God gave Jacob the new name "Israel" after Jacob wrestled all night with an angel. The name Israel means "wrestles with God." My imperfect relationship with God has been messy and angry. But God's love is eternal, and He desires all his children to keep wrestling with life's biggest questions.

May God bless each of us on our journeys of wrestling, stewardship, and healing.

Acknowledgments

First and foremost, I am grateful to our loving, eternal God. It is God from whom all blessings flow, from whom all written words, all stories, and all love are derived. I'm grateful that God held me in the moments of sorrow and the moments of triumph. As the gospel song says, "God on the mountain is still God in the valley."

I am grateful to my family, whom I love eternally. I believe any sorrow or grief we all experienced on this earth will be healed and remembered no more through our Savior, who provides a "new Heaven and a new Earth."

I'm grateful to my literary agent, Jonathan Bronitsky, and the entire team at ATHOS and Hachette Book Group. Jonathan's belief in this project was the genesis for what you're reading today. I also express heartfelt gratitude for Kathryn Riggs, my primary Center Street imprint editor. In moments of writer's block and discouragement around this project, her enthusiasm for the impact and purpose of this storytelling carried me along.

I've been blessed with wonderful professional mentors and friends who shepherded me in life and career over the years, including Prof. Joel Campbell at Brigham Young University, Dr. Richard Parker at Harvard University, Edward Conard, Lisa Goldstein, Clay Aiken, Annie Dickerson, Carrie Lukas, Joan Lindsey, Jennifer Schubert-Akin, Adele Malpass, Penny Nance, Clayton Banks, Leslie Bradshaw, and Ellen Walter.

Thank you to Summer Riffaud, who encouraged me to freedom. Women's minister Karen Smith Hetzler and Matthew Bennett, founder of Christian Union, along with Dr. Deepak Chopra, Dr. Charles Epstein, Jonathan and Carly Graham, Solange Nelson, Alicé Nascimento, Sarah Elizabeth Hill, Natalie Ann Sanchez Lopez, Dr. David Andersen of New York Media Initiative, and fellow fibromyalgia warrior Scott Seligman pulled me along through some sorrowful valleys, and I'm forever grateful for their wisdom and support.

Thank you to my spiritual mentors, figurative Jedi masters, who guided me through my walk of darkness and anger into a journey of light, forgiveness, and peace. That list includes Presiding Bishop Michael Curry; the Reverend Canon Charles K. Robertson; Reverend Canon Carl D. Turner, rector; and Matthew Moretz, vicar of Saint Thomas Church in Manhattan; and Reverend Joel C. Daniels, who baptized me. I'm also grateful to the late Rick Woolworth of Telemachus Network, Reverend Anthony B. Thompson, Pastor A. R. Bernard, Pastor Darrell Scott, Pastor Dimas Salaberrios, Kirsten Haglund, Carla M. Moore, Giovanna Cugnasca, Yordanos Eyoel, Carol M. Swain, Pastor Brian and Janine Weaver, Maria Brazda, and Ben Scott Jr. Though I haven't yet had the honor of meeting him, I'm deeply thankful for the late Pastor Tim Keller, a light to the nations whose books and speaking are profoundly inspiring.

Endnotes

1. "Obituary: James Black," *Deseret News*, March 5, 2000, https://www.deseret .com/2000/3/5/19494439/obituary-james-black.
2. Ralph Sheffield, "The Miracle of the Bookmark," Bright Horizon America, 1988, http://brighthorizon.us/Miracle.htm.
3. Sandra Gonzalez and Sonia Moghe, "Johnny Depp and Amber Heard React to Trial Verdicts: Read Their Full Statements," CNN, June 1, 2022, https://www .cnn.com/2022/06/01/entertainment/depp-heard-trial-verdict-reaction /index.html.
4. Ben Ashford, " 'See how many people believe you.' Listen As Amber Heard Scoffs at Johnny Depp for Claiming He's a Domestic Violence Victim, Suggesting Court Would Take Her Side Because She's a Slender Woman in Explosive Audio," *Daily Mail*, February 5, 2020, https://www.dailymail .co.uk/news/article-7966723/Amber-Heard-ridicules-Johnny-Depp-claiming -hes-domestic-violence-victim.html.
5. Jen Juneau, "Johnny Depp Says His Mom Was 'Violent' During His Childhood: 'Tried to Stay Out of the Line of Fire,' " *People*, April 19, 2022, https:// people.com/movies/johnny-depp-says-mom-betty-sue-palmer-violent -cruel-during-his-childhood-defamation-trial/.
6. "Child Abuse Linked to Risk of Suicide in Later Life," *ScienceDaily*, January 9, 2019, www.sciencedaily.com/releases/2019/01/190109192533.htm.
7. Ioannis Angelakis, Emma Louise Gillespie, and Maria Panagiotti, "Childhood Maltreatment and Adult Suicidality: A Comprehensive Systematic Review with Meta-Analysis," *Psychological Medicine* 49, no. 7 (May 2019): 1057–1078, https://doi.org/10.1017/S0033291718003823.
8. Elizabeth Scott, "What Is a Highly Sensitive Person (HSP)?" VeryWell Mind, Updated November 7, 2022, https://www.verywellmind.com/highly -sensitive-persons-traits-that-create-more-stress-4126393.
9. Elaine N. Aron, "Are You Highly Sensitive?" The Highly Sensitive Person, 1996, https://hsperson.com/test/highly-sensitive-test/.

10. Elizabeth Cady Stanton, Susan Brownell Anthony, Matilda Joslyn Gage, and Ida Husted Harper, *History of Woman Suffrage: 1883–1900* (Indianapolis: Hollenbeck Press, 1902), 263.

11. "Religions: Christadelphians," BBC, Updated June 25, 2009, https://www.bbc.co.uk/religion/religions/christianity/subdivisions/christadelphians_1.shtml.

12. Sheffield, "The Miracle of the Bookmark."

13. T.I., "Live Your Life," featuring Rihanna, *Paper Trail*, released September 30, 2008, https://genius.com/Ti-live-your-life-lyrics.

14. Ramon Amira, "Conquistador Suite," Classical Guitar, August 14, 2010, https://www.classicalguitardelcamp.com/viewtopic.php?t=52034.

15. Gene Weingarten, "Pearls Before Breakfast: Can One of the Nation's Great Musicians Cut through the Fog of a D.C. Rush Hour? Let's Find Out," *Washington Post*, April 8, 2007, https://www.washingtonpost.com/lifestyle/magazine/pearls-before-breakfast-can-one-of-the-nations-great-musicians-cut-through-the-fog-of-a-dc-rush-hour-lets-find-out/2014/09/23/8a6d46da-4331-11e4-b47c-f5889e061e5f_story.html.

16. Andrew Fletcher, "An Account of a Conversation Concerning a Right Regulation of Governments for the Common Good of Mankind: In a Letter to the Marquiss of Montrose, the Earls of Rothes, Roxburg and Haddington, from London the First of December, 1703," Farmington Hills: Gale Ecco, 2010.

17. Jessie L. Embry, "Mormons or Samoans?: Congregational and Ethnic Organizations Among Mormon Samoans in Independence, Missouri," *John Whitmer Historical Association Journal*, 20 (2000): 147–54, http://www.jstor.org/stable/43200137.

18. Kelly Phillips Erb, "Al Capone Convicted on This Day in 1931 After Boasting, 'They Can't Collect Legal Taxes from Illegal Money,'" *Forbes*, October 17, 2020, https://www.forbes.com/sites/kellyphillipserb/2020/10/17/al-capone-convicted-on-this-day-in-1931-after-boasting-they-cant-collect-legal-taxes-from-illegal-money/?sh=7b91648a1435.

19. Barry Bearak, "Eyes on Glory: Pied Pipers of Heaven's Gate," *New York Times*, April 28, 1997, https://www.nytimes.com/1997/04/28/us/eyes-on-glory-pied-pipers-of-heaven-s-gate.html.

20. Bearak, "Eyes on Glory."

21. Lee Davidson, "Census: Utah Is Unique, but Changing," *Salt Lake Tribune*, September 29, 2010, https://archive.sltrib.com/article.php?id=50370926&itype=CMSID.

22. "Steve Young's Mental Struggle Off the Playing Field," *CBS News Sunday Morning*, February 5, 2017, https://www.cbsnews.com/news/steve-youngs-mental-struggle-off-the-playing-field/.

23. "Brigham Young: Family Life," The Church of Jesus Christ of Latter-Day Saints, https://www.churchofjesuschrist.org/study/history/topics/brigham-young?lang=eng.

24. Brenda Kelley Kim, "Brain Activity during a Religious Experience," LabRoots, January 2, 2017, https://www.labroots.com/trending/neuroscience/4932/brain-activity-religious-experience.

25. Roland R. Griffiths et al., "Survey of Subjective 'God Encounter Experiences': Comparisons Among Naturally Occurring Experiences and those Occasioned by the Classic Psychedelics Psilocybin, LSD, Ayahuasca, or DMT," *PLOS One* 14, no. 4 (2019): e0214377, https://www.ncbi.nlm.nih.gov/pmc/articles/PMC6478303/.

26. René J. Muller, "Neurotheology: Are We Hardwired for God?" *Psychiatric Times* 25, no. 6, https://www.psychiatrictimes.com/view/neurotheology-are-we-hardwired-god.

27. "Read Martin Luther King Jr.'s 'I Have a Dream' Speech in its Entirety," NPR, Updated January 16, 2023, https://www.npr.org/2010/01/18/122701268/i-have-a-dream-speech-in-its-entirety.

28. Briana O'Higgins, "How Troost Became a Major Divide in Kansas City," KCUR, March 27, 2014, https://www.kcur.org/community/2014-03-27/how-troost-became-a-major-divide-in-kansas-city.

29. Robert Fink, "The Dozens Game," *Encyclopaedia Britannica*, https://www.britannica.com/topic/the-dozens.

30. Amuzie Chimezie, "The Dozens: An African-Heritage Theory," *Journal of Black Studies* 6, no. 4 (June 1976): 401–20, https://www.jstor.org/stable/2783770.

31. Harry Lefever, "'Playing the Dozens': A Mechanism for Social Control," *Phylon* 42, no. 1 (Spring 1981): 73–85.

32. "Education" *U.S. News & World Report*, https://www.usnews.com/news/best-states/rankings/education.

33. "KC Middle School of the Arts (Closed 2011)," *Public School Review*, https://www.publicschoolreview.com/k-c-middle-school-of-the-arts-profile#:~:text=The%20percentage%20of%20students%20achieving,the%202009%2D10%20school%20year.

34. "Suicide Rate for People with Schizophrenia Spectrum Disorders Over 20 Times Higher than the General Population," Centre for Addiction and Mental

Health, June 18, 2020, https://www.camh.ca/en/camh-news-and-stories
/suicide-rate-for-people-with-schizophrenia-spectrum-disorders.

35. William Shakespeare, *All's Well That Ends Well*, act 3, scene 5, Folger Shake-speare Library, https://www.folger.edu/explore/shakespeares-works/alls-well
-that-ends-well/read/3/5/.

36. "The White Horse Prophecy," Faithful Answers, Informed Response,
https://www.fairlatterdaysaints.org/answers/The_White_Horse
_prophecy.

37. Wilford Woodruff, "Official Declaration 1," Doctrine and Covenants,
https://www.churchofjesuschrist.org/study/scriptures/dc-testament
/od/1?lang=eng.

38. "Election 2010: Missouri 5th District Profile," *New York Times*, https://www
.nytimes.com/elections/2010/house/missouri/5.html.

39. Charlotte Brontë, *Jane Eyre* (Cornhill: Smith Elder and Co., 1847), chapter
XXIII.

40. Craig R. Frogley, "On the Sacred Act of Raising Your Arm to the Square," *Merid-ian Magazine*, May 7, 2018, https://latterdaysaintmag.com/on-the-sacred-act
-of-raising-your-arm-to-the-square/.

41. The Beatles, "Eleanor Rigby," *Revolver*, released August 5, 1966, https://
genius.com/The-beatles-eleanor-rigby-lyrics.

42. "Why It's So Difficult to Leave: All Too Often the Question 'Why Do Peo-ple Stay in Abusive Relationships?' Is Posed to Survivors, Implying that
They Are to Blame for the Abuse," *Women Against Abuse*, https://www
.womenagainstabuse.org/education-resources/learn-about-abuse/why
-its-so-difficult-to-leave.

43. Frank Darabont, dir. *The Shawshank Redemption*, released September 10,
1994, https://www.imdb.com/title/tt0111161/characters/nm0706554.

44. NIV.

45. Jay E. Jensen, "Do You Know How to Repent?" *New Era*, November 1999, https://
www.churchofjesuschrist.org/study/new-era/1999/11/do-you-know-how
-to-repent?lang=eng.

46. Nancy Schimelpfening, "How Self-Esteem Influences Teen Sex Behavior,"
Verywell Mind, Updated May 28, 2022, https://www.verywellmind.com
/teen-self-esteem-and-risky-sexual-behavior-1065482.

47. Aldous Huxley, *Brave New World* (London: Chatto & Windus, 1932), chapter
17, https://www.huxley.net/bnw/seventeen.html.

48. "The Old Mormon Fort: Birthplace of Las Vegas, Nevada (Teaching with
Historic Places)," US National Park Services, https://www.nps.gov/articles
/the-old-mormon-fort-birthplace-of-las-vegas-nevada-teaching-with

-historic-places.htm#:~:text=The%20history%20of%20the%20Las,in%20
the%20Las%20Vegas%20Valley.

49. NIV.

50. NIV.

51. Carrie Sheffield, "Cheslie Kryst's Heartbreaking Struggles Are All Too Common in Pageantry," *New York Post*, January 31, 2022, https://nypost.com
/2022/01/31/cheslie-krysts-struggles-are-all-too-common-in-pageantry/.

52. Leonard Cohen, "Hallelujah," *Various Positions*, released December 11,
1984, https://genius.com/Leonard-cohen-hallelujah-lyrics.

53. Amber Stegall, "Craigslist Killers: 86 Murders Linked to Popular Classifieds
Website," WAFB, April 9, 2015; Updated December 16, 2015, https://www
.wafb.com/story/28761189/craigslist-killers-86-murders-linked-to-popular
-classifieds-website/.

54. "Singles Awareness Day," National Today, https://nationaltoday.com
/singles-awareness-day/.

55. "Marine Corps Marathon—Results," Marathon Guide, October 29, 2006,
http://www.marathonguide.com/results/browse.cfm?MIDD=41061029.

56. Victoria E. Freile, "9 Reasons to Run a Marathon," *USA Today*, September 10,
2015, https://www.usatoday.com/story/news/nation-now/2015/09/10/run
-marathon-health-goals/72009114/.

57. Louise Perry, "How the Sexual Revolution Has Hurt Women," *Wall Street
Journal*, August 19, 2022, https://www.wsj.com/articles/how-the-sexual
-revolution-has-hurt-women-11660921139.

58. Arthur Brooks, "How to Stop Dating People Who Are Wrong for You,"
Atlantic, June 23, 2022, https://www.theatlantic.com/family/archive/2022
/06/dating-advice-failed-relationships/661238/.

59. Evan Marc Katz, "You're Attracted to the Wrong Men," blog, https://www
.evanmarckatz.com/blog/chemistry/youre-attracted-to-the-wrong-men.

60. "Darkest Hour—Churchill's Memorable Quotes Prompt Applause in Cin-
emas," ITV News, January 17, 2018, https://www.itv.com/news/anglia
/2018-01-17/darkest-hour-churchills-memorable-quotes-prompt-applause
-in-cinemas.

61. Lydia Saad, "Socialism and Atheism Still U.S. Political Liabilities," Gallup,
February 11, 2020, https://news.gallup.com/poll/285563/socialism-atheism
-political-liabilities.aspx; Saad, "In U.S., 22% Are Hesitant to Support a Mormon in 2012," Gallup, June 20, 2011, https://news.gallup.com/poll/148100
/hesitant-support-mormon-2012.aspx.

62. "Christian Persecution 'At Near Genocide Levels,'" BBC, May 3, 2019,
https://www.bbc.com/news/uk-48146305.

63. Doug Bandow, "Christianity Is the World's Most Persecuted Religion, Confirms New Report," Acton Institute, March 7, 2022, https://rlo.acton.org/archives/123127-christianity-is-the-worlds-most-persecuted-religion-confirms-new-report.html.

64. Donald Robertson, *The Philosophy of Cognitive Behavioural Therapy: Stoic Philosophy as Rational and Cognitive Psychotherapy* (New York: Routledge, 2010), 81, https://www.google.com/books/edition/The_Philosophy_of_Cognitive_Behavioural/_x6yDwAAQBAJ?hl=en&gbpv=1&dq=inauthor:%22Donald+Robertson%22&printsec=frontcover.

65. "Personality Disorders," Mayo Clinic, https://www.mayoclinic.org/diseases-conditions/personality-disorders/symptoms-causes/syc-20354463#:~:text=Cluster%20B%20personality%20disorders%20are,disorder%20and%20narcissistic%20personality%20disorder.

66. NKJV.

67. Corbin Volluz, "Jesus Christ as Elder Brother," *BYU Studies Quarterly* 45, no. 2 (2006): 141, https://byustudies.byu.edu/article/jesus-christ-as-elder-brother/.

68. Natalie Gochnour, "Utah's Economic Exceptionalism," *American Affairs* IV, no. 4 (Winter 2020), https://americanaffairsjournal.org/2020/11/utahs-economic-exceptionalism/.

69. "In U.S., Decline of Christianity Continues at Rapid Pace," Pew Research Center, October 17, 2019, https://www.pewresearch.org/religion/2019/10/17/in-u-s-decline-of-christianity-continues-at-rapid-pace/.

70. "Lift Up Thine Eyes," Civilization at the BYU Museum of Art, https://moa.byu.edu/civilization-at-the-byu-museum-of-art/lift-up-thine-eyes.

71. KJV.

72. "Memorial of Saint Thomas Aquinas, Priest and Doctor of the Church," Saint Boniface Catholic Church, https://stboniface-lunenburg.org/memorial-of-saint-thomas-aquinas-priest-and-doctor-of-the-church.

73. NIV.

74. Psychology Today Staff, "From Here to Eternity," *Psychology Today*, March 1, 1993; Reviewed June 9, 2016, https://www.psychologytoday.com/us/articles/199303/here-eternity.

75. Psychology Today Staff, "From Here to Eternity."

76. Geneva Pittman, "Fibromyalgia Comes with a Suicide Risk: Study," Reuters, July 16, 2010, https://www.reuters.com/article/us-fibromyalgia-suicide/fibromyalgia-comes-with-a-suicide-risk-study-idUSTRE66F3JJ20100716.

77. Larry Chang, ed. *Wisdom for the Soul: Five Millennia of Prescriptions for Spiritual Healing* (Washington, DC: Gnosophia Publishers, 2006), 764.

78. "Diseases & Conditions: Fibromyalgia," American College of Rheumatology, https://rheumatology.org/patients/fibromyalgia.

79. NIV.

80. NKJV.

81. "Shooting Victims' Families to Dylann Roof: We 'Forgive You,'" *USA Today*, June 19, 2015, https://www.youtube.com/watch?v=Fc8yRyBll-Q.

82. Leah Silverman, "15 of Billy Graham's Most Powerful Quotes," *Town & Country*, February 21, 2018, https://www.townandcountrymag.com/leisure /arts-and-culture/a18564816/billy-graham-quotes/.

83. KJV.

84. BGEA Admin, "Answers," Billy Graham Evangelistic Association, May 11, 2019, https://billygraham.org/answer/my-mom-and-i-dont-get-along-whats -the-answer-to-difficult-relationships/.

85. Elevation Worship and Maverick City Music, "Jireh," *Old Church Basement*, released April 30, 2021, https://genius.com/Elevation-worship-and-maverick -city-music-jireh-lyrics.

86. "People & Ideas: Frederick Douglass," PBS, https://www.pbs.org/wgbh /pages/frontline/godinamerica/people/frederick-douglass.html.

87. "Americans Have Positive Views about Religion's Role in Society, But Want It Out of Politics," Pew Research Center, November 15, 2019, https://www .pewresearch.org/religion/2019/11/15/many-in-u-s-see-religious-organiza tions-as-forces-for-good-but-prefer-them-to-stay-out-of-politics/.

88. "Few Americans Blame God or Say Faith Has Been Shaken Amid Pandemic, Other Tragedies," Pew Research Center, November 23, 2021, https://www .pewresearch.org/religion/2021/11/23/few-americans-blame-god-or-say -faith-has-been-shaken-amid-pandemic-other-tragedies/.

89. "Regularly Attending Religious Services Associated with Lower Risk of Deaths of Despair," Harvard T.H. Chan School of Public Health, May 6, 2020, https://www.hsph.harvard.edu/news/press-releases/regularly-attending -religious-services-associated-with-lower-risk-of-deaths-of-despair/.

90. Tyler Giles, Daniel M. Hungerman, and Tamar Oostrom, "Opiates of the Masses? Deaths of Despair and the Decline of American Religion," *NBER Working Paper Series*, no. 30840, DOI 10.3386/w30840, https://www.nber .org/system/files/working_papers/w30840/w30840.pdf.

91. KJV.

92. Cecil B. DeMille, "The Ten Commandments and You," BYU Speeches, May 31, 1957, https://speeches.byu.edu/talks/cecil-b-demille/ten-commandments -and-you/.

93. KJV.

94. Robert Waldinger and Marc Schulz, "The Lifelong Power of Close Relation-
    ships," *Wall Street Journal*, January 13, 2023, https://www.wsj.com/articles
    /the-lifelong-power-of-close-relationships-11673625450.

95. MEV.

96. NIV.

97. "Lincoln and Thanksgiving," US National Park Service, https://www.nps
    .gov/liho/learn/historyculture/lincoln-and-thanksgiving.htm.

98. "It Is the Greatest of All Mistakes, To Do Nothing Because You Can Only
    Do Little," Quote Investigator, https://quoteinvestigator.com/2020/01/31
    /little/.

99. NIV.